The Story of the Trapper

Agnes C. Laut

Alpha Editions

This edition published in 2024

ISBN : 9789362995131

Design and Setting By
Alpha Editions
www.alphaedis.com
Email - info@alphaedis.com

As per information held with us this book is in Public Domain.
This book is a reproduction of an important historical work. Alpha Editions uses the best technology to reproduce historical work in the same manner it was first published to preserve its original nature. Any marks or number seen are left intentionally to preserve its true form.

Contents

EDITOR'S PREFACE ....- 1 -

THE STORY OF THE TRAPPER PART I ....- 5 -

CHAPTER I GAMESTERS OF THE WILDERNESS ....- 7 -

CHAPTER II THREE COMPANIES IN CONFLICT ....- 11 -

CHAPTER III THE NOR' WESTERS' COUP ....- 19 -

CHAPTER IV THE ANCIENT HUDSON'S BAY COMPANY WAKENS UP ....- 23 -

CHAPTER V MR. ASTOR'S COMPANY ENCOUNTERS NEW OPPONENTS ....- 29 -

CHAPTER VI THE FRENCH TRAPPER ....- 36 -

CHAPTER VII THE BUFFALO-RUNNERS ....- 46 -

CHAPTER VIII THE MOUNTAINEERS ....- 57 -

PART II ....- 69 -

CHAPTER IX THE TAKING OF THE BEAVER ....- 71 -

CHAPTER X THE MAKING OF THE MOCCASINS .... - 80 -

CHAPTER XI THE INDIAN TRAPPER .... - 87 -

CHAPTER XII BA'TISTE, THE BEAR HUNTER .... - 97 -

CHAPTER XIII JOHN COLTER—FREE TRAPPER .... - 106 -

CHAPTER XIV THE GREATEST FUR COMPANY OF THE WORLD .... - 119 -

CHAPTER XV KOOT AND THE BOB-CAT .... - 135 -

CHAPTER XVI .... - 145 -

CHAPTER XVII THE RARE FURS— HOW THE TRAPPER TAKES SAKWASEW THE MINK, NEKIK THE OTTER, WUCHAK THE FISHER, AND WAPISTAN THE MARTEN I .... - 158 -

CHAPTER XVIII UNDER THE NORTH STAR—WHERE FOX AND ERMINE RUN I .... - 170 -

CHAPTER XIX WHAT THE TRAPPER STANDS FOR .... - 180 -

APPENDIX .... - 183 -

FOOTNOTES: .... - 186 -

EDITOR'S PREFACE

The picturesque figure of the trapper follows close behind the Indian in the unfolding of the panorama of the West. There is the explorer, but the trapper himself preceded the explorers—witness Lewis's and Clark's meetings with trappers on their journey. The trapper's hard-earned knowledge of the vast empire lying beyond the Missouri was utilized by later comers, or in a large part died with him, leaving occasional records in the documents of fur companies, or reports of military expeditions, or here and there in the name of a pass, a stream, a mountain, or a fort. His adventurous warfare upon the wild things of the woods and streams was the expression of a primitive instinct old as the history of mankind. The development of the motives which led the first pioneer trappers afield from the days of the first Eastern settlements, the industrial organizations which followed, the commanding commercial results which were evolved from the trafficking of Radisson and Groseillers in the North, the rise of the great Hudson's Bay Company, and the American enterprise which led, among other results, to the foundation of the Astor fortunes, would form no inconsiderable part of a history of North America. The present volume aims simply to show the type-character of the Western trapper, and to sketch in a series of pictures the checkered life of this adventurer of the wilderness.

The trapper of the early West was a composite figure. From the Northeast came a splendid succession of French explorers like La Vérendrye, with coureurs des bois, and a multitude of daring trappers and traders pushing west and south. From the south the Spaniard, illustrated in figures like Garces and others, held out hands which rarely grasped the waiting commerce. From the north and northeast there was the steady advance of the sturdy Scotch and English, typified in the deeds of the Henrys, Thompson, MacKenzie, and the leaders of the organized fur trade, explorers, traders, captains of industry, carrying the flags of the Hudson's Bay and North-West Fur companies across Northern America to the Pacific. On the far Northwestern coast the Russian appeared as fur trader in the middle of the eighteenth century, and the close of the century saw the merchants of Boston claiming their share of the fur traffic of that coast. The American trapper becomes a conspicuous figure in the early years of the nineteenth century. The emporium of his traffic was St. Louis, and the period of its greatest importance and prosperity began soon after the Louisiana Purchase and continued for forty years. The complete history of the American fur trade of the far West has been written by Captain H. M. Chittenden in volumes which will be included among the classics of early

Western history. Although his history is a publication designed for limited circulation, no student or specialist in this field can fail to appreciate the value of his faithful and comprehensive work.

In The Story of the Trapper there is presented for the general reader a vivid picture of an adventurous figure, which is painted with a singleness of purpose and a distinctness impossible of realization in the large and detailed histories of the American fur trade and the Hudson's Bay and North-West companies, or the various special relations and journals and narratives. The author's wilderness lore and her knowledge of the life, added to her acquaintance with its literature, have borne fruit in a personification of the Western and Northern trappers who live in her pages. It is the man whom we follow not merely in the evolution of the Western fur traffic, but also in the course of his strange life in the wilds, his adventures, and the contest of his craft against the cunning of his quarry. It is a most picturesque figure which is sketched in these pages with the etcher's art that selects essentials while boldly disregarding details. This figure as it is outlined here will be new and strange to the majority of readers, and the relish of its piquant flavour will make its own appeal. A strange chapter in history is outlined for those who would gain an insight into the factors which had to do with the building of the West. Woodcraft, exemplified in the calling of its most skilful devotees, is painted in pictures which breathe the very atmosphere of that life of stream and forest which has not lost its appeal even in these days of urban centralization. The flash of the paddle, the crack of the rifle, the stealthy tracking of wild beasts, the fearless contest of man against brute and savage, may be followed throughout a narrative which is constant in its fresh and personal interest.

The Hudson's Bay Company still flourishes, and there is still an American fur trade; but the golden days are past, and the heroic age of the American trapper in the West belongs to a bygone time. Even more than the cowboy, his is a fading figure, dimly realized by his successors. It is time to tell his story, to show what manner of man he was, and to preserve for a different age the adventurous character of a Romany of the wilderness, fascinating in the picturesqueness and daring of his primeval life, and also, judged by more practical standards, a figure of serious historical import in his relations to exploration and commerce, and even affairs of politics and state.

If, therefore, we take the trapper as a typical figure in the early exploitation of an empire, his larger significance may be held of far more consequence to us than the excesses and lawlessness so frequent in his life. He was often an adventurer pure and simple. The record of his dealings with the red man and with white competitors is darkened by many stains. His return from his lonely journeys afield brought an outbreak of license like that of the cowboy fresh from the range, but with all this the stern life of the old frontier bred a race of men who did their work. That work was the development of the only natural resources of vast regions in this country and to the Northward, which were utilized for long periods. There was also the task of exploration, the breaking the way for others, and as pioneer and as builder of commerce the trapper's part in our early history has a significance which cloaks the frailties characteristic of restraintless life in untrodden wilds.

THE STORY OF THE TRAPPER
PART I

CHAPTER I
GAMESTERS OF THE WILDERNESS

Fearing nothing, stopping at nothing, knowing no law, ruling his stronghold of the wilds like a despot, checkmating rivals with a deviltry that beggars parallel, wassailing with a shamelessness that might have put Rome's worst deeds to the blush, fighting—fighting—fighting, always fighting with a courage that knew no truce but victory, the American trapper must ever stand as a type of the worst and the best in the militant heroes of mankind.

Each with an army at his back, Wolfe and Napoleon won victories that upset the geography of earth. The fur traders never at any time exceeded a few thousands in number, faced enemies unbacked by armies and sallied out singly or in pairs; yet they won a continent that has bred a new race.

Like John Colter,[1] whom Manuel Lisa met coming from the wilds a hundred years ago, the trapper strapped a pack to his back, slung a rifle over his shoulder, and, without any fanfare of trumpets, stepped into the pathless shade of the great forests. Or else, like Williams of the Arkansas, the trapper left the moorings of civilization in a canoe, hunted at night, hid himself by day, evaded hostile Indians by sliding down-stream with muffled paddles, slept in mid-current screened by the branches of driftwood, and if a sudden halloo of marauders came from the distance, cut the strap that held his craft to the shore and got away under cover of the floating tree. Hunters crossing the Cimarron desert set out with pack-horses, and, like Captain Becknell's party, were often compelled to kill horses and dogs to keep from dying of thirst. Frequently their fate was that of Rocky Mountain Smith, killed by the Indians as he stooped to scoop out a drinking-hole in the sand. Men who brought down their pelts to the mountain rendezvous of Pierre's Hole, or went over the divide like Fraser and Thompson of the North-West Fur Company, had to abandon both horses and canoes, scaling cañon walls where the current was too turbulent for a canoe and the precipice too sheer for a horse, with the aid of their hunting-knives stuck in to the haft.[2] Where the difficulties were too great for a few men, the fur traders clubbed together under a master-mind like John Jacob Astor of the Pacific Company, or Sir Alexander MacKenzie of the Nor' Westers. Banded together, they thought no more of coasting round the sheeted antarctics, or slipping down the ice-jammed current of the MacKenzie River under the midnight sun of the arctic circle, than people to-day think of running from New York to Newport. When the conflict of 1812 cut off communication between western fur posts and New York by the overland route, Farnham, the Green Mountain boy, didn't think himself a hero at all for sailing to Kamtchatka and crossing the whole width of Asia, Europe, and the Atlantic, to reach Mr. Astor.

The American fur trader knew only one rule of existence—to go ahead without any heroics, whether the going cost his own or some other man's life. That is the way the wilderness was won; and the winning is one of the most thrilling pages in history.

About the middle of the seventeenth century Pierre Radisson and Chouart Groseillers, two French adventurers from Three Rivers, Quebec, followed the chain of waterways from the Ottawa and Lake Superior northwestward to the region of Hudson Bay.[3] Returning with tales of fabulous wealth to be had in the fur trade of the north, they were taken in hand by members of the British Commission then in Boston, whose influence secured the Hudson's Bay Company charter in 1670; and that ancient and honourable body—as the company was called—reaped enormous profits from the bartering of pelts. But the bartering went on in a prosy, half-alive way, the traders sitting snugly in their forts on Rupert and Severn Rivers, or at York Factory (Port Nelson) and Churchill (Prince of Wales). The French governor down in Quebec issued only a limited number of licenses for the fur trade in Canada; and the old English company had no fear of rivalry in the north. It never sought inland tribes, but waited with serene apathy for the Indians to come down to its fur posts on the bay. Young Le Moyne d'Iberville[4] might march overland from Quebec to the bay, catch the English company nodding, scale the stockades, capture its forts, batter down a wall or two, and sail off like a pirate with ship-loads of booty for Quebec. What did the ancient company care? European treaties restored its forts, and the honourable adventurers presented a bill of damages to their government for lost furs.

But came a sudden change. Great movements westward began simultaneously in all parts of the east.

This resulted from two events—England's victory over France at Quebec, and the American colonies' Declaration of Independence. The downfall of French ascendency in America meant an end to that license system which limited the fur trade to favourites of the governor. That threw an army of some two thousand men—voyageurs, coureurs des bois, mangeurs de lard,[5] famous hunters, traders, and trappers—on their own resources. The MacDonalds and MacKenzies and MacGillivrays and Frobishers and MacTavishes—Scotch merchants of Quebec and Montreal—were quick to seize the opportunity. Uniting under the names of North-West Fur

Company and X. Y. Fur Company, they re-engaged the entire retinue of cast-off Frenchmen, woodcraftsmen who knew every path and stream from Labrador to the Rocky Mountains. Giving higher pay and better fare than the old French traders, the Scotch merchants prepared to hold the field against all comers in the Canadas. And when the X. Y. amalgamated with the larger company before the opening of the nineteenth century, the Nor' Westers became as famous for their daring success as their unscrupulous ubiquity.

But at that stage came the other factor—American Independence. Locked in conflict with England, what deadlier blow to British power could France deal than to turn over Louisiana with its million square miles and ninety thousand inhabitants to the American Republic? The Lewis and Clark exploration up the Missouri, over the mountains, and down the Columbia to the Pacific was a natural sequel to the Louisiana Purchase, and proved that the United States had gained a world of wealth for its fifteen million dollars. Before Lewis and Clark's feat, vague rumours had come to the New England colonies of the riches to be had in the west. The Russian Government had organized a strong company to trade for furs with the natives of the Pacific coast. Captain Vancouver's report of the north-west coast was corroborated by Captain Grey, who had stumbled into the mouth of the Columbia; and before 1800 nearly thirty Boston vessels yearly sailed to the Northern Pacific for the fur trade.

Eager to forestall the Hudson's Bay Company, now beginning to rub its eyes and send explorers westward to bring Indians down to the bay,[6] Alexander MacKenzie of the Nor' Westers pushed down the great river named after him,[7] and forced his way across the northern Rockies to the Pacific. Flotillas of North-West canoes quickly followed MacKenzie's lead north to the arctics, south-west down the Columbia. At Michilimackinac—one of the most lawless and roaring of the fur posts—was an association known as the Mackinaw Company, made up of old French hunters under English management, trading westward from the Lakes to the Mississippi. Hudson Bay, Nor' Wester, and Mackinaw were daily pressing closer and closer to that vast unoccupied Eldorado—the fur country between the Missouri and the Saskatchewan, bounded eastward by the Mississippi, west by the Pacific.

Possession is nine points out of ten. The question was who would get possession first.

Unfortunately that question presented itself to three alert rivals at the same time and in the same light. And the war began.

The Mackinaw traders had all they could handle from the Lakes to the Mississippi. Therefore they did little but try to keep other traders out of the western preserve. The Hudson's Bay remained in its somnolent state till the very extremity of outrage brought such a mighty awakening that it put its rivals to an eternal sleep. But the Nor' Westers were not asleep. And John Jacob Astor of New York, who had accumulated what was a gigantic fortune in those days as a purchaser of furs from America and a seller to Europe, was not asleep. And Manual Lisa, a Spaniard, of New Orleans, engaged at St. Louis in fur trade with the Osage tribes, was not asleep.

CHAPTER II
THREE COMPANIES IN CONFLICT

If only one company had attempted to take possession of the vast fur country west of the Mississippi, the fur trade would not have become international history; but three companies were at strife for possession of territory richer than Spanish Eldorado, albeit the coin was "beaver"—not gold. Each of three companies was determined to use all means fair or foul to exclude its rivals from the field; and a fourth company was drawn into the strife because the conflict menaced its own existence.

From their Canadian headquarters at Fort William on Lake Superior, the Nor' Westers had yearly moved farther down the Columbia towards the mouth, where Lewis and Clark had wintered on the Pacific. In New York, Mr. Astor was formulating schemes to add to his fur empire the territory west of the Mississippi. At St. Louis was Manuel Lisa, the Spanish fur trader, already reaching out for the furs of the Missouri. And leagues to the north on the remote waters of Hudson Bay, the old English company lazily blinked its eyes open to the fact that competition was telling heavily on its returns, and that it would be compelled to take a hand in the merry game of a fur traders' war, though the real awakening had not yet come.

Lisa was the first to act on the information brought back by Lewis and Clark. Forming a partnership with Morrison and Menard of Kaskaskia, Ill., and engaging Drouillard, one of Lewis and Clark's men, as interpreter, he left St. Louis with a heavily laden keel-boat in the spring of 1807. Against the turbulent current of the Missouri in the full flood-tide of spring this unwieldy craft was slowly hauled or "cordelled," twenty men along the shore pulling the clumsy barge by means of a line fastened high enough on the mast to be above brushwood. Where the water was shallow the voyageurs poled single file, facing the stern and pushing with full chest strength. In deeper current oars were used.

Launched for the wilderness, with no certain knowledge but that the wilderness was peopled by hostiles, poor Bissonette deserted when they were only at the Osage River. Lisa issued orders for Drouillard to bring the deserter back dead or alive—orders that were filled to the letter, for the poor fellow was brought back shot, to die at St. Charles. Passing the mouth of the Platte, the company descried a solitary white man drifting downstream in a dugout. When it was discovered that this lone trapper was John Colter, who had left Lewis and Clark on their return trip and remained to hunt on the Upper Missouri, one can imagine the shouts that welcomed him. Having now been in the upper country for three years, he was the one man fitted to guide Lisa's party, and was promptly persuaded to turn back with the treasure-seekers.

Past Blackbird's grave, where the great chief of the Omahas had been buried astride his war-horse high on the crest of a hill that his spirit might see the canoes of the French voyageurs going up and down the river; past the lonely grave of Floyd,[8] whose death, like that of many a New World hero marked another milestone in the westward progress of empire; past the Aricaras, with their three hundred warriors gorgeous in vermilion, firing volleys across the keel-boat with fusees got from rival traders;[9] past the Mandans, threatening death to the intruders; past five thousand Assiniboine hostiles massed on the bank with weapons ready; up the Yellowstone to the mouth of the Bighorn—went Lisa, stopping in the very heart of the Crow tribe, those thieves and pirates and marauders of the western wilderness. Stockades were hastily stuck in the ground, banked up with a miniature parapet, flanked with the two usual bastions that could send a raking fire along all four walls; and Lisa was ready for trade.

In 1808 the keel-boat returned to St. Louis, loaded to the water-line with furs. The Missouri Company was formally organized,[10] and yearly expeditions were sent not only to the Bighorn, but to the Three Forks of the Missouri, among the ferocious Blackfeet. Of the two hundred and fifty men employed, fifty were trained riflemen for the defence of the trappers; but this did not prevent more than thirty men losing their lives at the hands of the Blackfeet within two years. Among the victims was Drouillard, struck down wheeling his horse round and round as a shield, literally torn to pieces by the exasperated savages and eaten according to the hideous superstition that the flesh of a brave man imparts bravery. All the plundered clothing, ammunition, and peltries were carried to the Nor' Westers' trading posts north of the boundary.[11] Not if the West were to be baptized in blood would the traders retreat. Crippled, but not beaten, the Missouri men under Andrew Henry's leadership moved south-west over the mountains into the region that was to become famous as Pierre's Hole.

Meanwhile neither the Nor' Westers nor Mr. Astor remained idle. The same year that Lisa organized his Missouri Fur Company Mr. Astor obtained a charter from the State of New York for the American Fur Company. To lessen competition in the great scheme gradually framing itself in his mind, he bought out that half of the Mackinaw Company's trade[12] which was within the United States, the posts in the British dominions falling into the hands of the all-powerful Nor' Westers. Intimate with the leading partners of the Nor' Westers, Mr. Astor proposed to avoid rivalry on the Pacific coast by giving the Canadians a third interest in his plans for the capture of the Pacific trade.

Lords of their own field, the Nor' Westers rejected Mr. Astor's proposal with a scorn born of unshaken confidence, and at once prepared to anticipate American possession of the Pacific coast. Mr. Astor countered by engaging the best of the dissatisfied Nor' Westers for his Pacific Fur Company. Duncan MacDougall, a little pepper-box of a Scotchman, with a bumptious idea of authority which was always making other eyes smart, was to be Mr. Astor's proxy on the ship to round the Horn and at the headquarters of the company on the Pacific. Donald MacKenzie was a relative of Sir Alexander of the Nor' Westers, and must have left the northern traders from some momentary pique; for he soon went back to the Canadian companies, became chief factor at Fort Garry,[13] the headquarters of the Hudson's Bay Company, and was for a time governor of Red River. Alexander MacKay had accompanied Sir Alexander MacKenzie on his famous northern trips, and was one Nor' Wester who served Mr. Astor with fidelity to the death. The elder Stuart was a rollicking winterer from The Labrador, with the hail-fellow-well-met-air of an equal among the mercurial French-Canadians. The younger Stuart was of the game, independent spirit that made Nor' Westers famous.

Of the Tonquin's voyage round the Horn—with its crew of twenty, and choleric Captain Thorn, and four[14] partners headed by the fussy little MacDougall in mutiny against the captain's discipline, and twelve clerks always getting their landlubber clumsiness in the sailors' way, and thirteen voyageurs ever grumbling at the ocean swell that gave them qualms unknown on inland waters—little need be said. Washington Irving has told this story; and what Washington Irving leaves untold, Captain Chittenden has recently unearthed from the files of the Missouri archives.

The Tonquin sailed from New York, September 6, 1810. The captain had been a naval officer, and cursed the partners for their easy familiarity with the men before the mast, and the note-writing clerks for a lot of scribbling blockheads, and the sea-sick voyageurs for a set of fresh-water braggarts. And the captain's amiable feelings were reciprocated by every Nor' Wester on board.

Cape Horn was doubled on Christmas Day, Hawaii sighted in February, some thirty Sandwich Islanders engaged for service in the new company, and the Columbia entered at the end of March, 1811. Eight lives were lost attempting to run small boats against the turbulent swell of tide and current. The place to land, the site to build, details of the new fort, Astoria—all were subjects for the jangling that went on between the fuming little Scotchman MacDougall and Captain Thorn, till the Tonquin weighed anchor on the 1st of June and sailed away to trade on the north coast, accompanied by only one partner, Alexander MacKay, and one clerk, James Lewis.

The obstinacy that had dominated Captain Thorn continued to dictate a wrong-headed course. In spite of Mr. Astor's injunction to keep Indians off the ship and MacKay's warning that the Nootka tribes were treacherous, the captain allowed natives to swarm over his decks. Once, when MacKay was on shore, Thorn lost his temper, struck an impertinent chief in the face with a bundle of furs, and expelled the Indian from the ship. When MacKay came back and learned what had happened, he warned the captain of Indian vengeance and urged him to leave the harbour. These warnings the captain scorned, welcoming back the Indians, and no doubt exulting to see that they had become almost servile.

One morning, when Thorn, and MacKay were yet asleep, a pirogue with twenty Indians approached the ship. The Indians were unarmed, and held up furs to trade. They were welcomed on deck. Another canoe glided near and another band mounted the ship's ladder. Soon the vessel was completely surrounded with canoes, the braves coming aboard with furs, the squaws laughing and chatting and rocking their crafts at the ship's side. This day the Indians were neither pertinacious nor impertinent in their trade. Matters went swimmingly till some of the Tonquin's crew noticed with alarm that all the Indians were taking knives and other weapons in exchange for their furs and that groups were casually stationing themselves at positions of wonderful advantage on the deck. MacKay and Thorn were quickly called.

This is probably what the Indians were awaiting.

MacKay grasped the fearful danger of the situation and again warned the captain. Again Thorn slighted the warning. But anchors were hoisted. The Indians thronged closer, as if in the confusion of hasty trade. Then the dour-headed Thorn understood. With a shout he ordered the decks cleared. His shout was answered by a counter-shout—the wild, shrill shriekings of the Indian war-cry! All the newly-bought weapons flashed in the morning sun. Lewis, the clerk, fell first, bending over a pile of goods, and rolled down the companion-way with a mortal stab in his back. MacKay was knocked from his seat on the taffrail by a war-club and pitched overboard to the canoes, where the squaws received him on their knives. Thorn had been roused so suddenly that he had no weapon but his pocket-knife. With this he was trying to fight his way to the firearms of the cabin, when he was driven, faint from loss of blood, to the wheel-house. A tomahawk clubbed down, and he, too, was pitched overboard to the knives of the squaws.

While the officers were falling on the quarter-deck, sailors and Sandwich Islanders were fighting to the death elsewhere. The seven men who had been sent up the ratlins to rig sails came shinning down ropes and masts to gain the cabin. Two were instantly killed. A third fell down the main hatch fatally wounded; and the other four got into the cabin, where they broke holes and let fly with musket and rifle. This sent the savages scattering overboard to the waiting canoes. The survivors then fired charge after charge from the deck cannon, which drove the Indians to land with tremendous loss of life.

All day the Indians watched the Tonquin's sails flapping to the wind; but none of the ship's crew appeared on the deck. The next morning the Tonquin still lay rocking to the tide; but no white men emerged from below. Eager to plunder the apparently deserted ship, the Indians launched their canoes and cautiously paddled near. A white man—one of those who had fallen down the hatch wounded—staggered up to the deck, waved for the natives to come on board, and dropped below. Gluttonous of booty, the savages beset the sides of the Tonquin like flocks of carrion-birds. Barely were they on deck when sea and air were rent with a terrific explosion as of ten thousand cannon! The ship was blown to atoms, bodies torn asunder, and the sea scattered with bloody remnants of what had been living men but a moment before.

The mortally wounded man, thought to be Lewis, the clerk,[15] had determined to effect the death of his enemies on his own pyre. Unable to escape with the other four refugees under cover of night, he had put a match to four tons of powder in the hold. But the refugees might better have perished with the Tonquin; for head-winds drove them ashore, where they were captured and tortured to death with all the prolonged cruelty that savages practise. Between twenty and thirty lives were lost in this disaster to the Pacific Fur Company; and MacDougall was left at Astoria with but a handful of men and a weakly-built fort to wait the coming of the overland traders whom Mr. Astor was sending by way of the Missouri and Columbia.

Indian runners brought vague rumours of thirty white men building a fort on the Upper Columbia. If these had been the overland party, they would have come on to Astoria. Who they were, MacDougall, who had himself been a Nor' Wester, could easily guess. As a countercheck, Stuart of Labrador was preparing to go up-stream and build a fur post for the Pacific Company; but Astoria was suddenly electrified by the apparition of nine white men in a canoe flying a British flag.

The North-West Company arrived just three months too late!

David Thompson, the partner at the head of the newcomers, had been delayed in the mountains by the desertion of his guides. Much to the disgust of Labrador Stuart, who might change masters often but was loyal to only one master at a time, MacDougall and Thompson hailed each other as old friends. Every respect is due Mr. Thompson as an explorer, but to the Astorians living under the ruthless code of fur-trading rivalry, he should have been nothing more than a North-West spy, to be guardedly received in a Pacific Company fort. As a matter of fact, he was welcomed with open arms, saw everything, and set out again with a supply of Astoria provisions.

History is not permitted to jump at conclusions, but unanswered questions will always cling round Thompson's visit. Did he bear some message from the Nor' Westers to MacDougall? Why was Stuart, an honourable, fair-minded man, in such high dudgeon that he shook free of Thompson's company on their way back up the Columbia? Why did MacDougall lose his tone of courage with such surprising swiftness? How could the next party of Nor' Westers take him back into the fold and grant him a partnership ostensibly without the knowledge of the North-West annual council, held in Fort William on Lake Superior?

Early in August wandering tribes brought news of the Tonquin's destruction, and Astoria bestirred itself to strengthen pickets, erect bastions, mount four-pounders, and drill for war. MacDougall's North-West training now came out, and he entered on a policy of conciliation with the Indians that culminated in his marrying Comcomly's daughter. He also perpetrated the world-famous threat of letting small-pox out of a bottle exhibited to the chiefs unless they maintained good behaviour. Traders established inland posts, the schooner Dolly was built, and New Year's Day of 1812 ushered in with a firing of cannon and festive allowance of rum. On January 18th arrived the forerunners of the overland party, ragged, wasted, starving, with a tale of blundering and mismanagement that must have been gall to MacKenzie, the old Nor' Wester accompanying them. The main body under Hunt reached Astoria in February, and two other detachments later.

The management of the overlanders had been intrusted to Wilson Price Hunt of New Jersey, who at once proceeded to Montreal with Donald MacKenzie, the Nor' Wester. Here the fine hand of the North-West Company was first felt. Rum, threats, promises, and sudden orders whisking them away prevented capable voyageurs from enlisting under the Pacific Company. Only worthless fellows could be engaged, which explains in part why these empty braggarts so often failed Mr. Hunt. Pushing up the Ottawa in a birch canoe, Hunt and MacKenzie crossed the lake to Michilimackinac.

Here the hand of the North-West Company was again felt. Tattlers went from man to man telling yarns of terror to frighten engagés back. Did a man enlist? Sudden debts were remembered or manufactured, and the bill presented to Hunt. Was a voyageur on the point of embarking? A swarm of naked brats with a frouzy Indian wife set up a howl of woe. Hunt finally got off with thirty men, accompanied by Mr. Ramsay Crooks, a distinguished Nor' Wester, who afterward became famous as the president of the American Fur Company. Going south by way of Green Bay and the Mississippi, Hunt reached St. Louis, where the machinations of another rival were put to work.

Having rejected Mr. Astor's suggestion to take part in the Pacific Company, Mr. Manuel Lisa of the Missouri traders did not propose to see his field invaded. The same difficulties were encountered at St. Louis in engaging men as at Montreal, and when Hunt was finally ready in March, 1811, to set out with his sixty men up the Missouri, Lisa resurrected a liquor debt against Pierre Dorion, Hunt's interpreter, with the fluid that cheers a French-Canadian charged at ten dollars a quart. Pierre slipped Lisa's coil by going overland through the woods and meeting Hunt's party farther upstream, beyond the law.

Whatever his motive, Lisa at once organized a search party of twenty picked voyageurs to go up the Missouri to the rescue of that Andrew Henry who had fled from the Blackfeet over the mountains to Snake River. Traders too often secured safe passage through hostile territory in those lawless days by giving the savages muskets enough to blow out the brains of the next comers. Lisa himself was charged with this by Crooks and MacLellan.[16] Perhaps that was his reason for pushing ahead at all speed to overtake Hunt before either party had reached Sioux territory.

Hunt got wind of the pursuit. The faster Lisa came, the harder Hunt fled. This curious race lasted for a thousand miles and ended in Lisa coming up with the Astorians on June 2d. For a second time the Spaniard tampered with Dorion. Had not two English travellers intervened, Hunt and Lisa would have settled their quarrel with pistols for two. Thereafter the rival parties proceeded in friendly fashion, Lisa helping to gather horses for Hunt's party to cross the mountains.

That overland journey was one of the most pitiful, fatuous, mismanaged expeditions in the fur trade. Why a party of sixty-four well-armed, well-provisioned men failed in doing what any two voyageurs or trappers were doing every day, can only be explained by comparison to a bronco in a blizzard. Give the half-wild prairie creature the bit, and it will carry its rider through any storm. Jerk it to right, to left, east, and west till it loses its confidence, and the bronco is as helpless as the rider. So with the voyageur. Crossing the mountains alone in his own way, he could evade famine and danger and attack by lifting a brother trader's cache—hidden provisions—

or tarrying in Indian lodges till game crossed his path, or marrying the daughter of a hostile chief, or creeping so quietly through the woods neither game nor Indian scout could detect his presence. With a noisy cavalcade of sixty-four all this was impossible. Broken into detachments, weak, emaciated, stripped naked, on the verge of dementia and cannibalism, now shouting to each other across a roaring cañon, now sinking in despair before a blind wall, the overlanders finally reached Astoria after nearly a year's wanderings.

Mr. Astor's second ship, the Beaver, arrived with re-enforcements of men and provisions. More posts were established inland. After several futile attempts, despatches were sent overland to St. Louis. Under direction of Mr. Hunt, the Beaver sailed for Alaska to trade with the Russians. Word came from the North-West forts on the Upper Columbia of war with England. Mr. Astor's third ship, the Lark, was wrecked. Astoria was now altogether in the hands of men who had been Nor' Westers.

And what was the alert North-West Company doing?[17]

CHAPTER III
THE NOR' WESTERS' COUP

"It had been decided in council at Fort William that the company should send the Isaac Todd to the Columbia River, where the Americans had established Astoria, and that a party should proceed from Fort William (overland) to meet the ship on the coast," wrote MacDonald of Garth, a North-West partner, for the perusal of his children.

This was decided at the North-West council of 1812, held annually on the shores of Lake Superior. It was just a year from the time that Thompson had discovered the American fort in the hands of former Nor' Westers. At this meeting Thompson's report must have been read.

The overland party was to be led by the two partners, John George MacTavish and Alexander Henry, the sea expedition on the Isaac Todd by Donald MacTavish, who had actually been appointed governor of the American fort in anticipation of victory. On the Isaac Todd also went MacDonald of Garth.[18]

The overland expedition was to thread that labyrinth of water-ways connecting Lake Superior and the Saskatchewan, thence across the plains to Athabasca, over the northern Rockies, past Jasper House, through Yellow Head Pass, and down half the length of the Columbia through Kootenay plains to Astoria. One has only to recall the roaring cañons of the northern Rockies, with their sheer cataracts and bottomless precipices, to realize how much more hazardous this route was than that followed by Hunt from St. Louis to Astoria. Hunt had to cross only the plains and the width of the Rockies. The Nor' Westers not only did this, but passed down the middle of the Rockies for nearly a thousand miles.

Before doubling the Horn the Isaac Todd was to sail from Quebec to England for convoy of a war-ship. The Nor' Westers naïve assurance of victory was only exceeded by their utter indifference to danger, difficulty, and distance in the attainment of an end. In view of the terror which the Isaac Todd was alleged to have inspired in MacDougall's mind, it is interesting to know what the Nor' Westers thought of their ship. "A twenty-gun letter of marque with a mongrel crew," writes MacDonald of Garth, "a miserable sailor with a miserable commander and a rascally crew." On the way out MacDonald transferred to the British convoy Raccoon, leaving the frisky old Governor MacTavish with his gay barmaid Jane[19] drinking pottle deep on the Isaac Todd, where the rightly disgusted captain was not on speaking terms with his Excellency. "We were nearly six weeks before we could double Cape Horn, and were driven half-way to the Cape of Good Hope; ... at last doubled the cape under topsails, ... the deck one sheet of ice for six weeks, ... our sails one frozen sheet; ... lost sight of the Isaac Todd in a gale," wrote MacDonald on the Raccoon.

It will be remembered that Hunt's overlanders arrived at Astoria months after the Pacific Company's ship. Such swift coasters of the wilderness were the Nor' Westers, this overland party came sweeping down the Columbia, ten canoes strong, hale, hearty, singing as they paddled, a month before the Raccoon had come, six months before their own ship, the Isaac Todd.

And what did MacDougall do? Threw open his gates in welcome, let an army of eighty rivals camp under shelter of his fort guns, demeaned himself into a pusillanimous, little, running fetch-and-carry at the beck of the Nor' Westers, instead of keeping sternly inside his fort, starving rivals into surrender, or training his cannon upon them if they did not decamp.

Alexander Henry, the partner at the head of these dauntless Nor' Westers, says their provisions were "nearly all gone." But, oh! the bragging voyageurs told those quaking Astorians terrible things of what the Isaac Todd would do. There were to be British convoys and captures and prize-money and prisoners of war carried off to Sainte Anne alone knew where. The American-born scorned these exaggerated yarns, knowing their purpose, but not so MacDougall. All his pot-valiant courage sank at the thought of the Isaac Todd, and when the campers ran up a British flag he forbade the display of American colours above Astoria. The end of it was that he sold out Mr. Astor's interests at forty cents on the dollar, probably salving his conscience with the excuse that he had saved that percentage of property from capture by the Raccoon.

At the end of November a large ship was sighted standing in over the bar with all sails spread but no ensign out. Three shots were fired from Astoria. There was no answer. What if this were the long-lost Mr. Hunt coming back from Alaskan trade on the Beaver? The doughty Nor' Westers hastily packed their furs, ninety-two bales in all, and sent their voyageurs scampering up-stream to hide and await a signal. But MacDougall was equal to the emergency. He launched out for the ship, prepared to be an American if it were the Beaver with Mr. Hunt, a Nor' Wester if it were the Raccoon with a company partner.

It was the Raccoon, and the British captain addressed the Astorians in words that have become historic: "Is this the fort I've heard so much about? D—— me, I could batter it down in two hours with a four-pounder!"

Two weeks later the Union Jack was hoisted above Astoria, with traders and marines drawn up under arms to fire a volley. A bottle of Madeira was broken against the flagstaff, the country pronounced a British possession by the captain, cheers given, and eleven guns fired from the bastions.

At this stage all accounts, particularly American accounts, have rung down the curtain on the catastrophe, leaving the Nor' Westers intoxicated with success. But another act was to complete the disasters of Astoria, for the very excess of intoxication brought swift judgment on the revelling Nor' Westers.

The Raccoon left on the last day of 1813. MacDougall had been appointed partner in the North-West Company, and the other Canadians re-engaged under their own flag. When Hunt at last arrived in the Pedler, which he had chartered after the wreck of Mr. Astor's third vessel, the Lark, it was too late to do more than carry away those Americans still loyal to Mr. Astor. Farnham was left at Kamtchatka, whence he made his way to Europe. The others were captured off California and they afterward scattered to all parts of the world. Early in April, 1814, a brigade of Nor' Westers, led by MacDonald of Garth and the younger MacTavish, set out for the long journey across the mountains and prairie to the company's headquarters at Port William. In the flotilla of ten canoes went many of the old Astorians. Two weeks afterward came the belated Isaac Todd with the Nor' Westers' white flag at its foretop and the dissolute old Governor MacTavish holding a high carnival of riot in the cabin.

No darker picture exists than that of Astoria—or Fort George, as the British called it—under Governor MacTavish's régime. The picture is from the hand of a North-West partner himself. "Not in bed till 2 A. M.; ... the gentlemen and the crew all drunk; ... famous fellows for grog they are; ... diced for articles belonging to Mr. M.," Alexander Henry had written when the Raccoon was in port; and now under Governor MacTavish's vicious example every pretence to decency was discarded.

"Avec les loups il faut hurler" was a common saying among Nor' Westers, and perhaps that very assimilation to the native races which contributed so much to success also contributed to the trader's undoing. White men and Indians vied with each other in mutual debasement. Chinook and Saxon and Frenchmen alike lay on the sand sodden with corruption; and if one died from carousals, companions weighted neck and feet with stones and pushed the corpse into the river. Quarrels broke out between the wassailing governor and the other partners. Emboldened, the underlings and hangers-on indulged in all sorts of theft. "All the gentlemen were intoxicated," writes one who was present; seven hours rowing one mile, innocently states the record of another day, the tide running seven feet high past the fort.

The spring rains had ceased. Mountain peaks emerged from the empurpled horizon in domes of opal above the clouds, and the Columbia was running its annual mill-race of spring floods, waters milky from the silt of countless glaciers and turbulent from the rush of a thousand cataracts. Governor MacTavish[20] and Alexander Henry had embarked with six voyageurs to cross the river. A blustering wind caught the sail. A tidal wave pitched amidships. The craft filled and sank within sight of the fort.

So perished the conquerors of Astoria!

CHAPTER IV
THE ANCIENT HUDSON'S BAY COMPANY WAKENS UP

Those eighty[21] Astorians and Nor' Westers who set inland with their ten canoes and boats under protection of two swivels encountered as many dangers on the long trip across the continent as they had left at Fort George.

Following the wandering course of the Columbia, the traders soon passed the international boundary northward into the Arrow Lakes with their towering sky-line of rampart walls, on to the great bend of the Columbia where the river becomes a tumultuous torrent milky with glacial sediment, now raving through a narrow cañon, now teased into a white whirlpool by obstructing rocks, now tumbling through vast shadowy forests, now foaming round the green icy masses of some great glacier, and always mountain-girt by the tent-like peaks of the eternal snows.

"A plain, unvarnished tale, my dear Bellefeuille," wrote the mighty MacDonald of Garth in his eighty-sixth year for a son; but the old trader's tale needed no varnish of rhetoric. "Nearing the mountains we got scarce of provisions; ... bought horses for beef.... Here (at the Great Bend) we left canoes and began a mountain pass (Yellow Head Pass).... The river meanders much, ... and we cut across, ... holding by one another's hands, ... wading to the hips in water, dashing in, frozen at one point, thawed at the next, ... frozen before we dashed in, ... our men carrying blankets and provisions on their heads; ... four days' hard work before we got to Jasper House at the source of the Athabasca, sometimes camping on snow twenty feet deep, so that the fires we made in the evening were fifteen or twenty feet below us in the morning."

They had now crossed the mountains, and taking to canoes again paddled down-stream to the portage between Athabasca River and the Saskatchewan. Tramping sixty miles, they reached Fort Augustus (Edmonton) on the Saskatchewan, where canoes were made on the spot, and the voyageurs launched down-stream a trifling distance of two thousand miles by the windings of the river, past Lake Winnipeg southward to Fort William, the Nor' Westers' headquarters on Lake Superior.

Here the capture of Astoria was reported, and bales to the value of a million dollars in modern money sent east in fifty canoes with an armed guard of three hundred men.[22] Coasting along the north shore of Lake

Superior, the voyageurs came to the Sault and found Mr. Johnston's establishment a scene of smoking ruins. It was necessary to use the greatest caution not to attract the notice of warring parties on the Lakes.

Indian voyageurs "packing" over long portage, each packet containing from fifty to one hundred pounds.

"Overhauled a canoe going eastward, ... a Mackinaw trader and four Indians with a dozen fresh American scalps," writes MacDonald, showing to what a pass things had come. Two days later a couple of boats were overtaken and compelled to halt by a shot from MacDonald's swivels. The strangers proved to be the escaping crew of a British ship which had been captured by two American schooners, and the British officer bore bad news. The American schooners were now on the lookout for the rich prize of furs being taken east in the North-West canoes. Slipping under the nose of these schooners in the dark, the officer hurried to Mackinac, leaving the Nor' Westers hidden in the mouth of French River. William MacKay, a Nor' West partner, at once sallied out to the defence of the furs.

Determined to catch the brigade, one schooner was hovering about the Sault, the other cruising into the countless recesses of the north shore. Against the latter the Mackinaw traders directed their forces, boarding her, and, as MacDonald tells with brutal frankness, "pinning the crew with fixed bayonets to the deck." Lying snugly at anchor, the victors awaited the coming of the other unsuspecting schooner, let her cast anchor, bore down upon her, poured in a broadside, and took both schooners to Mackinac. Freed from all apprehension of capture, the North-West brigade proceeded eastward to the Ottawa River, and without further adventure came to Montreal, where all was wild confusion from another cause.

At the very time when war endangered the entire route of the Nor' Westers from Montreal to the Pacific, the Hudson's Bay Company awakened from its long sleep. While Mr. Astor was pushing his schemes in the United States, Lord Selkirk was formulating plans for the control of all Canada's fur trade. Like Mr. Astor, he too had been the guest at the North-West banquets in the Beaver Club, Montreal, and had heard fabulous things from those magnates of the north about wealth made in the fur trade. Returning to England, Lord Selkirk bought up enough stock of the Hudson's Bay Company to give him full control, and secured from the shareholders an enormous grant of land surrounding the mouths of the Red and Assiniboine rivers.

Where the Assiniboine joins the northern Red were situated Fort Douglas (later Fort Garry, now Winnipeg), the headquarters of the Hudson's Bay Company, and Fort Gibraltar, the North-West post whence supplies were sent all the way from the Mandans on the Missouri to the Eskimo in the arctics.

Not satisfied with this coup, Lord Selkirk engaged Colin Robertson, an old Nor' Wester, to gather a brigade of voyageurs two hundred strong at Montreal and proceed up the Nor' Westers' route to Athabasca, MacKenzie River, and the Rockies. This was the noisy, blustering, bragging company of gaily-bedizened fellows that had turned the streets of Montreal into a roistering booth when the Astorians came to the end of their long eastward journey. Poor, fool-happy revellers! Eighteen of them died of starvation in the far, cold north, owing to the conflict between Fort Douglas and Gibraltar, which delayed supplies.

Beginning in 1811, Lord Selkirk poured a stream of colonists to his newly-acquired territory by way of Churchill and York Factory on Hudson Bay. These people were given lands, and in return expected to defend the Hudson's Bay Company from Nor' Westers. The Nor' Westers struck back by discouraging the colonists, shipping them free out of the country, and getting possession of their arms.

Miles MacDonell, formerly of the King's Royal Regiment, New York, governor of the Hudson's Bay Company at Fort Douglas, at once issued proclamations forbidding Indians to trade furs with Nor' Westers and ordering Nor' Westers from the country. On the strength of these proclamations two or three outlying North-West forts were destroyed and North-West fur brigades rifled. Duncan Cameron,[23] the North-West partner at Fort Gibraltar, countered by letting his Bois-Brûlés, a ragged half-breed army of wild plain rangers under Cuthbert Grant, canter across the two miles that separated the rival forts, and pour a volley of musketry into the Hudson Bay houses. To save the post for the Hudson's Bay Company, Miles MacDonell gave himself up and was shipped out of the country.

But the Hudson's Bay fort was only biding its time till the valiant North-West defenders had scattered to their winter posts. Then an armed party seized Duncan Cameron not far from the North-West fort, and with pistol cocked by one man, publicly horsewhipped the Nor' Wester. Afterward, when Semple, the new Hudson's Bay governor, was absent from Fort Douglas and could not therefore be held responsible for consequences, the Hudson's Bay men, led by the same Colin Robertson who had brought the large brigade from Montreal, marched across the prairie to Fort Gibraltar, captured Mr. Cameron, plundered all the Nor' Westers' stores, and burned the fort to the ground. By way of retaliation for MacDonell's expulsion, the North-West partner was shipped down to Hudson Bay, where he might as well have been on Devil's Island for all the chance of escape.

One company at fault as often as the other, similar outrages were perpetrated in all parts of the north fur country, the blood of rival traders being spilt without a qualm of conscience or thought of results. The effect of this conflict among white men on the bloodthirsty red-skins one may guess. The Bois-Brûlés were clamouring for Cuthbert Grant's permission to wipe the English—meaning the Hudson's Bay men—off the earth; and the Swampy Crees and Saulteaux under Chief Peguis were urging Governor Semple to let them defend the Hudson's Bay—meaning kill the Nor' Westers.

The crisis followed sharp on the destruction of Fort Gibraltar. That post had sent all supplies to North-West forts. If Fort Douglas of the Hudson's Bay Company, past which North-West canoes must paddle to turn westward to the plains, should intercept the incoming brigade of Nor' Westers' supplies, what would become of the two thousand North-West traders and voyageurs and engagés inland? Whether the Hudson's Bay had such intentions or not, the Nor' Westers were determined to prevent the possibility.

Like the red cross that called ancient clans to arms, scouts went scouring across the plains to rally the Bois-Brûlés from Portage la Prairie and Souris and Qu'Appelle.[24] Led by Cuthbert Grant, they skirted north of the Hudson's Bay post to meet and disembark supplies above Fort Douglas. It was but natural for the settlers to mistake this armed cavalcade, red with paint and chanting war-songs, for hostiles.

Rushing to Fort Douglas, the settlers gave the alarm. Ordering a field-piece to follow, Governor Semple marched out with a little army of twenty-eight Hudson's Bay men. The Nor' Westers thought that he meant to obstruct their way till his other forces had captured their coming canoes. The Hudson's Bay thought that Cuthbert Grant meant to attack the Selkirk settlers.

It was in the evening of June 19, 1816. The two parties met at the edge of a swamp beside a cluster of trees, since called Seven Oaks. Nor' Westers say that Governor Semple caught the bridle of their scout and tried to throw him from his horse. The Hudson's Bay say that the governor had no sooner got within range than the half-breed scout leaped down and fired from the shelter of his horse, breaking Semple's thigh.

It is well known how the first blood of battle has the same effect on all men of whatever race. The human is eclipsed by that brute savagery which comes down from ages when man was a creature of prey. In a trice twenty-one of the Hudson's Bay men lay dead. While Grant had turned to obtain carriers to bear the wounded governor off the field, poor Semple was brutally murdered by one of the Deschamps family, who ran from body to body, perpetrating the crimes of ghouls. It was in vain for Grant to expostulate. The wild blood of a savage race had been roused. The soft velvet night of the summer prairie, with the winds crooning the sad monotone of a limitless sea, closed over a scene of savages drunk with slaughter, of men gone mad with the madness of murder, of warriors thinking to gain courage by drinking the blood of the slain.

Grant saved the settlers' lives by sending them down-stream to Lake Winnipeg, where dwelt the friendly Chief Peguis. On the river they met the indomitable Miles MacDonell, posting back to resume authority. He brought news that must have been good cheer. Moved by the expelled governor's account of disorders, Lord Selkirk was hastening north, armed with the authority of a justice of the peace, escorted by soldiers in full regalia as became his station, with cannon mounted on his barges and stores of munition that ill agreed with the professions of a peaceful justice.

The time has gone past for quibbling as to the earl's motives in pushing north armed like a lord of war. MacDonell hastened back and met him with his army of Des Meurons[25] at the Sault. In August Lord Selkirk appeared before Fort William with uniformed soldiers in eleven boats. The justice of the peace set his soldiers digging trenches opposite the Nor' Westers' fort. As for the Nor' Westers, they had had enough of blood. They capitulated without one blow. Selkirk took full possession.

Six months later (1817), when ice had closed the rivers, he sent Captain d'Orsennens overland westward to Red River, where Fort Douglas was captured back one stormy winter night by the soldiers scaling the fort walls during a heavy snowfall. The conflict had been just as ruthless on the Saskatchewan. Nor' Westers were captured as they disembarked to pass Grand Rapids and shipped down to York Factory, where Franklin the explorer saw four Nor' Westers maltreated. One of them was the same John George MacTavish who had helped to capture Astoria; another, Frobisher, a partner, was ultimately done to death by the abuse. The Deschamps murderers of Seven Oaks fled south, where their crimes brought terrible vengeance from American traders.

Victorious all along the line, the Hudson's Bay Company were in a curious quandary. Suits enough were pressing in the courts to ruin both companies; and for the most natural reason in the world, neither Hudson Bay nor Nor'

Wester could afford to have the truth told and the crimes probed. There was only one way out of the dilemma. In March, 1821, the companies amalgamated under the old title of Hudson's Bay. In April, 1822, a new fort was built half-way between the sites of Gibraltar and Fort Douglas, and given the new name of Fort Garry by Sir George Simpson, the governor, to remove all feeling of resentment. The thousand men thrown out of employment by the union at once crossed the line and enlisted with American traders.

The Hudson's Bay was now strong with the strength that comes from victorious conflict—so strong, indeed, that it not only held the Canadian field, but in spite of the American law[26] forbidding British traders in the United States, reached as far south as Utah and the Missouri, where it once more had a sharp brush with lusty rivals.

CHAPTER V
MR. ASTOR'S COMPANY ENCOUNTERS NEW OPPONENTS

That Andrew Henry whom Lisa had sought when he pursued the Astorians up the Missouri continued to be dogged by misfortune on the west side of the mountains. Game was scarce and his half-starving followers were scattered, some to the British posts in the north, some to the Spaniards in the south, and some to the nameless graves of the mountains. Henry forced his way back over the divide and met Lisa in the Aricara country. The British war broke out and the Missouri Company were compelled to abandon the dangerous territory of the Blackfeet, who could purchase arms from the British traders, raid the Americans, and scurry back to Canada.

When Lisa died in 1820 more than three hundred Missouri men were again in the mountains; but they suffered the same ill luck. Jones and Immel's party were annihilated by the Blackfeet; and Pilcher, who succeeded to Lisa's position and dauntlessly crossed over to the Columbia, had all his supplies stolen, reaching the Hudson's Bay post, Fort Colville, almost destitute. The British rivals received him with that hospitality for which they were renowned when trade was not involved, and gave him escort up the Columbia, down the Athabasca and Saskatchewan to Red River, thence overland to the Mandan country and St. Louis.

These two disasters marked the wane of the Missouri Company.

But like the shipwrecked sailor, no sooner safe on land than he must to sea again, the indomitable Andrew Henry linked his fortunes with General Ashley of St. Louis. Gathering to the new standard Campbell, Bridger, Fitzpatrick, Beckworth, Smith, and the Sublettes—men who made the Rocky Mountain trade famous—Ashley and Henry led one hundred men to the mountains the first year and two hundred the next. In that time not less than twenty-five lives were lost among Aricaras and Blackfeet. Few pelts were obtained and the expeditions were a loss.

But in 1824 came a change. Smith met Hudson's Bay trappers loaded with beaver pelts in the Columbia basin, west of the Rockies. They had become separated from their leader, Alexander Ross, an old Astorian. Details of this bargain will never be known; but when Smith came east he had the Hudson's Bay furs. This was the first brush between Rocky Mountain men and the Hudson's Bay, and the mountain trappers scored.

Henceforth, to save time, the active trappers met their supplies annually at a rendezvous in the mountains, in Pierre's Hole, a broad valley below the Tetons, or Jackson's Hole, east of the former, or Ogden's Hole at Salt Lake. Seventeen Rocky Mountain men had been massacred by the Snake Indians in the Columbia basin; but that did not deter General Ashley himself from going up the Platte, across the divide to Salt Lake. Here he found Peter Ogden, a Hudson's Bay trapper, with an enormous prize of beaver pelts. When the Hudson's Bay man left Salt Lake, he had no furs; and when General Ashley came away, his packers were laden with a quarter of a million dollars worth of pelts. This was the second brush between Rocky Mountain and Hudson's Bay, and again the mountaineers scored.

The third encounter was more to the credit of both companies. After three years' wanderings, Smith found himself stranded and destitute at the British post of Fort Vancouver. Fifteen of his men had been killed, his horses taken and peltries stolen. The Hudson's Bay sent a punitive force to recover his property, gave him a $20,000 draft for the full value of the recovered furs, and sent him up the Columbia. Thenceforth Rocky Mountain trappers and Hudson's Bay respected each other's rights in the valley of the Columbia, but southward the old code prevailed. Fitzpatrick, a Rocky Mountain trader, came on the same poor Peter Ogden at Salt Lake trading with the Indians, and at once plied the argument of whisky so actively that the furs destined for Red River went over the mountains to St. Louis.

The trapper probably never heard of a Nemesis; but a curious retribution seemed to follow on the heels of outrage.

Lisa had tried to balk the Astorians, and the Missouri Company went down before Indian hostility. The Nor' Westers jockeyed the Astorians out of their possessions and were in league with murderers at the massacre of Seven Oaks; but the Nor' Westers were jockeyed out of existence by the Hudson's Bay under Lord Selkirk. The Hudson's Bay had been guilty of rank outrage—particularly on the Saskatchewan, where North-West partners were seized, manacled, and sent to a wilderness—and now the Hudson's Bay were cheated, cajoled, overreached by the Rocky Mountain trappers. And the Rocky Mountain trappers, in their turn, met a rival that could outcheat their cheatery.

In 1831 the mountains were overrun with trappers from all parts of America. Men from every State in the Union, those restless spirits who have pioneered every great movement of the race, turned their faces to the wilderness for furs as a later generation was to scramble for gold.

In the summer of 1832, when the hunters came down to Pierre's Hole for their supplies, there were trappers who had never before summered away from Detroit and Mackinaw and Hudson Bay.[27] There were half-wild

Frenchmen from Quebec who had married Indian wives and cast off civilization as an ill-fitting garment. There were Indian hunters with the mellow, rhythmic tones that always betray native blood. There were lank New Englanders under Wyeth of Boston, erect as a mast pole, strong of jaw, angular of motion, taking clumsily to buckskins. There were the Rocky Mountain men in tattered clothes, with unkempt hair and long beards, and a trick of peering from their bushy brows like an enemy from ambush. There were probably odd detachments from Captain Bonneville's adventurers on the Platte, where a gay army adventurer was trying his luck as fur trader and explorer. And there was a new set of men, not yet weather-worn by the wilderness, alert, watchful, ubiquitous, scattering themselves among all groups where they could hear everything, see all, tell nothing, always shadowing the Rocky Mountain men who knew every trail of the wilds and should be good pilots to the best hunting-grounds. By the middle of July all business had been completed, and the trappers spent a last night round camp-fires, spinning yarns of the hunt.

Early in the morning when the Rocky Mountain men were sallying from the valley, they met a cavalcade of one hundred and fifty Blackfeet. Each party halted to survey its opponent. In less than ten years the Rocky Mountain men had lost more than seventy comrades among hostiles. Even now the Indians were flourishing a flag captured from murdered Hudson's Bay hunters.

The number of whites disconcerted the Indians. Their warlike advance gave place to friendliness. One chief came forward with the hand of comity extended. The whites were not deceived. Many a time had Rocky Mountain trappers been lured to their death by such overtures.

No excuse is offered for the hunters. The code of the wilderness never lays the unction of a hypocritical excuse to conscience. The trappers sent two scouts to parley with the detested enemy. One trapper, with Indian blood in his veins and Indian thirst for the avengement of a kinsman's death in his heart, grasped the chief's extended hand with the clasp of a steel trap. On the instant the other scout fired. The powerless chief fell dead; and using their horses as a breastwork, the Blackfeet hastily threw themselves behind some timber, cast up trenches, and shot from cover.

All the trappers at the rendezvous spurred to the fight, priming guns, casting off valuables, making their wills as they rode. The battle lasted all day; and when under cover of night the Indians withdrew, twelve men lay dead on the trappers' side, as many more were wounded; and the Blackfeet's loss was twice as great. For years this tribe exacted heavy atonement for the death of warriors behind the trenches of Pierre's Hole.

Leaving Pierre's Hole the mountaineers scattered to their rocky fastnesses, but no sooner had they pitched camp on good hunting-grounds than the strangers who had shadowed them at the rendezvous came up. Breaking camp, the Rocky Mountain men would steal away by new and unknown passes to another valley. A day or two later, having followed by tent-poles dragging the ground, or brushwood broken by the passing packers, the pertinacious rivals would reappear. This went on persistently for three months.

Infuriated by such tactics, the mountaineers planned to lead the spies a dance. Plunging into the territory of hostiles they gave their pursuers the slip. Neither party probably intended that matters should become serious; but that is always the fault of the white man when he plays the dangerous game of war with Indians. The spying party was ambushed, the leader slain, his flesh torn from his body and his skeleton thrown into the river. A few months later the Rocky Mountain traders paid for this escapade. Fitzpatrick, the same trapper who had "lifted" Ogden's furs and led this game against the spies, was robbed among Indians instigated by white men of the American Fur Company. This marked the beginning of the end with the Rocky Mountain trappers.

The American Fur Company, which Mr. Astor had organized and stuck to through good repute and evil repute, was now officered by Ramsay Crooks and Farnham and Robert Stuart, who had remained loyal to Mr. Astor in Astoria and been schooled in a discipline that offered no quarter to enemies. The purchase of the Mackinaw Company gave the American Company all those posts between the Great Lakes and the height of land dividing the Mississippi and Missouri. When Congress excluded foreign traders in 1816, all the Nor' Westers' posts south of the boundary fell to the American Fur Company; and sturdy old Nor' Westers, who had been thrown out by the amalgamation with the Hudson's Bay, also added to the Americans' strength. Kenneth MacKenzie, with Laidlaw, Lament, and Kipp, had a line of posts from Green Bay to the Missouri held by an American to evade the law, but known as the Columbia Company.

This organization[28] the American Fur Company bought out, placing MacKenzie at the mouth of the Yellowstone, where he built Fort Union and became the Pooh-Bah of the whole region, living in regal style like his ancestral Scottish chiefs. "King of the Missouri" white men called him, "big Indian me" the Blackfeet said; and "big Indian me" he was to them, for he was the first trader to win both their friendship and the Crows'.

Here MacKenzie entertained Prince Maximilian of Wied and Catlin the artist and Audubon the naturalist, and had as his constant companion Hamilton, an English nobleman living in disguise and working for the fur company. Many an unmeant melodrama was enacted under the walls of Union in MacKenzie's reign.

Once a free trapper came floating down the Missouri with his canoe full of beaver-pelts, which he quickly exchanged for the gay attire to be obtained at Fort Union. Oddly enough, though the fellow was a French-Canadian, he had long, flaxen hair, of which he was inordinately vain. Strutting about the court-yard, feeling himself a very prince of importance, he saw MacKenzie's pretty young Indian wife. Each paid the other the tribute of adoration that was warmer than it was wise. The dénouement was a vision of the flaxen-haired Siegfried sprinting at the top of his speed through the fort gate, with the irate MacKenzie flourishing a flail to the rear. The matter did not end here. The outraged Frenchman swore to kill MacKenzie on sight, and haunted the fort gates with a loaded rifle till MacKenzie was obliged to hire a mulatto servant to "wing" the fellow with a shot in the shoulder, when he was brought into the fort, nursed back to health, and sent away.

At another time two Rocky Mountain trappers built an opposition fort just below Union and lay in wait for the coming of the Blackfeet to trade with the American Fur Company. MacKenzie posted a lookout on his bastion. The moment the Indians were descried, out sallied from Fort Union a band in full regalia, with drum and trumpet and piccolo and fife—wonders that would have lured the astonished Indians to perdition. Behind the band came gaudy presents for the savages, and what was not supposed to be in the Indian country—liquor. When these methods failed to outbuy rivals, MacKenzie did not hesitate to pay twelve dollars for a beaver-skin not worth two. The Rocky Mountain trappers were forced to capitulate, and their post passed over to the American Fur Company.

In the ruins of their post was enacted a fitting finale to the turbulent conflicts of the American traders. The Deschamps family, who had perpetrated the worst butcheries on the field of Seven Oaks, in the fight between Hudson's Bay and Nor' Westers, had acted as interpreters for the Rocky Mountain trappers. Boastful of their murderous record in Canada, the father, mother, and eight grown children were usually so violent in their carousals that Hamilton, the English gentleman, used to quiet their outrage and prevent trouble by dropping laudanum in their cups. Once they slept so heavily that the whole fort was in a panic lest their sleep lasted to eternity; but the revellers came to life defiant as ever. At Union was a very handsome young half-breed fellow by the name of Gardepie, whose life the Deschamps harpies attempted to take from sheer jealousy and love of crime. Joined by two free trappers, Gardepie killed the elder Deschamps one morning at breakfast with all the gruesome mutilation of Indian custom. He at the same time wounded a younger son. Spurred by the haglike mother and nerved to the deed with alcohol, the Deschamps undertook to avenge their father's death by killing all the whites of the fur post. One man had fallen when the alarm was carried to Fort Union.

Twice had the Deschamps robbed Fort Union. Many trappers had been assassinated by a Deschamps. Indians had been flogged by them for no other purpose than to inflict torture. Beating on the doors of Fort Union, the wife of their last victim called out that the Deschamps were on the warpath.

The traders of Fort Union solemnly raised hands and took an oath to exterminate the murderous clan. The affair had gone beyond MacKenzie's control. Seizing cannon and ammunition, the traders crossed the prairie to the abandoned fort of the Rocky Mountain trappers, where the murderers were intrenched. All valuables were removed from the fort. Time was given for the family to prepare for death. Then the guns were turned on the house. Suddenly that old harpy of crime, the mother, rushed out, holding forward the Indian pipe of peace and begging for mercy.

She got all the mercy that she had ever given, and fell shot through the heart.

At last the return firing ceased. Who would enter and learn if the Deschamps were all dead? Treachery was feared. The assailants set fire to the fort. In the light of the flames one man was espied crouching in the bastion. A trader rushed forward exultant to shoot the last of the Deschamps; but a shot from the bastion sent him leaping five feet into the air to fall back dead, and a yell of fiendish victory burst from the burning tower.[29]

Again the assailants fired a volley. No answering shot came from the fort. Rushing through the smoke the traders found François Deschamps backed up in a corner like a beast at bay, one wrist broken and all ammunition gone. A dozen rifle-shots cracked sharp. The fellow fell and his body was thrown into the flames. The old mother was buried without shroud or coffin in the clay bank of the river. A young boy mortally wounded was carried from the ruins to die in Union.

This dark act marked the last important episode in the long conflict among traders. A decline of values followed the civil war. Settlers were rushing overland to Oregon, and Fort Union went into the control of the militia. To-day St. Louis is still a centre of trade in manufactured furs, and St. Paul yet receives raw pelts from trappers who wander through the forests of Minnesota and Idaho and the mountains. Only a year ago the writer employed as guides in the mountains three trappers who have spent their lives ranging the northern wilds and the Upper Missouri; but outside the mountain and forest wastes, the vast hunting-grounds of the famous old trappers have been chalked off by the fences of settlers.

In Canada, too, bloodshed marked the last of the conflict—once in the seventies when Louis Riel, a half-breed demagogue, roused the Metis against the surveyors sent to prepare Red River for settlement, and again in 1885 when this unhanged rascal incited the half-breeds of the Saskatchewan to rebellion over title-deeds to their lands. Though the Hudson's Bay Company had nothing to do with either complaint, the conflict waged round their forts.

In the first affair the ragged army of rebels took possession of Fort Garry, and for no other reason than the love of killing that riots in savage blood as in a wolf's, shot down Scott outside the fort gates. In the second rebellion Riel's allies came down on the far-isolated Fort Pitt three hundred strong, captured the fort, and took the factor, Mr. MacLean, and his family to northern wastes, marching them through swamps breast-high with spring floods, where General Middleton's troops could not follow. The children of the family had been in the habit of bribing old Indian gossips into telling stories by gifts of tobacco; and the friendship now stood the white family in good stead. Day and night in all the weeks of captivity the friendly Indians never left the side of the trader's family, slipping between the hostiles and the young children, standing guard at the tepee door, giving them weapons of defence till all were safely back among the whites.

This time Riel was hanged, and the Hudson's Bay Company resumed its sway of all that realm between Labrador and the Pacific north of the Saskatchewan.

Traders' lives are like a white paper with a black spot. The world looks only at the black spot.

In spite of his faults when in conflict with rivals, it has been the trader living alone, unprotected and unfearing, one voice among a thousand, who has restrained the Indian tribes from massacres that would have rolled back the progress of the West a quarter of a century.

CHAPTER VI
THE FRENCH TRAPPER

To live hard and die hard, king in the wilderness and pauper in the town, lavish to-day and penniless to-morrow—such was the life of the most picturesque figure in America's history.

Take a map of America. Put your finger on any point between the Gulf of Mexico and Hudson Bay, or the Great Lakes and the Rockies. Ask who was the first man to blaze a trail into this wilderness; and wherever you may point, the answer is the same—the French trapper.

Impoverished English noblemen of the seventeenth century took to freebooting, Spanish dons to piracy and search for gold; but for the young French noblesse the way to fortune was by the fur trade. Freedom from restraint, quick wealth, lavish spending, and adventurous living all appealed to a class that hated the menial and slow industry of the farm. The only capital required for the fur trade was dauntless courage. Merchants were keen to supply money enough to stock canoes with provisions for trade in the wilderness. What would be equivalent to $5,000 of modern money was sufficient to stock four trappers with trade enough for two years.

At the end of that time the sponsors looked for returns in furs to the value of eight hundred per cent on their capital. The original investment would be deducted, and the enormous profit divided among the trappers and their outfitters. In the heyday of the fur trade, when twenty beaver-skins were got for an axe, it was no unusual thing to see a trapper receive what would be equivalent to $3,000 of our money as his share of two years' trapping. But in the days when the French were only beginning to advance up the Missouri from Louisiana and across from Michilimackinac to the Mississippi vastly larger fortunes were made.

Two partners[30] have brought out as much as $200,000 worth of furs from the great game preserve between Lake Superior and the head waters of the Missouri after eighteen months' absence from St. Louis or from Montreal. The fur country was to the young French nobility what a treasure-ship was to a pirate. In vain France tried to keep her colonists on the land by forbidding trade without a license. Fines, the galleys for life, even death for repeated offence, were the punishments held over the head of the illicit trader. The French trapper evaded all these by staying in the wilds till he amassed fortune enough to buy off punishment, or till he had lost taste for civilized life and remained in the wilderness, coureur des bois, voyageur, or leader of a band of half-wild retainers whom he ruled like a feudal baron, becoming a curious connecting link between the savagery of the New World and the noblesse of the Old.

Duluth, of the Lakes region; La Salle, of the Mississippi; Le Moyne d'Iberville, ranging from Louisiana to Hudson Bay; La Mothe Cadillac in Michilimackinac, Detroit, and Louisiana; La Vérendrye exploring from Lake Superior to the Rockies; Radisson on Hudson Bay—all won their fame as explorers and discoverers in pursuit of the fur trade. A hundred years before any English mind knew of the Missouri, French voyageurs had gone beyond the Yellowstone. Before the regions now called Minnesota, Dakota, and Wisconsin were known to New Englanders, the French were trapping about the head waters of the Mississippi; and two centuries ago a company of daring French hunters went to New Mexico to spy on Spanish trade.

East of the Mississippi were two neighbours whom the French trapper shunned—the English colonists and the Iroquois. North of the St. Lawrence was a power that he shunned still more—the French governor, who had legal right to plunder the peltries of all who traded and trapped without license. But between St. Louis and MacKenzie River was a great unclaimed wilderness, whence came the best furs.

Naturally, this became the hunting-ground of the French trapper.

There were four ways by which he entered his hunting-ground: (1) Sailing from Quebec to the mouth of the Mississippi, he ascended the river in pirogue or dugout, but this route was only possible for a man with means to pay for the ocean voyage. (2) From Detroit overland to the Illinois, or Ohio, which he rafted down to the Mississippi, and then taking to canoe turned north. (3) From Michilimackinac, which was always a grand rendezvous for the French and Indian hunters, to Green Bay on Lake Michigan, thence up-stream to Fox River, overland to the Wisconsin, and down-stream to the Mississippi. (4) Up the Ottawa through "the Soo" to Lake Superior and westward to the hunting-ground. Whichever way he went his course was mainly up-stream and north: hence the name Pays d'en Haut vaguely designated the vast hunting-ground that lay between the Missouri and the MacKenzie River.

The French trapper was and is to-day as different from the English as the gamester is from the merchant. Of all the fortunes brought from the Missouri to St. Louis, or from the Pays d'en Haut to Montreal, few escaped the gaming-table and dram-shop. Where the English trader saves his returns, Pierre lives high and plays high, and lords it about the fur post till he must pawn the gay clothing he has bought for means to exist to the opening of the next hunting season.

It is now that he goes back to some birch tree marked by him during the preceding winter's hunt, peels the bark off in a great seamless rind, whittles out ribs for a canoe from cedar, ash, or pine, and shapes the green bark to the curve of a canoe by means of stakes and stones down each side. Lying on his back in the sun spinning yarns of the great things he has done and will do, he lets the birch harden and dry to the proper form, when he fits the gunwales to the ragged edge, lines the inside of the keel with thin pine boards, and tars the seams where the bark has crinkled and split at the junction with the gunwale.

It is in the idle summer season that he and his squaw—for the Pierre adapts, or rather adopts, himself to the native tribes by taking an Indian wife—design the wonderfully bizarre costumes in which the French trapper appears: the beaded toque for festive occasions, the gay moccasins, the buckskin suit fringed with horse-hair and leather in lieu of the Indian scalp-locks, the white caribou capote with horned head-gear to deceive game on the hunter's approach, the powder-case made of a buffalo-horn, the bullet bag of a young otter-skin, the musk-rat or musquash cap, and great gantlets coming to the elbow.

None of these things does the English trader do. If he falls a victim to the temptations awaiting the man from the wilderness in the dram-shop of the trading-post, he takes good care not to spend his all on the spree. He does not affect the hunter's decoy dress, for the simple reason that he prefers to let the Indians do the hunting of the difficult game, while he attends to the trapping that is gain rather than game. For clothes, he is satisfied with cheap material from the shops. And if, like Pierre, the Englishman marries an Indian wife, he either promptly deserts her when he leaves the fur country for the trading-post or sends her to a convent to be educated up to his own level. With Pierre the marriage means that he has cast off the last vestige of civilization and henceforth identifies himself with the life of the savage.

After the British conquest of Canada and the American Declaration of Independence came a change in the status of the French trapper. Before, he had been lord of the wilderness without a rival. Now, powerful English companies poured their agents into his hunting-grounds. Before, he had been a partner in the fur trade. Now, he must either be pushed out or enlist as servant to the newcomer. He who had once come to Montreal and St. Louis with a fortune of peltries on his rafts and canoes, now signed with the great English companies for a paltry one, two, and three hundred dollars a year.

It was but natural in the new state of things that the French trapper, with all his knowledge of forest and stream, should become coureur des bois and voyageur, while the Englishman remained the barterer. In the Mississippi basin the French trappers mainly enlisted with four companies: the Mackinaw Company, radiating from Michilimackinac to the Mississippi; the American Company, up the Missouri; the Missouri Company, officered by St. Louis merchants, westward to the Rockies; and the South-West Company, which was John Jacob Astor's amalgamation of the American and Mackinaw. In Canada the French sided with the Nor' Westers and X. Y.'s, who had sprung up in opposition to the great English Hudson's Bay Company.

Though he had become a burden-carrier for his quondam enemies, the French trapper still saw life through the glamour of la gloire and noblesse, still lived hard and died game, still feasted to-day and starved to-morrow, gambled the clothes off his back and laughed at hardship; courted danger and trolled off one of his chansons brought over to America by ancestors of Normandy, uttered an oath in one breath at the whirlpool ahead and in the next crossed himself reverently with a prayer to Sainte Anne, the voyageurs' saint, just before his canoe took the plunge.

Your Spanish grandee of the Missouri Company, like Manuel Lisa of St. Louis, might sit in a counting-house or fur post adding up rows of figures, and your Scotch merchant chaffer with Indians over the value of a beaver-skin. As for Pierre, give him a canoe sliding past wooded banks with a throb of the keel to the current and the whistle of wild-fowl overhead; clear sky above with a feathering of wind clouds, clear sky below with a feathering of wind clouds, and the canoe between like a bird at poise. Sometimes a fair wind livens the pace; for the voyageurs hoist a blanket sail, and the canoe skims before the breeze like a seagull.

Where the stream gathers force and whirls forward in sharp eddies and racing leaps each voyageur knows what to expect. No man asks questions. The bowman stands up with his eyes to the fore and steel-shod pole ready. Every eye is on that pole. Presently comes a roar, and the green banks begin to race. The canoe no longer glides. It vaults—springs—bounds, with a shiver of live waters under the keel and a buoyant rise to her prow that mounts the crest of each wave fast as wave pursues wave. A fanged rock thrusts up in mid-stream. One deft push of the pole. Each paddler takes the cue; and the canoe shoots past the danger straight as an arrow, righting herself to a new course by another lightning sweep of the pole and paddles.

But the waters gather as if to throw themselves forward. The roar becomes a crash. As if moved by one mind the paddlers brace back. The lightened bow lifts. A white dash of spray. She mounts as she plunges; and the voyageurs are whirling down-stream below a small waterfall. Not a word is spoken to indicate that it is anything unusual to sauter les rapides, as the voyageurs say. The men are soaked. Now, perhaps, some one laughs; for Jean, or Ba'tiste, or the dandy of the crew, got his moccasins wet when the canoe took water. They all settle forward. One paddler pauses to bail out water with his hat.

Traders running a mackinaw or keel-boat down the rapids of Slave River without unloading.

Thus the lowest waterfalls are run without a portage. Coming back this way with canoes loaded to the water-line, there must be a disembarking. If the rapids be short, with water enough to carry the loaded canoe high above rocks that might graze the bark, all hands spring out in the water, but one man who remains to steady the craft; and the canoe is "tracked" up-stream, hauled along by ropes. If the rapids be at all dangerous, each voyageur lands, with pack on his back and pack-straps across his forehead, and runs along the shore. A long portage is measured by the number of pipes the voyageur smokes, each lighting up meaning a brief rest; and a portage of many "pipes" will be taken at a running gait on the hottest days without one word of complaint. Nine miles is the length of one famous portage opposite the Chaudière Falls on the Ottawa.

In winter the voyageur becomes coureur des bois to his new masters. Then for six months endless reaches, white, snow-padded, silent; forests wreathed and bossed with snow; nights in camp on a couch of pines or rolled in robes with a roaring fire to keep the wolves off, melting snow steaming to the heat, meat sputtering at the end of a skewered stick; sometimes to the marche donc! marche donc! of the driver, with crisp tinkling of dog-bells in frosty air, a long journey overland by dog-sled to the trading-post; sometimes that blinding fury which sweeps over the northland, turning earth and air to a white darkness; sometimes a belated traveller cowering under a snow-drift for warmth and wrapping his blanket about him to cross life's Last Divide.

These things were the every-day life of the French trapper.

At present there is only one of the great fur companies remaining—the Hudson's Bay of Canada. In the United States there are only two important centres of trade in furs which are not imported—St. Paul and St. Louis. For both the Hudson's Bay Company and the fur traders of the Upper Missouri the French trapper still works as his ancestors did for the great companies a hundred years ago.

The roadside tramp of to-day is a poor representative of Robin Hoods and Rob Roys; and the French trapper of shambling gait and baggy clothes seen at the fur posts of the north to-day is a poor type of the class who used to stalk through the baronial halls[31] of Montreal's governor like a lord and set the rafters of Fort William's council chamber ringing, and make the wine and the money and the brawls of St. Louis a by-word.

And yet, with all his degeneracy, the French trapper retains a something of his old traditions. A few years ago I was on a northern river steamer going to one of the Hudson's Bay trading-posts. A brawl seemed to sound from the steerage passengers. What was the matter? "Oh," said the captain, "the French trappers going out north for the winter, drunk as usual!"

As he spoke, a voice struck up one of those chansons populaires, which have been sung by every generation of voyageurs since Frenchmen came to America, A La Claire Fontaine, a song which the French trappers' ancestors brought from Normandy hundreds of years ago, about the fickle lady and the faded roses and the vain regrets. Then—was it possible?—these grizzled fellows, dressed in tinkers' tatters, were singing—what? A song of the Grand Monarque which has led armies to battle, but not a song which one would expect to hear in northern wilds—

"Malbrouck s'on va-t-en guerre
Mais quand reviendra a-t-il?"

Three foes assailed the trapper alone in the wilds. The first danger was from the wolf-pack. The second was the Indian hostile egged on by rival traders. This danger the French trapper minimized by identifying himself more completely with the savage than any other fur trader succeeded in doing. The third foe was the most perverse and persevering thief known outside the range of human criminals.

Perhaps the day after the trapper had shot his first deer he discovered fine footprints like a child's hand on the snow around the carcass. He recognises the trail of otter or pekan or mink. It would be useless to bait a deadfall with meat when an unpolluted feast lies on the snow. The man takes one of his small traps and places it across the line of approach. This trap is buried beneath snow or brush. Every trace of man-smell is obliterated. The fresh hide of a deer may be dragged across the snow. Pomatum or castoreum may be daubed on everything touched. He may even handle the trap with deer-hide. Pekan travel in pairs. Besides, the dead deer will be likely to attract more than one forager; so the man sets a circle of traps round the carcass.

The next morning he comes back with high hope. Very little of the deer remains. All the flesh-eaters of the forest, big and little, have been there. Why, then, is there no capture? One trap has been pulled up, sprung, and partly broken. Another carried a little distance off and dumped into a hollow. A third had caught a pekan; but the prisoner had been worried and torn to atoms. Another was tampered with from behind and exposed for very deviltry. Some have disappeared altogether.

Among forest creatures few are mean enough to kill when they have full stomachs, or to eat a trapped brother with untrapped meat a nose-length away.

The French trapper rumbles out some maledictions on le sacré carcajou. Taking a piece of steel like a cheese-tester's instrument, he pokes grains of strychnine into the remaining meat. He might have saved himself the trouble. The next day he finds the poisoned meat mauled and spoiled so that no animal will touch it. There is nothing of the deer but picked bones. So the trapper tries a deadfall for the thief. Again he might have spared himself the trouble. His next visit shows the deadfall torn from behind and robbed without danger to the thief.

Several signs tell the trapper that the marauder is the carcajou or wolverine. All the stealing was done at night; and the wolverine is nocturnal. All the traps had been approached from behind. The wolverine will not cross man's track. The poison in the meat had been scented. Whether the wolverine knows poison, he is too wary to experiment on doubtful diet. The exposing of the traps tells of the curiosity which characterizes the wolverine. Other creatures would have had too much fear. The tracks run back to cover, and not across country like the badger's or the fox's.

Fearless, curious, gluttonous, wary, and suspicious, the mischief-maker and the freebooter and the criminal of the animal world, a scavenger to save the northland from pollution of carrion, and a scourge to destroy wounded, weaklings, and laggards—the wolverine has the nose of a fox, with long, uneven, tusk-like teeth that seem to be expressly made for tearing. The eyes are well set back, greenish, alert with almost human intelligence of the type that preys. Out of the fulness of his wrath one trapper gave a perfect description of the wolverine. He didn't object, he said, to being outrun by a wolf, or beaten by a respectable Indian, but to be outwitted by a little beast the size of a pig with the snout of a fox, the claws of a bear, and the fur of a porcupine's quills, was more than he could stand.

In the economy of nature the wolverine seems to have but one design—destruction. Beaver-dams two feet thick and frozen like rock yield to the ripping onslaught of its claws. He robs everything: the musk-rats' haycock houses; the gopher burrows; the cached elk and buffalo calves under hiding of some shrub while the mothers go off to the watering-place; the traps of his greatest foe, man; the cached provisions of the forest ranger; the graves of the dead; the very tepees and lodges and houses of Indian, half-breed, and white man. While the wolverine is averse to crossing man's track, he will follow it for days, like a shark behind a ship; for he knows as well as the man knows there will be food in the traps when the man is in his lodge, and food in the lodge when the man is at the traps.

But the wolverine has two characteristics by which he may be snared—gluttony and curiosity.

After the deer has disappeared the trapper finds that the wolverine has been making as regular rounds of the traps as he has himself. It is then a question whether the man or the wolverine is to hold the hunting-ground. A case is on record at Moose Factory, on James Bay, of an Indian hunter and his wife who were literally brought to the verge of starvation by a wolverine that nightly destroyed their traps. The contest ended by the starving Indians travelling a hundred miles from the haunts of that "bad devil—oh—he—bad devil—carcajou!" Remembering the curiosity and gluttony of his enemy, the man sets out his strongest steel-traps. He takes some strong-smelling meat, bacon or fish, and places it where the wolverine tracks run. Around this he sets a circle of his traps, tying them securely to poles and saplings and stakes. In all likelihood he has waited his chance for a snowfall which will cover traces of the man-smell.

Night passes. In the morning the man comes to his traps. The meat has been taken. All else is as before. Not a track marks the snow; but in midwinter meat does not walk off by itself. The man warily feels for the hidden traps. Then he notices that one of the stakes has been pulled up and carried off. That is a sign. He prods the ground expectantly. It is as he thought. One trap is gone. It had caught the wolverine; but the cunning beast had pulled with all his strength, snapped the attached sapling, and escaped. A fox or beaver would have gnawed the imprisoned limb off. The wolverine picks the trap up in his teeth and hobbles as hard as three legs will carry him to the hiding of a bush, or better still, to the frozen surface of a river, hidden by high banks, with glare ice which will not reveal a trail. But on the river the man finds only a trap wrenched out of all semblance to its proper shape, with the spring opened to release the imprisoned leg.

The wolverine had been caught, and had gone to the river to study out the problem of unclinching the spring.

One more device remains to the man. It is a gun trick. The loaded weapon is hidden full-cock under leaves or brush. Directly opposite the barrel is the bait, attached by a concealed string to the trigger. The first pull will blow the thief's head off.

The trap experience would have frightened any other animals a week's run from man's tracks; but the wolverine grows bolder, and the trapper knows he will find his snares robbed until carcajou has been killed.

Perhaps he has tried the gun trick before, to have the cord gnawed through and the bait stolen. A wolverine is not to be easily tricked; but its gluttony and curiosity bring it within man's reach.

The man watches until he knows the part of the woods where the wolverine nightly gallops. He then procures a savoury piece of meat heavy enough to balance a cocked trigger, not heavy enough to send it off. The gun is suspended from some dense evergreen, which will hide the weapon. The bait hangs from the trigger above the wolverine's reach.

Then a curious game begins.

One morning the trapper sees the wolverine tracks round and round the tree as if determined to ferret out the mystery of the meat in mid-air.

The next morning the tracks have come to a stand below the meat. If the wolverine could only get up to the bait, one whiff would tell him whether the man-smell was there. He sits studying the puzzle till his mark is deep printed in the snow.

The trapper smiles. He has only to wait.

The rascal may become so bold in his predatory visits that the man may be tempted to chance a shot without waiting.

But if the man waits Nemesis hangs at the end of the cord. There comes a night when the wolverine's curiosity is as rampant as his gluttony. A quick clutch of the ripping claws and a blare of fire-smoke blows the robber's head into space.

The trapper will hold those hunting-grounds.

He has got rid of the most unwelcome visitor a solitary man ever had; but for the consolation of those whose sympathies are keener for the animal than the man, it may be said that in the majority of such contests it is the wolverine and not the man that wins.

CHAPTER VII
THE BUFFALO-RUNNERS

If the trapper had a crest like the knights of the wilderness who lived lives of daredoing in olden times, it should represent a canoe, a snow-shoe, a musket, a beaver, and a buffalo. While the beaver was his quest and the coin of the fur-trading realm, the buffalo was the great staple on which the very existence of the trapper depended.

Bed and blankets and clothing, shields for wartime, sinew for bows, bone for the shaping of rude lance-heads, kettles and bull-boats and saddles, roof and rug and curtain wall for the hunting lodge, and, most important of all, food that could be kept in any climate for any length of time and combined the lightest weight with the greatest nourishment—all these were supplied by the buffalo.

From the Gulf of Mexico to the Saskatchewan and from the Alleghanies to the Rockies the buffalo was to the hunter what wheat is to the farmer. Moose and antelope and deer were plentiful in the limited area of a favoured habitat. Provided with water and grass the buffalo could thrive in any latitude south of the sixties, with a preference for the open ground of the great central plains except when storms and heat drove the herds to the shelter of woods and valleys.

Besides, in that keen struggle for existence which goes on in the animal world, the buffalo had strength to defy all enemies. Of all the creatures that prey, only the full-grown grisly was a match against the buffalo; and according to old hunting legends, even the grisly held back from attacking a beast in the prime of its power and sneaked in the wake of the roving herds, like the coyotes and timber-wolves, for the chance of hamstringing a calf, or breaking a young cow's neck, or tackling some poor old king worsted in battle and deposed from the leadership of the herd, or snapping up some lost buffalo staggering blind on the trail of a prairie fire. The buffalo, like the range cattle, had a quality that made for the persistence of the species. When attacked by a beast of prey, they would line up for defence, charge upon the assailant, and trample life out. Adaptability to environment, strength excelling all foes, wonderful sagacity against attack—these were factors that partly explained the vastness of the buffalo herds once roaming this continent.

Proofs enough remain to show that the size of the herds simply could not be exaggerated. In two great areas their multitude exceeded anything in the known world. These were: (1) between the Arkansas and the Missouri, fenced in, as it were, by the Mississippi and the Rockies; (2) between the Missouri and the Saskatchewan, bounded by the Rockies on the west and on the east, that depression where lie Lakes Winnipeg, Manitoba, and Winnipegoosis. In both regions the prairie is scarred by trails where the buffalo have marched single file to their watering-places—trails trampled by such a multitude of hoofs that the groove sinks to the depth of a rider's stirrup or the hub of a wagon-wheel. At fording-places on the Qu'Appelle and Saskatchewan in Canada, and on the Upper Missouri, Yellowstone, and Arkansas in the Western States, carcasses of buffalo have been found where the stampeding herd trampled the weak under foot, virtually building a bridge of the dead over which the vast host rushed.

Then there were "the fairy rings," ruts like the water trail, only running in a perfect circle, with the hoofprints of countless multitudes in and outside the ring. Two explanations were given of these. When the calves were yet little, and the wild animals ravenous with spring hunger, the bucks and old leaders formed a cordon round the mothers and their young. The late Colonel Bedson of Stony Mountain, Manitoba, who had the finest private collection of buffalo in America until his death ten years ago, when the herd was shipped to Texas, observed another occasion when the buffalo formed a circle. Of an ordinary winter storm the herd took small notice except to turn backs to the wind; but if to a howling blizzard were added a biting north wind, with the thermometer forty degrees below zero, the buffalo lay down in a crescent as a wind-break to the young. Besides the "fairy rings" and the fording-places, evidences of the buffaloes' numbers are found at the salt-licks, alkali depressions on the prairie, soggy as paste in spring, dried hard as rock in midsummer and retaining footprints like a plaster cast; while at the wallows, where the buffalo have been taking mud-baths as a refuge from vermin and summer heat, the ground is scarred and ploughed as if for ramparts.

The comparison of the buffalo herds to the northland caribou has become almost commonplace; but it is the sheerest nonsense. From Hearne, two hundred years ago, to Mr. Tyrrel or Mr. Whitney in the Barren Lands in 1894-'96, no mention is ever made of a caribou herd exceeding ten thousand. Few herds of one thousand have ever been seen.

What are the facts regarding the buffalo?

In the thirties, when the American Fur Company was in the heyday of its power, there were sent from St. Louis alone in a single year one hundred thousand robes. The company bought only the perfect robes. The hunter usually kept an ample supply for his own needs; so that for every robe bought by the company, three times as many were taken from the plains. St. Louis was only one port of shipment. Equal quantities of robes were being sent from Mackinaw, Detroit, Montreal, and Hudson Bay. A million would not cover the number of robes sent east each year in the thirties and forties. In 1868 Inman, Sheridan, and Custer rode continuously for three days through one herd in the Arkansas region. In 1869 trains on the Kansas Pacific were held from nine in the morning till six at night to permit the passage of one herd across the tracks. Army officers related that in 1862 a herd moved north from the Arkansas to the Yellowstone that covered an area of seventy by thirty miles. Catlin and Inman and army men and employees of the fur companies considered a drove of one hundred thousand buffalo a common sight along the line of the Santa Fé trail. Inman computes that from St. Louis alone the bones of thirty-one million buffalo were shipped between 1868 and 1881. Northward the testimony is the same. John MacDonell, a partner of the North-West Company, tells how at the beginning of the last century a herd stampeded across the ice of the Qu'Appelle valley. In some places the ice broke. When the thaw came, a continuous line of drowned buffalo drifted past the fur post for three days. Mr. MacDonell counted up to seven thousand three hundred and sixty: there his patience gave out. And the number of the drowned was only a fringe of the travelling herd.

To-day where are the buffalo? A few in the public parks of the United States and Canada. A few of Colonel Bedson's old herd on Lord Strathcona's farm in Manitoba and the rest on a ranch in Texas. The railway more than the pot-hunter was the power that exterminated the buffalo. The railway brought the settlers; and the settlers fenced in the great ranges where the buffalo could have galloped away from all the pot-hunters of earth combined. Without the railway the buffalo could have resisted the hunter as they resisted Indian hunters from time immemorial; but when the iron line cut athwart the continent the herds only stampeded from one quarter to rush into the fresh dangers of another.

Much has been said about man's part in the destruction of the buffalo; and too much could not be said against those monomaniacs of slaughter who went into the buffalo-hunt from sheer love of killing, hiring the Indians to drive a herd over an embankment or into soft snow, while the valiant hunters sat in some sheltered spot, picking off the helpless quarry. This was not hunting. It was butchery, which none but hungry savages and white barbarians practised. The plains-man—who is the true type of the buffalo-runner—entered the lists on a fair field with the odds a hundred to one against himself, and the only advantages over brute strength the dexterity of his own aim.

Man was the least cruel of the buffalo's foes. Far crueler havoc was worked by the prairie fire and the fights for supremacy in the leadership of the herd and the sleuths of the trail and the wild stampedes often started by nothing more than the shadow of a cloud on the prairie. Natural history tells of nothing sadder than a buffalo herd overtaken by a prairie fire. Flee as they might, the fiery hurricane was fleeter; and when the flame swept past, the buffalo were left staggering over blackened wastes, blind from the fire, singed of fur to the raw, and mad with a thirst they were helpless to quench.

In the fights for leadership of the herd old age went down before youth. Colonel Bedson's daughter has often told the writer of her sheer terror as a child when these battles took place among the buffalo. The first intimation of trouble was usually a boldness among the young fellows of maturing strength. On the rove for the first year or two of their existence these youngsters were hooked and butted back into place as a rear-guard; and woe to the fellow whose vanity tempted him within range of the leader's sharp, pruning-hook horns! Just as the wolf aimed for the throat or leg sinews of a victim, so the irate buffalo struck at the point most vulnerable to his sharp, curved horn—the soft flank where a quick rip meant torture and death.

Comes a day when the young fellows refuse to be hooked and hectored to the rear! Then one of the boldest braces himself, circling and guarding and wheeling and keeping his lowered horns in line with the head of the older rival. That is the buffalo challenge! And there presently follows a bellowing like the rumbling of distant thunder, each keeping his eye on the other, circling and guarding and countering each other's moves, like fencers with foils. When one charges, the other wheels to meet the charge straight in front; and with a crash the horns are locked. It is then a contest of strength against strength, dexterity against dexterity. Not unusually the older brute goes into a fury from sheer amazement at the younger's presumption. His guarded charges become blind rushes, and he soon finds himself on the end of a pair of piercing horns. As soon as the rumbling and pawing began, Colonel Bedson used to send his herders out on the fleetest buffalo ponies to part the contestants; for, like the king of beasts that he is, the buffalo does not know how to surrender. He fights till he can fight no more; and if he is not killed, is likely to be mangled, a deposed king, whipped and broken-spirited and relegated to the fag-end of the trail, where he drags lamely after the subjects he once ruled.

Some day the barking of a prairie-dog, the rustle of a leaf, the shadow of a cloud, startles a giddy young cow. She throws up her head and is off. There is a stampede—myriad forms lumbering over the earth till the ground rocks and nothing remains of the buffalo herd but the smoking dust of the far horizon—nothing but the poor, old, deposed king, too weak to keep up the pace, feeble with fear, trembling at his own shadow, leaping in terror at a leaf blown by the wind.

After that the end is near, and the old buffalo must realize that fact as plainly as a human being would. Has he roamed the plains and guarded the calves from sleuths of the trail and seen the devourers leap on a fallen comrade before death has come, and yet does not know what those vague, gray forms are, always hovering behind him, always sneaking to the crest of a hill when he hides in the valley, always skulking through the prairie grass when he goes to a lookout on the crest of the hill, always stopping when he stops, creeping closer when he lies down, scuttling when he wheels, snapping at his heels when he stoops for a drink? If the buffalo did not know what these creatures meant, he would not have spent his entire life from calfhood guarding against them. But he does know; and therein lies the tragedy of the old king's end. He invariably seeks out some steep background where he can take his last stand against the wolves with a face to the foe.

But the end is inevitable.

While the main pack baits him to the fore, skulkers dart to the rear; and when, after a struggle that lasts for days, his hind legs sink powerless under him, hamstrung by the snap of some vicious coyote, he still keeps his face to the foe. But in sheer horror of the tragedy the rest is untellable; for the hungry creatures that prey do not wait till death comes to the victim.

Poor old king! Is anything that man has ever done to the buffalo herd half as tragically pitiful as nature's process of deposing a buffalo leader?

Catlin and Inman and every traveller familiar with the great plains region between the Arkansas and Saskatchewan testify that the quick death of the bullet was, indeed, the mercy stroke compared to nature's end of her wild creatures. In Colonel Bedson's herd the fighters were always parted before either was disabled; but it was always at the sacrifice of two or three ponies' lives.

In the park specimens of buffalo a curious deterioration is apparent. On Lord Strathcona's farm in Manitoba, where the buffalo still have several hundred acres of ranging-ground and are nearer to their wild state than elsewhere, they still retain their leonine splendour of strength in shoulders and head; but at Banff only the older ones have this appearance, the younger generation, like those of the various city parks, gradually assuming more dwarfed proportions about the shoulders, with a suggestion of a big, round-headed, clumsy sheep.

Between the Arkansas and the Saskatchewan buffalo were always plentiful enough for an amateur's hunt; but the trapper of the plains, to whom the hunt meant food and clothing and a roof for the coming year, favoured two seasons: (1) the end of June, when he had brought in his packs to the fur post and the winter's trapping was over and the fort full of idle hunters keen for the excitement of the chase; (2) in midwinter, when that curious lull came over animal life, before the autumn stores had been exhausted and before the spring forage began.

In both seasons the buffalo-robes were prime: sleek and glossy in June before the shedding of the fleece, with the fur at its greatest length; fresh and clean and thick in midwinter. But in midwinter the hunters were scattered, the herds broken in small battalions, the climate perilous for a lonely man who might be tempted to track fleeing herds many miles from a known course. South of the Yellowstone the individual hunter pursued the buffalo as he pursued deer—by still-hunting; for though the buffalo was keen of scent, he was dull of sight, except sideways on the level, and was not easily disturbed by a noise as long as he did not see its cause.

Behind the shelter of a mound and to leeward of the herd the trapper might succeed in bringing down what would be a creditable showing in a moose or deer hunt; but the trapper was hunting buffalo for their robes. Two or three robes were not enough from a large herd; and before he could get more there was likely to be a stampede. Decoy work was too slow for the trapper who was buffalo-hunting. So was tracking on snow-shoes, the way the Indians hunted north of the Yellowstone. A wounded buffalo at close range was quite as vicious as a wounded grisly; and it did not pay the trapper to risk his life getting a pelt for which the trader would give him only four or five dollars' worth of goods.

The Indians hunted buffalo by driving them over a precipice where hunters were stationed on each side below, or by luring the herd into a pound or pit by means of an Indian decoy masking under a buffalo-hide. But the precipice and pit destroyed too many hides; and if the pound were a sort of cheval-de-frise or corral converging at the inner end, it required more hunters than were ever together except at the incoming of the spring brigades.

When there were many hunters and countless buffalo, the white blood of the plains' trapper preferred a fair fight in an open field—not the indiscriminate carnage of the Indian hunt; so that the greatest buffalo-runs took place after the opening of spring. The greatest of these were on the Upper Missouri. This was the Mandan country, where hunters of the Mackinaw from Michilimackinac, of the Missouri from St. Louis, of the Nor' Westers from Montreal, of the Hudson Bay from Fort Douglas (Winnipeg), used to congregate before the War of 1812, which barred out Canadian traders.

At a later date the famous, loud-screeching Red River ox-carts were used to transport supplies to the scene of the hunt; but at the opening of the last century all hunters, whites, Indians, and squaws, rode to field on cayuse ponies or broncos, with no more supplies than could be stowed away in a saddle-pack, and no other escort than the old-fashioned muskets over each white man's shoulder or attached to his holster.

The Indians were armed with bow and arrow only. The course usually led north and westward, for the reason that at this season the herds were on their great migrations north, and the course of the rivers headed them westward. From the first day out the hunter best fitted for the captainship was recognised as leader, and such discipline maintained as prevented unruly spirits stampeding the buffalo before the cavalcade had closed near enough for the wild rush.

At night the hunters slept under open sky with horses picketed to saddles, saddles as pillows, and musket in hand. When the course led through the country of hostiles, sentinels kept guard; but midnight usually saw all hunters in the deep sleep of outdoor life, bare faces upturned to the stars, a little tenuous stream of uprising smoke where the camp-fire still glowed red, and on the far, shadowy horizon, with the moonlit skyline meeting the billowing prairie in perfect circle, vague, whitish forms—the coyotes keeping watch, stealthy and shunless as death.

The northward movement of the buffalo began with the spring. Odd scattered herds might have roamed the valleys in the winter; but as the grass grew deeper and lush with spring rains, the reaches of the prairie land became literally covered with the humpback, furry forms of the roving herds. Indian legend ascribed their coming directly to the spirits. The more prosaic white man explained that the buffalo were only emerging from winter shelter, and their migration was a search for fresh feeding-ground.

Be that as it may, northward they came, in straggling herds that covered the prairie like a flock of locusts; in close-formed battalions, with leaders and scouts and flank guards protecting the cows and the young; in long lines, single file, leaving the ground, soft from spring rains, marked with a rut like a ditch; in a mad stampede at a lumbering gallop that roared like an ocean tide up hills and down steep ravines, sure-footed as a mountain-goat, thrashing through the swollen water-course of river and slough, up embankments with long beards and fringed dewlaps dripping—on and on and on—till the tidal wave of life had hulked over the sky-line beyond the heaving horizon. Here and there in the brownish-black mass were white and gray forms, light-coloured buffalo, freaks in the animal world.

The age of the calves in each year's herd varied. The writer remembers a sturdy little buffalo that arrived on the scene of this troublous life one freezing night in January, with a howling blizzard and the thermometer at forty below—a combination that is sufficient to set the teeth of the most mendacious northerner chattering. The young buffalo spent the first three days of his life in this gale and was none the worse, which seems to prove that climatic apology, "though it is cold, you don't feel it." Another spindly-legged, clumsy bundle of fawn and fur in the same herd counted its natal day from a sweltering afternoon in August.

Many signs told the buffalo-runners which way to ride for the herd. There was the trail to the watering-place. There were the salt-licks and the wallows and the crushed grass where two young fellows had been smashing each other's horns in a trial of strength. There were the bones of the poor old deposed king, picked clear by the coyotes, or, perhaps, the lonely outcast himself, standing at bay, feeble and frightened, a picture of dumb woe! To such the hunter's shot was a mercy stroke. Or, most interesting of all signs and surest proof that the herd was near—a little bundle of fawn-coloured fur lying out flat as a door-mat under hiding of sage-brush, or against a clay mound, precisely the colour of its own hide.

Poke it! An ear blinks, or a big ox-like eye opens! It is a buffalo calf left cached by the mother, who has gone to the watering-place or is pasturing with the drove. Lift it up! It is inert as a sack of wool. Let it go! It drops to earth flat and lifeless as a door-mat. The mother has told it how to escape the coyotes and wolverines; and the little rascal is "playing dead." But if you fondle it and warm it—the Indians say, breathe into its face—it forgets all about the mother's warning and follows like a pup.

At the first signs of the herd's proximity the squaws parted from the cavalcade and all impedimenta remained behind. The best-equipped man was the man with the best horse, a horse that picked out the largest buffalo from one touch of the rider's hand or foot, that galloped swift as wind in pursuit, that jerked to a stop directly opposite the brute's shoulders and leaped from the sideward sweep of the charging horns. No sound came from the hunters till all were within close range. Then the captain gave the signal, dropped a flag, waved his hand, or fired a shot, and the hunters charged.

**The buffalo-hunt.
After a contemporary print.**

Arrows whistled through the air, shots clattered with the fusillade of artillery volleys. Bullets fell to earth with the dull ping of an aim glanced aside by the adamant head bones or the heaving shoulder fur of the buffalo. The Indians shouted their war-cry of "Ah—oh, ah—oh!" Here and there French voices screamed "Voilà! Les b[oe]ufs! Les b[oe]ufs! Sacré! Tonnerre! Tir—tir—tir—donc! By Gar!" And Missouri traders called out plain and less picturesque but more forcible English.

Sometimes the suddenness of the attack dazed the herd; but the second volley with the smell of powder and smoke and men started the stampede. Then followed such a wild rush as is unknown in the annals of any other kind of hunting, up hills, down embankments, over cliffs, through sloughs, across rivers, hard and fast and far as horses had strength to carry riders in a boundless land!

Riders were unseated and went down in the mêlée; horses caught on the horns of charging bulls and ripped from shoulder to flank; men thrown high in mid-air to alight on the back of a buffalo; Indians with dexterous aim bringing down the great brutes with one arrow; unwary hunters trampled to death under a multitude of hoofs; wounded buffalo turning with fury on their assailants till the pursuer became pursued and only the fleetness of the pony saved the hunter's life.

A retired officer of the North-West mounted police, who took part in a Missouri buffalo-run forty years ago, described the impression at the time as of an earthquake. The galloping horses, the rocking mass of fleeing buffalo, the rumbling and quaking of the ground under the thunderous pounding, were all like a violent earthquake. The same gentleman tells how he once saw a wounded buffalo turn on an Indian hunter. The man's horse took fright. Instead of darting sideways to give him a chance to send a last finishing shot home, the horse became wildly unmanageable and fled. The buffalo pursued. Off they raced, rider and buffalo, the Indian craning over his horse's neck, the horse blown and fagged and unable to gain one pace ahead of the buffalo, the great beast covered with foam, his eyes like fire, pounding and pounding—closer and closer to the horse till rider and buffalo disappeared over the horizon.

"To this day I have wondered what became of that Indian," said the officer, "for the horse was losing and the buffalo gaining when they went over the bluff."

The incident illustrates a trait seldom found in wild animals—a persistent vindictiveness.

In a word, buffalo-hunting was not all boys' play.

After the hunt came the gathering of skins and meat. The tongue was first taken as a delicacy for the great feast that celebrated every buffalo-hunt. To this was sometimes added the fleece fat or hump. White hunters have been accused of waste, because they used only the skin, tongue, and hump of the buffalo. But what the white hunter left the Indian took, making pemmican by pounding the meat with tallow, drying thinly-shaved slices into "jerked" meat, getting thread from the buffalo sinews and implements of the chase from the bones.

The gathering of the spoils was not the least dangerous part of the buffalo-hunt. Many an apparently lifeless buffalo has lunged up in a death-throe that has cost the hunter dear. The mounted police officer of whom mention has been made was once camping with a patrol party along the international line between Idaho and Canada. Among the hunting stories told over the camp-fire was that of the Indian pursued by the wounded buffalo. Scarcely had the colonel finished his anecdote when a great hulking buffalo rose to the crest of a hillock not a gunshot away.

"Come on, men! Let us all have a shot," cried the colonel, grasping his rifle.

The buffalo dropped at the first rifle-crack, and the men scrambled pell-mell up the hill to see whose bullet had struck vital. Just as they stooped over the fallen buffalo it lunged up with an angry snort.

The story of the pursued Indian was still fresh in all minds. The colonel is the only man of the party honest enough to tell what happened next. He declares if breath had not given out every man would have run till he dropped over the horizon, like the Indian and the buffalo.

And when they plucked up courage to go back, the buffalo was dead as a stone.

CHAPTER VIII
THE MOUNTAINEERS

It was in the Rocky Mountains that American trapping attained its climax of heroism and dauntless daring and knavery that out-herods comparison.

The War of 1812 had demoralized the American fur trade. Indians from both sides of the international boundary committed every depredation, and evaded punishment by scampering across the line to the protection of another flag. Alexander MacKenzie of the North-West Company had been the first of the Canadian traders to cross the Rockies, reaching the Pacific in 1793. The result was that in less than fifteen years the fur posts of the North-West and Hudson's Bay Companies were dotted like beads on a rosary down the course of the mountain rivers to the boundary. Of the American traders, the first to follow up Lewis and Clark's lead from the Missouri to the Columbia were Manuel Lisa the Spaniard and Major Andrew Henry, the two leading spirits of the Missouri Company. John Jacob Astor sent his Astorians of the Pacific Company across the continent in 1811, and a host of St. Louis firms had prepared to send free trappers to the mountains when the war broke out. The end of the war saw Astoria captured by the Nor' Westers, the Astorians scattered to all parts of the world, Lisa driven down the Missouri to Council Bluffs, Andrew Henry a fugitive from the Blackfeet of the Yellowstone, and all the free trappers like an idle army waiting for a captain.

Their captain came.

Mr. Astor's influence secured the passage of a law barring out British fur traders from the United States. That threw all the old Hudson's Bay and North-West posts south of the boundary into the hands of Mr. Astor's American Fur Company. He had already bought out the American part of the Mackinaw Company's posts, stretching west from Michilimackinac beyond the Mississippi towards the head waters of the Missouri. And now to his force came a tremendous accession—all those dissatisfied Nor' Westers thrown out of employment when their company amalgamated with the Hudson's Bay.

If Mr. Astor alone had held the American fur trade, there would have been none of that rivalry which ended in so much bloodshed. But St. Louis, lying like a gateway to the mountain trade, had always been jealous of those fur traders with headquarters in New York. Lisa had refused to join Mr. Astor's Pacific Company, and doubtless the Spaniard chuckled over his own wisdom when that venture failed with a loss of nearly half a million to its founder. When Lisa died the St. Louis traders still held back from the American Fur Company. Henry and Ashley and the Sublettes and Campbell and Fitzpatrick and Bridger—subsequently known as the Rocky Mountain traders—swept up the Missouri with brigades of one hundred, two hundred, and three hundred men, and were overrunning the mountains five years before the American Company's slowly extending line of forts had reached as far west as the Yellowstone. A clash was bound to ensue when these two sets of rivals met on a hunting-field which the Rocky Mountain men regarded as pre-empted by themselves.

The clash came from the peculiarities of the hunting-ground.

It was two thousand miles by trappers' trail from the reach of law. It was too remote from the fur posts for trappers to go down annually for supplies. Supplies were sent up by the fur companies to a mountain rendezvous, to Pierre's Hole under the Tetons, or Jackson's Hole farther east, or Ogden's Hole at Salt Lake, sheltered valleys with plenty of water for men and horses when hunters and traders and Indians met at the annual camp.

Elsewhere the hunter had only to follow the windings of a river to be carried to his hunting-ground. Here, streams were too turbulent for canoes; and boats were abandoned for horses; and mountain cañons with sides sheer as a wall drove the trapper back from the river-bed to interminable forests, where windfall and underbrush and rockslide obstructed every foot of progress. The valley might be shut in by a blind wall which cooped the hunter up where was neither game nor food. Out of this valley, then, he must find a way for himself and his horses, noting every peak so that he might know this region again, noting especially the peaks with the black rock walls; for where the rock is black snow has not clung, and the mountain face will not change; and where snow cannot stick, a man cannot climb; and the peak is a good one for the trapper to shun.

One, two, three seasons have often slipped away before the mountaineers found good hunting-ground. Ten years is a short enough time to learn the lie of the land in even a small section of mountains. It was twenty years from the time Lewis and Clark first crossed the mountains before the traders of St. Louis could be sure that the trappers sent into the Rockies would find their way out. Seventy lives were lost in the first two years of mountain trapping, some at the hands of the hostile Blackfeet guarding the entrance to the mountains at the head waters of the Missouri, some at the hands of the Snakes on the Upper Columbia, others between the Platte and Salt Lake. Time and money and life it cost to learn the hunting-grounds of the Rockies; and the mountaineers would not see knowledge won at such a cost wrested away by a spying rival.

Then, too, the mountains had bred a new type of trapper, a new style of trapping.

Only the most daring hunters would sign contracts for the "Up-Country," or Pays d'en Haut as the French called it. The French trappers, for the most part, kept to the river valleys and plains; and if one went to the mountains for a term of years, when he came out he was no longer the smug, indolent, laughing, chattering voyageur. The great silences of a life hard as the iron age had worked a change. To begin with, the man had become a horseman, a climber, a scout, a fighter of Indians and elements, lank and thin and lithe, silent and dogged and relentless.

In other regions hunters could go out safely in pairs or even alone, carrying supplies enough for the season in a canoe, and drifting down-stream with a canoe-load of pelts to the fur post. But the mountains were so distant and inaccessible, great quantities of supplies had to be taken. That meant long cavalcades of pack-horses, which Blackfeet were ever on the alert to stampede. Armed guards had to accompany the pack-train. Out of a party of a hundred trappers sent to the mountains by the Rock Mountain Company, thirty were always crack rifle-shots for the protection of the company's property. One such party, properly officered and kept from crossing the animal's tracks, might not drive game from a valley. Two such bands of rival traders keen to pilfer each other's traps would result in ruin to both.

That is the way the clash came in the early thirties of the last century.

All winter bands of Rocky Mountain trappers under Fitzpatrick and Bridger and Sublette had been sweeping, two hundred strong, like foraging bandits, from the head waters of the Missouri, where was one mountain pass to the head waters of the Platte, where was a second pass much used by the mountaineers. Summer came with the heat that wakens all the mountain silences to a roar of rampant life. Summer came with the fresh-loosened rocks clattering down the mountain slopes in a landslide, and the avalanches booming over the precipices in a Niagara of snow, and the swollen torrents shouting to each other in a thousand voices till the valleys vibrated to that grandest of all music—the voice of many waters. Summer came with the heat that drives the game up to the cool heights of the wind-swept peaks; and the hunters of the game began retracing their way from valley to valley, gathering the furs cached during the winter hunt.

Then the cavalcade set out for the rendezvous: grizzled men in tattered buckskins, with long hair and unkempt beards and bronzed skin, men who rode as if they were part of the saddle, easy and careless but always with eyes alert and one hand near the thing in their holsters; long lines of packhorses laden with furs climbing the mountains in a zigzag trail like a spiral stair, crawling along the face of cliffs barely wide enough to give a horse footing, skirting the sky-line between lofty peaks in order to avoid the detour round the broadened bases, frequently swimming raging torrents whose force carried them half a mile off their trail; always following the long slopes, for the long slopes were most easily climbed; seldom following a water-course, for mountain torrents take short cuts over precipices; packers scattering to right and left at the fording-places, to be rounded back by the collie-dog and the shouting drivers, and the old bell-mare darting after the bolters with her ears laid flat.

Not a sign by the way escaped the mountaineer's eye. Here the tumbling torrent is clear and sparkling and cold as champagne. He knows that stream comes from snow. A glacial stream would be milky blue or milky green from glacial silts; and while game seeks the cool heights in summer, the animals prefer the snow-line and avoid the chill of the iced masses in a glacier. There will be game coming down from the source of that stream when he passes back this way in the fall. Ah! what is that little indurated line running up the side of the cliff—just a displacement of the rock chips here, a hardening of the earth that winds in and out among the devil's-club and painter's-brush and mountain laurel and rock crop and heather?

"Something has been going up and down here to a drinking-place," says the mountaineer.

Punky yellow logs lie ripped open and scratched where bruin has been enjoying a dainty morsel of ants' eggs; but the bear did not make that track. It is too dainty, and has been used too regularly. Neither has the bighorn made it; for the mountain-sheep seldom stay longer above tree-line, resting in the high, meadowed Alpine valleys with the long grasses and sunny reaches and larch shade.

Presently the belled leader tinkles her way round an elbow of rock where a stream trickles down. This is the drinking-place. In the soft mould is a little cleft footprint like the ace of hearts, the trail of the mountain-goat feeding far up at the snow-line where the stream rises.

Then the little cleft mark unlocks a world of hunter's yarns: how at such a ledge, where the cataract falls like wind-blown mist, one trapper saw a mother goat teaching her little kid to take the leap, and how when she scented human presence she went jump—jump—jump—up and up and up the rock wall, where the man could not follow, bleating and calling the kid; and how the kid leaped and fell back and leaped, and cried as pitifully as a child, till the man, having no canned milk to bring it up, out of very sympathy went away.

Then another tells how he tried to shoot a goat running up a gulch, but as fast as he sighted his rifle—"drew the bead"—the thing jumped from side to side, criss-crossing up the gulch till she got above danger and away. And some taciturn oracle comes out with the dictum that "men hadn't ought to try to shoot goat except from above or in front."

Every pack-horse of the mountains knows the trick of planting legs like stanchions and blowing his sides out in a balloon when the men are tightening cinches. No matter how tight girths may be, before every climb and at the foot of every slope there must be re-tightening. And at every stop the horses come shouldering up for the packs to be righted, or try to scrape the things off under some low-branched tree.

Night falls swiftly in the mountains, the long, peaked shadows etching themselves across the valleys. Shafts of sunlight slant through the mountain gaps gold against the endless reaches of matted forest, red as wine across the snowy heights. With the purpling shadows comes a sudden chill, silencing the roar of mountain torrents to an all-pervading ceaseless prolonged h—u—s—h—!

Mountaineers take no chances on the ledges after dark. It is dangerous enough work to skirt narrow precipices in daylight; and sunset is often followed by a thick mist rolling across the heights in billows of fog. These are the clouds that one sees across the peaks at nightfall like banners. How does it feel benighted among those clouds?

A few years ago I was saving a long detour round the base of a mountain by riding along the saddle of rock between two peaks. The sky-line rounded the convex edge of a sheer precipice for three miles. Midway the inner wall rose straight, the outer edge above blackness—seven thousand feet the mountaineer guiding us said it was, though I think it was nearer five. The guide's horse displaced a stone the size of a pail from the path. If a man had slipped in the same way he would have fallen to the depths; but when one foot slips, a horse has three others to regain himself; and with a rear-end flounder the horse got his footing. But down—down—down went the stone, bouncing and knocking and echoing as it struck against the precipice wall—down—down—down till it was no larger than a spool—then out of sight—and silence! The mountaineer looked back over his shoulder.

"Always throw both your feet over the saddle to the inner side of the trail in a place like this," he directed, with a curious meaning in his words.

"What do you do when the clouds catch you on this sort of a ledge?"

"Get off—knock ahead with your rifle to feel where the edge is—throw bits of rock through the fog so you can tell where you are by the sound."

"And when no sound comes back?"

"Sit still," said he. Then to add emphasis, "You bet you sit still! People can say what they like, but when no sound comes back, or when the sound's muffled as if it came from water below, you bet it gives you chills!"

So the mountaineers take no chances on the ledges after dark. The moon riding among the peaks rises over pack-horses standing hobbled on the lee side of a roaring camp-fire that will drive the sand-flies and mosquitoes away, on pelts and saddle-trees piled carefully together, on men sleeping with no pillow but a pack, no covering but the sky.

If a sharp crash breaks the awful stillness of a mountain night, the trapper is unalarmed. He knows it is only some great rock loosened by the day's thaw rolling down with a landslide. If a shrill, fiendish laugh shrieks through the dark, he pays no heed. It is only the cougar prowling cattishly through the under-brush perhaps still-hunting the hunter. The lonely call overhead is not the prairie-hawk, but the eagle lilting and wheeling in a sort of dreary enjoyment of utter loneliness.

Long before the sunrise has drawn the tented shadows across the valley the mountaineers are astir, with the pack-horses snatching mouthfuls of bunch-grass as they travel off in a way that sets the old leader's bell tinkling.

The mountaineers usually left their hunting-grounds early in May. They seldom reached their rendezvous before July or August. Three months travelling a thousand miles! Three hundred miles a month! Ten miles a day! It is not a record that shows well beside our modern sixty miles an hour—a thousand miles a day. And yet it is a better record; for if our latter-day fliers had to build the road as they went along, they would make slower time than the mountaineers of a century ago.

Rivers too swift to swim were rafted on pine logs, cut and braced together while the cavalcade waited. Muskegs where the industrious little beaver had flooded a valley by damming up the central stream often mired the horses till all hands were called to haul out the unfortunate; and where the mire was very treacherous and the surrounding mountains too steep for foothold, choppers went to work and corduroyed a trail across, throwing the logs on branches that kept them afloat, and overlaying with moss to save the horses' feet.

But the greatest cause of delay was the windfall, pines and spruce of enormous girth pitched down by landslide and storm into an impassable cheval-de-frise. Turn to the right! A matted tangle of underbrush higher than the horses' head bars the way! Turn to the left! A muskeg where horses sink through quaking moss to saddle-girths! If the horses could not be driven around the barrier, the mountaineers would try to force a high jump. The high jump failing except at risk of broken legs, there was nothing to do but chop a passage through.

And were the men carving a way through the wilderness only the bushwhackers who have pioneered other forest lands? Of the prominent men leading mountaineers in 1831, Vanderburgh of the American Fur Company was a son of a Fifth New York Regiment officer in the Revolutionary War, and himself a graduate of West Point. One of the Rocky Mountain leaders was a graduate from a blacksmith-shop. Another leader was a descendant of the royal blood of France. All grades of life supplied material for the mountaineer; but it was the mountains that bred the heroism, that created a new type of trapper—the most purely American type, because produced by purely American conditions.

Green River was the rendezvous for the mountaineers in 1831; and to Green River came trappers of the Columbia, of the Three Forks, of the Missouri, of the Bighorn and Yellowstone and Platte. From St. Louis came the traders to exchange supplies for pelts; and from every habitable valley of the mountains native tribes to barter furs, sell horses for transport, carouse at the merry meeting and spy on what the white hunters were doing. For a month all was the confusion of a gipsy camp or Oriental fair.

French-Canadian voyageurs who had come up to raft the season's cargo down-stream to St. Louis jostled shoulders with mountaineers from the Spanish settlements to the south and American trappers from the Columbia to the north and free trappers who had ranged every forest of America from Labrador to Mexico.[32] Merchants from St. Louis, like General Ashley, the foremost leader of Rocky Mountain trappers, descendants from Scottish nobility like Kenneth MacKenzie of Fort Union, miscellaneous gentlemen of adventure like Captain Bonneville, or Wyeth of Boston, or Baron Stuart—all with retinues of followers like mediæval lords—found themselves hobnobbing at the rendezvous with mighty Indian sachems, Crows or Pend d'Oreilles or Flat Heads, clad in little else than moccasins, a buffalo-skin blanket, and a pompous dignity.

Among the underlings was a time of wild revel, drinking daylight out and daylight in, decking themselves in tawdry finery for the one dress occasion of the year, and gambling sober or drunk till all the season's earnings, pelts and clothing and horses and traps, were gone.

The partners—as the Rocky Mountain men called themselves in distinction to the bourgeois of the French, the factors of the Hudson's Bay, the partisans of the American Fur Company—held confabs over crumpled maps, planning the next season's hunt, drawing in roughly the fresh information brought down each year of new regions, and plotting out all sections of the mountains for the different brigades.

This year a new set of faces appeared at the rendezvous, from thirty to fifty men with full quota of saddle-horses, pack-mules, and traps. On the traps were letters that afterward became magical in all the Up-Country—A. F. C.—American Fur Company. Leading these men were Vanderburgh, who had already become a successful trader among the Aricaras and had to his credit one victory over the Blackfeet; and Drips, who had been a member of the old Missouri Fur Company and knew the Upper Platte well. But the Rocky Mountain men, who knew the cost of life and time and money it had taken to learn the hunting-grounds of the Rockies, doubtless smiled at these tenderfeet who thought to trap as successfully in the hills as they had on the plains.

Two things counselled caution. Vanderburgh would stop at nothing. Drips had married a native woman of the Platte, whose tribe might know the hunting-grounds as well as the mountaineers. Hunters fraternize in friendship at holidaying; but they no more tell each other secrets than rival editors at a banquet. Mountaineers knowing the field like Bridger who had been to the Columbia with Henry as early as 1822 and had swept over the ranges as far south as the Platte, or Fitzpatrick[33] who had made the Salt Lake region his stamping-ground, might smile at the newcomers; but they took good care to give their rivals the slip when hunters left the rendezvous for the hills.

When the mountaineers scattered, Fitzpatrick led his brigade to the region between the Black Hills on the east and the Bighorn Mountains on the west. The first snowfall was powdering the hills. Beaver were beginning to house up for the winter. Big game was moving down to the valley. The hunters had pitched a central camp on the banks of Powder River, gathered in the supply of winter meat, and dispersed in pairs to trap all through the valley.

But forest rangers like Vanderburgh and Drips were not to be so easily foiled. Every axe-mark on windfall, every camp-fire, every footprint in the spongy mould, told which way the mountaineers had gone. Fitzpatrick's hunters wakened one morning to find traps marked A. F. C. beside their own in the valley. The trick was too plain to be misunderstood. The American Fur Company might not know the hunting-grounds of the Rockies, but they were deliberately dogging the mountaineers to their secret retreats.

Armed conflict would only bring ruin in lawsuits.

Gathering his hunters together under cover of snowfall or night, Fitzpatrick broke camp, slipped stealthily out of the valley, over the Bighorn range, across the Bighorn River, now almost impassable in winter, into the pathless foldings of the Wind River Mountains, with their rampart walls and endless snowfields, westward to Snake River Valley, three hundred miles away from the spies. Instead of trapping from east to west, as he had intended to do so that the return to the rendezvous would lead past the caches, Fitzpatrick thought to baffle the spies by trapping from west to east.

Having wintered on the Snake, he moved gradually up-stream. Crossing southward over a divide, they unexpectedly came on the very rivals whom they were avoiding, Vanderburgh and Drips, evidently working northward on the mountaineers' trail. By a quick reverse they swept back north in time for the summer rendezvous at Pierre's Hole.

Who had told Vanderburgh and Drips that the mountaineers were to meet at Pierre's Hole in 1832? Possibly Indians and fur trappers who had been notified to come down to Pierre's Hole by the Rocky Mountain men; possibly, too, paid spies in the employment of the American Fur Company.

Before supplies had come up from St. Louis for the mountaineers Vanderburgh and Drips were at the rendezvous. Neither of the rivals could flee away to the mountains till the supplies came. Could the mountaineers but get away first, Vanderburgh and Drips could no longer dog a fresh trail. Fitzpatrick at once set out with all speed to hasten the coming convoy. Four hundred miles eastward he met the supplies, explained the need to hasten provisions, and with one swift horse under him and another swift one as a relay, galloped back to the rendezvous.

But the Blackfeet were ever on guard at the mountain passes like cats at a mouse-hole. Fitzpatrick had ridden into a band of hostiles before he knew the danger. Vaulting to the saddle of the fresh horse, he fled to the hills, where he lay concealed for three days. Then he ventured out. The Indians still guarded the passes. They must have come upon him at a night camp when his horse was picketed, for Fitzpatrick escaped to the defiles of the mountains with nothing but the clothes on his back and a single ball in his rifle. By creeping from shelter to shelter of rugged declivities where the Indian ponies could not follow, he at last got across the divide, living wholly on roots and berries. Swimming one of the swollen mountain rivers, he lost his rifle. Hatless—for his hat had been cut up to bind his bleeding feet and protect them from the rocks—and starving, he at last fell in with some Iroquois hunters also bound for the rendezvous.

The convoy under Sublette had already arrived at Pierre's Hole.

The famous battle between white men and hostile Blackfeet at Pierre's Hole, which is told elsewhere, does not concern the story of rivalry between mountaineers and the American Fur Company. The Rocky Mountain men now realized that the magical A. F. C. was a rival to be feared and not to be lightly shaken. Some overtures were made by the mountaineers for an equal division of the hunting-ground between the two great companies. These Vanderburgh and Drips rejected with the scorn of utter confidence. Meanwhile provisions had not come for the American Fur Company. The mountaineers not only captured all trade with the friendly Indians, but in spite of the delay from the fight with the Blackfeet got away to their hunting-grounds two weeks in advance of the American Company.

What the Rocky Mountain men decided when the American Company rejected the offer to divide the hunting-ground can only be inferred from what was done.

Vanderburgh and Drips knew that Fitzpatrick and Bridger had led a picked body of horsemen northward from Pierre's Hole.

If the mountaineers had gone east of the lofty Tetons, their hunting-ground would be somewhere between the Yellowstone and the Bighorn. If they had gone south, one could guess they would round-up somewhere about Salt Lake where the Hudson's Bay[34] had been so often "relieved" of their furs by the mountaineers. If they had gone west, their destination must be on the Columbia or the Snake. If they went north, they would trap on the Three Forks of the Upper Missouri.

Therefore Vanderburgh and Drips cached all impedimenta that might hamper swift marching, smiled to themselves, and headed their horses for the Three Forks of the Missouri.

There were Blackfeet, to be sure, in that region; and Blackfeet hated Vanderburgh with deadly venom because he had once defeated them and slain a great warrior. Also, the Blackfeet were smarting from the fearful losses of Pierre's Hole.

But if the Rocky Mountain men could go unscathed among the Blackfeet, why, so could the American Fur Company!

And Vanderburgh and Drips went!

Rival traders might not commit murder. That led to the fearful ruin of the lawsuits that overtook Nor' Westers and Hudson's Bay in Canada only fifteen years before.

But the mountaineers knew that the Blackfeet hated Henry Vanderburgh!

Corduroyed muskeg where the mountaineers' long file of pack-horses had passed, fresh-chopped logs to make a way through blockades of fallen pine, the green moss that hangs festooned among the spruce at cloudline broken and swinging free as if a rider had passed that way, grazed bark where the pack-saddle had brushed a tree-trunk, muddy hoof-marks where the young packers had balked at fording an icy stream, scratchings on rotten logs where a mountaineer's pegged boot had stepped—all these told which way Fitzpatrick and Bridger had led their brigade.

Oh, it was an easy matter to scent so hot a trail! Here the ashes of a camp-fire! There a pile of rock placed a deal too carefully for nature's work—the cached furs of the fleeing rivals! Besides, what with cañon and whirlpool, there are so very few ways by which a cavalcade can pass through mountains that the simplest novice could have trailed Fitzpatrick and Bridger.

Doubtless between the middle of August when Vanderburgh and Drips set out on the chase and the middle of September when they ran down the fugitives the American Fur Company leaders had many a laugh at their own cleverness.

They succeeded in overtaking the mountaineers in the valley of the Jefferson, splendid hunting-grounds with game enough for two lines of traps, which Vanderburgh and Drips at once set out. No swift flight by forced marches this time! The mountaineers sat still for almost a week. Then they casually moved down the Jefferson towards the main Missouri.

The hunting-ground was still good. Weren't the mountaineers leaving a trifle too soon? Should the Americans follow or stay? Vanderburgh remained, moving over into the adjacent valley and spreading his traps along the Madison. Drips followed the mountaineers.

Two weeks' chase over utterly gameless ground probably suggested to Drips that even an animal will lead off on a false scent to draw the enemy away from the true trail. At the Missouri he turned back up the Jefferson.

Wheeling right about, the mountaineers at once turned back too, up the farthest valley, the Gallatin, then on the way to the first hunting-ground westward over a divide to the Madison, where—ill luck!—they again met their ubiquitous rival, Vanderburgh!

How Vanderburgh laughed at these antics one may guess!

Post-haste up the Madison went the mountaineers!

Should Vanderburgh stay or follow? Certainly the enemy had been bound back for the good hunting-grounds when they had turned to retrace their way up the Madison. If they meant to try the Jefferson, Vanderburgh would forestall the move. He crossed over to the valley where he had first found them.

Sure enough there were camp-fires on the old hunting-grounds, a dead buffalo, from which the hunters had just fled to avoid Vanderburgh! If Vanderburgh laughed, his laugh was short; for there were signs that the buffalo had been slain by an Indian.

The trappers refused to hunt where there were Blackfeet about. Vanderburgh refused to believe there was any danger of Blackfeet. Calling for volunteers, he rode forward with six men.

First they found a fire. The marauders must be very near. Then a dead buffalo was seen, then fresh tracks, unmistakably the tracks of Indians. But buffalo were pasturing all around undisturbed. There could not be many Indians.

Determined to quiet the fears of his men, Vanderburgh pushed on, entered a heavily wooded gulch, paused at the steep bank of a dried torrent, descried nothing, and jumped his horse across the bank, followed by the six volunteers.

Instantly the valley rang with rifle-shots. A hundred hostiles sprang from ambush. Vanderburgh's horse went down. Three others cleared the ditch at a bound and fled; but Vanderburgh was to his feet, aiming his gun, and coolly calling out: "Don't run! Don't run!" Two men sent their horses back over the ditch to his call, a third was thrown to be slain on the spot, and Vanderburgh's first shot had killed the nearest Indian, when another volley from the Blackfeet exacted deadly vengeance for the warrior Vanderburgh had slain years before.

Panic-stricken riders carried the news to the waiting brigade. Refuge was taken in the woods, where sentinels kept guard all night. The next morning, with scouts to the fore, the brigade retreated cautiously towards some of their caches. A second night was passed behind barriers of logs; and the third day a band of friendly Indians was encountered, who were sent to bury the dead.

The Frenchman they buried. Vanderburgh had been torn to pieces and his bones thrown into the river.

So ended the merry game of spying on the mountaineers.

As for the mountaineers, they fell into the meshes of their own snares; for on the way to Snake River, when parleying with friendly Blackfeet, the accidental discharge of Bridger's gun brought a volley of arrows from the Indians, one hooked barb lodging in Bridger's shoulder-blade, which he carried around for three years as a memento of his own trickery.

Fitzpatrick fared as badly. Instigated by the American Fur Company, the Crows attacked him within a year, stealing everything that he possessed.

PART II

CHAPTER IX
THE TAKING OF THE BEAVER

All summer long he had hung about the fur company trading-posts waiting for the signs.

And now the signs had come.

Foliage crimson to the touch of night-frosts. Crisp autumn days, spicy with the smell of nuts and dead leaves. Birds flying away southward, leaving the woods silent as the snow-padded surface of a frozen pond. Hoar-frost heavier every morning; and thin ice edged round stagnant pools like layers of mica.

Then he knew it was time to go. And through the Northern forests moved a new presence—the trapper.

Of the tawdry, flash clothing in which popular fancy is wont to dress him he has none. Bright colours would be a danger-signal to game. If his costume has any colour, it is a waist-belt or neck-scarf, a toque or bright handkerchief round his head to keep distant hunters from mistaking him for a moose. For the rest, his clothes are as ragged as any old, weather-worn garments. Sleeping on balsam boughs or cooking over a smoky fire will reduce the newness of blanket coat and buckskin jacket to the dun shades of the grizzled forest. A few days in the open and the trapper has the complexion of a bronzed tree-trunk.

Like other wild creatures, this foster-child of the forest gradually takes on the appearance and habits of woodland life. Nature protects the ermine by turning his russet coat of the grass season to spotless white for midwinter—except the jet tail-tip left to lure hungry enemies and thus, perhaps, to prevent the little stoat degenerating into a sloth. And the forest looks after her foster-child by transforming the smartest suit that ever stepped out of the clothier's bandbox to the dull tints of winter woods.

This is the seasoning of the man for the work. But the trapper's training does not stop here.

When the birds have gone south the silence of a winter forest on a windless day becomes tense enough to be snapped by either a man's breathing or the breaking of a small twig; and the trapper acquires a habit of moving through the brush with noiseless stealth. He must learn to see better than the caribou can hear or the wolf smell—which means that in keenness and accuracy his sight outdistances the average field-glass. Besides, the trapper has learned how to look, how to see, and seeing—discern; which the average man cannot do even through a field-glass. Then animals have a trick of deceiving the enemy into mistaking them for inanimate things by suddenly standing stock-still in closest peril, unflinching as stone; and to match himself against them the trapper must also get the knack of instantaneously becoming a statue, though he feel the clutch of bruin's five-inch claws.

And these things are only the a b c of the trapper's woodcraft.

One of the best hunters in America confessed that the longer he trapped the more he thought every animal different enough from the fellows of its kind to be a species by itself. Each day was a fresh page in the book of forest-lore.

It is in the month of May-goosey-geezee, the Ojibways' trout month, corresponding to the late October and early November of the white man, that the trapper sets out through the illimitable stretches of the forest land and waste prairie south of Hudson Bay, between Labrador and the Upper Missouri.

His birch canoe has been made during the summer. Now, splits and seams, where the bark crinkles at the gunwale, must be filled with rosin and pitch. A light sled, with only runners and cross frame, is made to haul the canoe over still water, where the ice first forms. Sled, provisions, blanket, and fish-net are put in the canoe, not forgetting the most important part of his kit—the trapper's tools. Whether he hunts from point to point all winter, travelling light and taking nothing but absolute necessaries, or builds a central lodge, where he leaves full store and radiates out to the hunting-grounds, at least four things must be in his tool-bag: a woodman's axe; a gimlet to bore holes in his snow-shoe frame; a crooked knife—not the sheathed dagger of fiction, but a blade crooked hook-shape, somewhat like a farrier's knife, at one end—to smooth without splintering, as a carpenter's plane; and a small chisel to use on the snow-shoe frames and wooden contrivances that stretch the pelts.

If accompanied by a boy, who carries half the pack, the hunter may take more tools; but the old trapper prefers to travel light. Fire-arms, ammunition, a common hunting-knife, steel-traps, a cotton-factory tepee, a large sheet of canvas, locally known as abuckwan, for a shed tent, complete the trapper's equipment. His dog is not part of the equipment: it is fellow-hunter and companion.

From the moose must come the heavy filling for the snow-shoes; but the snow-shoes will not be needed for a month, and there is no haste about shooting an unfound moose while mink and musk-rat and otter and beaver are waiting to be trapped. With the dog showing his wisdom by sitting motionless as an Indian bowman, the trapper steps into his canoe and pushes out.

Eye and ear alert for sign of game or feeding-place, where traps would be effective, the man paddles silently on. If he travels after nightfall, the chances are his craft will steal unawares close to a black head above a swimming body. With both wind and current meeting the canoe, no suspicion of his presence catches the scent of the sharp-nosed swimmer. Otter or beaver, it is shot from the canoe. With a leap over bow or stern—over his master's shoulder if necessary, but never sideways, lest the rebound cause an upset—the dog brings back his quarry. But this is only an aside, the hap-hazard shot of an amateur hunter, not the sort of trapping that fills the company's lofts with fur bales.

While ranging the forest the former season the trapper picked out a large birch-tree, free of knots and underbranching, with the full girth to make the body of a canoe from gunwale to gunwale without any gussets and seams. But birch-bark does not peel well in winter. The trapper scratched the trunk with a mark of "first-finder-first-owner," honoured by all hunters; and came back in the summer for the bark.

Perhaps it was while taking the bark from this tree that he first noticed the traces of beaver. Channels, broader than runnels, hardly as wide as a ditch, have been cut connecting pool with pool, marsh with lake. Here are runways through the grass, where beaver have dragged young saplings five times their own length to a winter storehouse near the dam. Trees lie felled miles away from any chopper. Chips are scattered about marked by teeth which the trapper knows—knows, perhaps, from having seen his dog's tail taken off at a nip, or his own finger amputated almost before he felt it. If the bark of a tree has been nibbled around, like the line a chopper might make before cutting, the trapper guesses whether his coming has not interrupted a beaver in the very act.

All these are signs which spell out the presence of a beaver-dam within one night's travelling distance; for the timid beaver frequently works at night, and will not go so far away that forage cannot be brought in before daylight. In which of the hundred water-ways in the labyrinth of pond and stream where beavers roam is this particular family to be found?

Realizing that his own life depends on the life of the game, no true trapper will destroy wild creatures when the mothers are caring for their young. Besides, furs are not at their prime when birch-bark is peeled, and the trapper notes the place, so that he may come back when the fall hunt begins. Beaver kittens stay under the parental roof for three years, but at the end of the first summer are amply able to look after their own skins.

Free from nursery duties, the old ones can now use all the ingenuity and craft which nature gave them for self-protection. When cold weather comes the beaver is fair game to the trapper. It is wit against wit. To be sure, the man has superior strength, a gun, and a treacherous thing called a trap. But his eyes are not equal to the beaver's nose. And he hasn't that familiarity with the woods to enable him to pursue, which the beaver has to enable it to escape. And he can't swim long enough under water to throw enemies off the scent, the way the beaver does.

Now, as he paddles along the network of streams which interlace Northern forests, he will hardly be likely to stumble on the beaver-dam of last summer. Beavers do not build their houses, where passers-by will stumble upon them. But all the streams have been swollen by fall rains; and the trapper notices the markings on every chip and pole floating down the full current. A chip swirls past white and fresh cut. He knows that the rains have floated it over the beaver-dam. Beavers never cut below their houses, but always above, so that the current will carry the poles down-stream to the dam.

Leaving his canoe-load behind, the trapper guardedly advances within sight of the dam. If any old beaver sentinel be swimming about, he quickly scents the man-smell, upends and dives with a spanking blow of his trowel tail on the water, which heliographs danger to the whole community. He swims with his webbed hind feet, the little fore paws being used as carriers or hanging limply, the flat tail acting the faintest bit in the world like a rudder; but that is a mooted question. The only definitely ascertained function of that bat-shaped appendage is to telegraph danger to comrades. The beaver neither carries things on his tail, nor plasters houses with it; for the simple reason that the joints of his caudal appurtenance admit of only slight sidelong wigglings and a forward sweep between his hind legs, as if he might use it as a tray for food while he sat back spooning up mouthfuls with his fore paws.

Having found the wattled homes of the beaver, the trapper may proceed in different ways. He may, after the fashion of the Indian hunter, stake the stream across above the dam, cut away the obstruction lowering the water, break the conical crowns of the houses on the south side, which is thinnest, and slaughter the beavers indiscriminately as they rush out. But such hunting kills the goose that lays the golden egg; and explains why it was necessary to prohibit the killing of beaver for some years. In the confusion of a wild scramble to escape and a blind clubbing of heads there was bootless destruction. Old and young, poor and in prime, suffered the same fate. The house had been destroyed; and if one beaver chanced to escape into some of the bank-holes under water or up the side channels, he could be depended upon to warn all beaver from that country. Only the degenerate white man practises bad hunting.

The skilled hunter has other methods.

If unstripped saplings be yet about the bank of the stream, the beavers have not finished laying up their winter stores in adjacent pools. The trapper gets one of his steel-traps. Attaching the ring of this to a loose trunk heavy enough to hold the beaver down and drown him, he places the trap a few inches under water at the end of a runway or in one of the channels. He then takes out a bottle of castoreum. This is a substance from the glands of a beaver which destroys all traces of the man-smell. For it the beavers have a curious infatuation, licking everything touched by it, and said, by some hunters, to be drugged into a crazy stupidity by the very smell. The hunter daubs this on his own foot-tracks.

Or, if he finds tracks of the beaver in the grass back from the bank, he may build an old-fashioned deadfall, with which the beaver is still taken in Labrador. This is the small lean-to, with a roof of branches and bark—usually covered with snow—slanting to the ground on one side, the ends either posts or logs, and the front an opening between two logs wide enough to admit half the animal's body. Inside, at the back, on a rectangular stick, one part of which bolsters up the front log, is the bait. All traces of the hunter are smeared over with the elusive castoreum. One tug at the bait usually brings the front log crashing down across the animal's back, killing it instantly.

But neither the steel-trap nor the deadfall is wholly satisfactory. When the poor beaver comes sniffing along the castoreum trail to the steel-trap and on the first splash into the water feels a pair of iron jaws close on his feet, he dives below to try and gain the shelter of his house. The log plunges after him, holding him down and back till he drowns; and his whereabouts are revealed by the upend of the tree.

But several chances are in the beaver's favour. With the castoreum licks, which tell them of some other beaver, perhaps looking for a mate or lost cub, they may become so exhilarated as to jump clear of the trap. Or, instead of diving down with the trap, they may retreat back up the bank and amputate the imprisoned foot with one nip, leaving only a mutilated paw for the hunter. With the deadfall a small beaver may have gone entirely inside the snare before the front log falls; and an animal whose teeth saw through logs eighteen inches in diameter in less than half an hour can easily eat a way of escape from a wooden trap. Other things are against the hunter. A wolverine may arrive on the scene before the trapper and eat the finest beaver ever taken; or the trapper may discover that his victim is a poor little beaver with worthless, ragged fur, who should have been left to forage for three or four years.

All these risks can be avoided by waiting till the ice is thick enough for the trapper to cut trenches. Then he returns with a woodman's axe and his dog. By sounding the ice, he can usually find where holes have been hollowed out of the banks. Here he drives stakes to prevent the beaver taking refuge in the shore vaults. The runways and channels, where the beaver have dragged trees, may be hidden in snow and iced over; but the man and his dog will presently find them.

The beaver always chooses a stream deep enough not to be frozen solid, and shallow enough for it to make a mud foundation for the house without too much work. Besides, in a deep, swift stream, rains would carry away any house the beaver could build. A trench across the upper stream or stakes through the ice prevent escape that way.

The trapper then cuts a hole in the dam. Falling water warns the terrified colony that an enemy is near. It may be their greatest foe, the wolverine, whose claws will rip through the frost-hard wall as easily as a bear delves for gophers; but their land enemies cannot pursue them into water; so the panic-stricken family—the old parents, wise from many such alarms; the young three-year-olds, who were to go out and rear families for themselves in the spring; the two-year-old cubbies, big enough to be saucy, young enough to be silly; and the baby kittens, just able to forage for themselves and know the soft alder rind from the tough old bark unpalatable as mud—pop pell-mell from the high platform of their houses into the water. The water is still falling. They will presently be high and dry. No use trying to escape up-stream. They see that in the first minute's wild scurry through the shallows. Besides, what's this across the creek? Stakes, not put there by any beaver; for there is no bark on. If they only had time now they might cut a passage through; but no—this wretched enemy, whatever it is, has ditched the ice across.

They sniff and listen. A terrible sound comes from above—a low, exultant, devilish whining. The man has left his dog on guard above the dam. At that the little beavers—always trembling, timid fellows—tumble over each other in a panic of fear to escape by way of the flowing water below the dam. But there a new terror assails them. A shadow is above the ice, a wraith of destruction—the figure of a man standing at the dam with his axe and club—waiting.

Where to go now? They can't find their bank shelters, for the man has staked them up. The little fellows lose their presence of mind and their heads and their courage, and with a blind scramble dash up the remaining open runway. It is a cul-de-sac. But what does that matter? They run almost to the end. They can crouch there till the awful shadow goes away. Exactly. That is what the man has been counting on. He will come to them afterward.

The old beavers make no such mistake. They have tried the hollow-log trick with an enemy pursuing them to the blind end, and have escaped only because some other beaver was eaten.

The old ones know that water alone is safety.

That is the first and last law of beaver life. They, too, see that phantom destroyer above the ice; but a dash past is the last chance. How many of the beaver escape past the cut in the dam to the water below, depends on the dexterity of the trapper's aim. But certainly, for the most, one blow is the end; and that one blow is less cruel to them than the ravages of the wolf or wolverine in spring, for these begin to eat before they kill.

A signal, and the dog ceases to keep guard above the dam. Where is the runway in which the others are hiding? The dog scampers round aimlessly, but begins to sniff and run in a line and scratch and whimper. The man sees that the dog is on the trail of sagging snow, and the sag betrays ice settling down where a channel has run dry. The trapper cuts a hole across the river end of the runway and drives down stakes. The young beavers are now prisoners.

The human mind can't help wondering why the foolish youngsters didn't crouch below the ice above the dam and lie there in safe hiding till the monster went away. This may be done by the hermit beavers—fellows who have lost their mates and go through life inconsolable; or sick creatures, infested by parasites and turned off to house in the river holes; or fat, selfish ladies, who don't want the trouble of training a family. Whatever these solitaries are—naturalists and hunters differ—they have the wit to keep alive; but the poor little beavers rush right into the jaws of death. Why do they? For the same reason probably, if they could answer, that people trample each other to death when there is an alarm in a crowd.

They cower in the terrible pen, knowing nothing at all about their hides being valued all the way from fifty cents to three dollars, according to the quality; nothing about the dignity of being a coin of the realm in the Northern wilderness, where one beaver-skin sets the value for mink, otter, marten, bear, and all other skins, one pound of tobacco, one kettle, five pounds of shot, a pint of brandy, and half a yard of cloth; nothing about the rascally Indians long ago bartering forty of their hides for a scrap of iron and a great company sending one hundred thousand beaver-skins in a single year to make hats and cloaks for the courtiers of Europe; nothing about the laws of man forbidding the killing of beaver till their number increase.

All the little beaver remembers is that it opened its eyes to daylight in the time of soft, green grasses; and that as soon as it got strong enough on a milk diet to travel, the mother led the whole family of kittens—usually three or four—down the slanting doorway of their dim house for a swim; and that she taught them how to nibble the dainty, green shrubs along the bank; and then the entire colony went for the most glorious, pell-mell splash up-stream to fresh ponds. No more sleeping in that stifling lodge; but beds in soft grass like a goose-nest all night, and tumbling in the water all day, diving for the roots of the lily-pads. But the old mother is always on guard, for the wolves and bears are ravenous in spring. Soon the cubs can cut the hardening bark of alder and willow as well as their two-year-old brothers; and the wonderful thing is—if a tooth breaks, it grows into perfect shape inside of a week.

By August the little fellows are great swimmers, and the colony begins the descent of the stream for their winter home. If unmolested, the old dam is chosen; but if the hated man-smell is there, new waterways are sought. Burrows and washes and channels and retreats are cleaned out. Trees are cut and a great supply of branches laid up for winter store near the lodge, not a chip of edible bark being wasted. Just before the frost they begin building or repairing the dam. Each night's frost hardens the plastered clay till the conical wattled roof—never more than two feet thick—will support the weight of a moose.

All work is done with mouth and fore paws, and not the tail. This has been finally determined by observing the Marquis of Bute's colony of beavers. If the family—the old parents and three seasons' offspring—be too large for the house, new chambers are added. In height the house is seldom more than five feet from the base, and the width varies. In building a new dam they begin under water, scooping out clay, mixing this with stones and sticks for the walls, and hollowing out the dome as it rises, like a coffer-dam, except that man pumps out water and the beaver scoops out mud. The domed roof is given layer after layer of clay till it is cold-proof. Whether the houses have one door or two is disputed; but the door is always at the end of a sloping incline away from the land side, with a shelf running round above, which serves as the living-room. Differences in the houses, breaks below water, two doors instead of one, platforms like an oven instead of a shelf, are probably explained by the continual abrasion of the current. By the time the ice forms the beavers have retired to their houses for the winter, only coming out to feed on their winter stores and get an airing.

But this terrible thing has happened; and the young beavers huddle together under the ice of the canal, bleating with the cry of a child. They are afraid to run back; for the crunch of feet can be heard. They are afraid to go forward; for the dog is whining with a glee that is fiendish to the little beavers. Then a gust of cold air comes from the rear and a pole prods forward.

The man has opened a hole to feel where the hiding beavers are, and with little terrified yelps they scuttle to the very end of the runway. By this time the dog is emitting howls of triumph. For hours he has been boxing up his wolfish ferocity, and now he gives vent by scratching with a zeal that would burrow to the middle of earth.

The trapper drives in more stakes close to the blind end of the channel, and cuts a hole above the prison of the beaver. He puts down his arm. One by one they are dragged out by the tail; and that finishes the little beaver—sacrificed, like the guinea-pigs and rabbits of bacteriological laboratories, to the necessities of man. Only, this death is swifter and less painful. A prolonged death-struggle with the beaver would probably rob the trapper of half his fingers. Very often the little beavers with poor fur are let go. If the dog attempts to capture the frightened runaways by catching at the conspicuous appendage to the rear, that dog is likely to emerge from the struggle minus a tail, while the beaver runs off with two.

Trappers have curious experiences with beaver kittens which they take home as pets. When young they are as easily domesticated as a cat, and become a nuisance with their love of fondling. But to them, as to the hunter, comes what the Indians call "the-sickness-of-long-thinking," the gipsy yearning for the wilds. Then extraordinary things happen. The beaver are apt to avenge their comrades' death. One old beaver trapper of New Brunswick related that by June the beavers became so restless, he feared their escape and put them in cages. They bit their way out with absurd ease.

He then tried log pens. They had eaten a hole through in a night. Thinking to get wire caging, he took them into his lodge, and they seemed contented enough while he was about; but one morning he wakened to find a hole eaten through the door, and the entire round of birch-bark, which he had staked out ready for the gunwales and ribbing of his canoe—bark for which he had travelled forty miles—chewed into shreds. The beavers had then gone up-stream, which is their habit in spring.

CHAPTER X
THE MAKING OF THE MOCCASINS

It is a grim joke of the animal world that the lazy moose is the moose that gives wings to the feet of the pursuer. When snow comes the trapper must have snow-shoes and moccasins. For both, moose supplies the best material.

Bees have their drones, beaver their hermits, and moose a ladified epicure who draws off from the feeding-yards of the common herd, picks out the sweetest browse of the forest, and gorges herself till fat as a gouty voluptuary. While getting the filling for his snow-shoes, the trapper also stocks his larder; and if he can find a spinster moose, he will have something better than shredded venison and more delicately flavoured than finest teal.

Sledding his canoe across shallow lakelets, now frozen like rock, still paddling where there is open way, the trapper continues to guide his course up the waterways. Big game, he knows, comes out to drink at sunrise and sunset; and nearly all the small game frequents the banks of streams either to fish or to prey on the fisher.

Each night he sleeps in the open with his dog on guard; or else puts up the cotton tepee, the dog curling outside the tent flap, one ear awake. And each night a net is set for the white-fish that are to supply breakfast, feed the dog, and provide heads for the traps placed among rocks in mid-stream, or along banks where dainty footprints were in the morning's hoar-frost. Brook trout can still be got in the pools below waterfalls; but the trapper seldom takes time now to use the line, depending on his gun and fish-net.

During the Indian's white-fish month—the white man's November—the weather has become colder and colder; but the trapper never indulges in the big log fire that delights the heart of the amateur hunter. That would drive game a week's tracking from his course. Unless he wants to frighten away nocturnal prowlers, a little, chip fire, such as the fishermen of the Banks use in their dories, is all the trapper allows himself.

First snow silences the rustling leaves. First frost quiets the flow of waters. Except for the occasional splitting of a sap-frozen tree, or the far howl of a wolf-pack, there is the stillness of death. And of all quiet things in the quiet forest, the trapper is the quietest.

As winter closes in the ice-skim of the large lakes cuts the bark canoe like a knife. The canoe is abandoned for snow-shoes and the cotton tepee for more substantial shelter.

If the trapper is a white man he now builds a lodge near the best hunting-ground he has found. Around this he sets a wide circle of traps at such distances their circuit requires an entire day, and leads the trapper out in one direction and back in another, without retracing the way. Sometimes such lodges run from valley to valley. Each cabin is stocked; and the hunter sleeps where night overtakes him. But this plan needs two men; for if the traps are not closely watched, the wolverine will rifle away a priceless fox as readily as he eats a worthless musk-rat. The stone fire-place stands at one end. Moss, clay, and snow chink up the logs. Parchment across a hole serves as window. Poles and brush make the roof, or perhaps the remains of the cotton tent stretched at a steep angle to slide off the accumulating weight of snow.

But if the trapper is an Indian, or the white man has a messenger to carry the pelts marked with his name to a friendly trading-post, he may not build a lodge; but move from hunt to hunt as the game changes feeding-ground. In this case he uses the abuckwan—canvas—for a shed tent, with one side sloping to the ground, banked by brush and snow, the other facing the fire, both tent and fire on such a slope that the smoke drifts out while the heat reflects in. Pine and balsam boughs, with the wood end pointing out like sheaves in a stook, the foliage converging to a soft centre, form the trapper's bed.

The snow is now too deep to travel without snow-shoes. The frames for these the trapper makes of ash, birch, or best of all, the mackikwatick—tamarack—curving the easily bent green wood up at one end, canoe shape, and smoothing the barked wood at the bend, like a sleigh runner, by means of the awkward couteau croche, as the French hunter calls his crooked knife.

In style, the snow-shoe varies with the hunting-ground. On forested, rocky, hummocky land, the shoe is short to permit short turns without entanglement. Oval and broad, rather than long and slim, it makes up in width what it lacks in length to support the hunter's weight above the snow. And the toe curve is slight; for speed is impossible on bad ground. To save the instep from jars, the slip noose may be padded like a cowboy's stirrup.

On the prairie, where the snowy reaches are unbroken as air, snow-shoes are wings to the hunter's heels. They are long, and curved, and narrow, and smooth enough on the runners for the hunter to sit on their rear ends and coast downhill as on a toboggan. If a snag is struck midway, the racquets may bounce safely over and glissade to the bottom; or the toe may catch, heels fly over head, and the hunter land with his feet noosed in frames sticking upright higher than his neck.

Any trapper can read the story of a hunt from snow-shoes. Bound and short: east of the Great Lakes. Slim and long: from the prairie. Padding for the instep: either rock ground or long runs. Filling of hide strips with broad enough interspaces for a small foot to slip through: from the wet, heavily packed, snow region of the Atlantic coast, for trapping only, never the chase, small game, not large. Lace ties, instead of a noose to hold the foot: the amateur hunter. Atibisc, a fine filling taken from deer or caribou for the heel and toe; with askimoneiab, heavy, closely interlaced, membraneous filling from the moose across the centre to bear the brunt of wear; long enough for speed, short enough to turn short: the trapper knows he is looking at the snow-shoe of the craftsman. This is the sort he must have for himself.

The first thing, then—a moose for the heavy filling; preferably a spinster moose; for she is too lazy to run from a hunter who is not yet a Mercury; and she will furnish him with a banquet fit for kings.

Neither moose call nor birch horn, of which wonders are told, will avail now. The mating season is well past. Even if an old moose responded to the call, the chances are his flesh would be unfit for food. It would be a wasted kill, contrary to the principles of the true trapper.

Every animal has a sign language as plain as print. The trapper has hardly entered the forest before he begins to read this language. Broad hoof-marks are on the muskeg—quaking bog, covered with moss—over which the moose can skim as if on snow-shoes, where a horse would sink to the saddle. Park-like glades at the heads of streams, where the moose have spent the summer browsing on twigs and wallowing in water holes to get rid of sand flies, show trampled brush and stripped twigs and rubbed bark.

Coming suddenly on a grove of quaking aspens, a saucy jay has fluttered up with a noisy call—an alarm note; and something is bounding off to hiding in a thicket on the far side of the grove. The wis-kat-jan, or whisky jack, as the white men call it, who always hangs about the moose herds, has seen the trapper and sounded the alarm.

In August, when the great, palmated horns, which budded out on the male in July, are yet in the velvet, the trapper finds scraps of furry hair sticking to young saplings. The vain moose has been polishing his antlers, preparatory to mating. Later, there is a great whacking of horns among the branches. The moose, spoiling for a fight, in moose language is challenging his rivals to battle. Wood-choppers have been interrupted by the apparition of a huge, palmated head through a thicket. Mistaking the axe for his rival's defiance, the moose arrives on the scene in a mood of blind rage that sends the chopper up a tree, or back to the shanty for his rifle.

But the trapper allows these opportunities to pass. He is not ready for his moose until winter compels the abandoning of the canoe. Then the moose herds are yarding up in some sheltered feeding-ground.

It is not hard for the trapper to find a moose yard. There is the tell-tale cleft footprint in the snow. There are the cast-off antlers after the battles have been fought—the female moose being without horns and entirely dependent on speed and hearing and smell for protection. There is the stripped, overhead twig, where a moose has reared on hind legs and nibbled a branch above. There is the bent or broken sapling which a moose pulled down with his mouth and then held down with his feet while he browsed. This and more sign language of the woods—too fine for the language of man—lead the trapper close on the haunts of a moose herd. But he does not want an ordinary moose. He is keen for the solitary track of a haughty spinster. And he probably comes on the print when he has almost made up his mind to chance a shot at one of the herd below the hill, where he hides. He knows the trail is that of a spinster. It is unusually heavy; and she is always fat. It drags clumsily over the snow; for she is lazy. And it doesn't travel straight away in a line like that of the roving moose; for she loiters to feed and dawdle out of pure indolence.

And now the trapper knows how a hound on a hot scent feels. He may win his prize with the ease of putting out his hand and taking it—sighting his rifle and touching the trigger. Or, by the blunder of a hair's breadth, he may daily track twenty weary miles for a week and come back empty at his cartridge-belt, empty below his cartridge-belt, empty of hand, and full, full of rage at himself, though his words curse the moose. He may win his prize in one of two ways: (1) by running the game to earth from sheer exhaustion; (2) or by a still hunt.

The straightaway hunt is more dangerous to the man than the moose. Even a fat spinster can outdistance a man with no snow-shoes. And if his perseverance lasts longer than her strength—for though a moose swings out in a long-stepping, swift trot, it is easily tired—the exhausted moose is a moose at bay; and a moose at bay rears on her hind legs and does defter things with the flattening blow of her fore feet than an exhausted man can do with a gun. The blow of a cleft hoof means something sharply split, wherever that spreading hoof lands. And if the something wriggles on the snow in death-throes, the moose pounds upon it with all four feet till the thing is still. Then she goes on her way with eyes ablaze and every shaggy hair bristling.

The contest was even and the moose won.

Apart from the hazard, there is a barbarism about this straightaway chase, which repels the trapper. It usually succeeds by bogging the moose in crusted snow, or a waterhole—and then, Indian fashion, a slaughter; and no trapper kills for the sake of killing, for the simple practical reason that his own life depends on the preservation of game.

A slight snowfall and the wind in his face are ideal conditions for a still hunt. One conceals him. The other carries the man-smell from the game.

Which way does the newly-discovered footprint run? More flakes are in one hole than the other. He follows the trail till he has an idea of the direction the moose is taking; for the moose runs straightaway, not circling and doubling back on cold tracks like the deer, but marching direct to the objective point, where it turns, circles slightly—a loop at the end of a line—and lies down a little off the trail. When the pursuer, following the cold scent, runs past, the moose gets wind and is off in the opposite direction like a vanishing streak.

Having ascertained the lie of the land, the trapper leaves the line of direct trail and follows in a circling detour. Here, he finds the print fresher, not an hour old. The moose had stopped to browse and the markings are moist on a twig. The trapper leaves the trail, advancing always by a detour to leeward. He is sure, now, that it is a spinster. If it had been any other, the moose would not have been alone. The rest would be tracking into the leader's steps; and by the fresh trail he knows for a certainty there is only one. But his very nearness increases the risk. The wind may shift. The snowfall is thinning. This time, when he comes back to the trail, it is fresher still. The hunter now gets his rifle ready. He dare not put his foot down without testing the snow, lest a twig snap. He parts a way through the brush with his hand and replaces every branch. And when next he comes back to the line of the moose's travel, there is no trail. This is what he expected. He takes off his coat; his leggings, if they are loose enough to rub with a leathery swish; his musk-rat fur cap, if it has any conspicuous colour; his boots, if they are noisy and given to crunching. If only he aim true, he will have moccasins soon enough. Leaving all impedimenta, he follows back on his own steps to the place where he last saw the trail. Perhaps the saucy jay cries with a shrill, scolding shriek that sends cold shivers down the trapper's spine. He wishes he could get his hands on its wretched little neck; and turning himself to a statue, he stands stone-still till the troublesome bird settles down. Then he goes on.

Here is the moose trail!

He dare not follow direct. That would lead past her hiding-place and she would bolt. He resorts to artifice; but, for that matter, so has the moose resorted to artifice. The trapper, too, circles forward, cutting the moose's magic guard with transverse zigzags. But he no longer walks. He crouches, or creeps, or glides noiselessly from shelter to shelter, very much the way a cat advances on an unwary mouse. He sinks to his knees and feels forward for snow-pads every pace. Then he is on all-fours, still circling. His detour has narrowed and narrowed till he knows she must be in that aspen thicket. The brush is sparser. She has chosen her resting-ground wisely. The man falls forward on his face, closing in, closing in, wiggling and watching till— he makes a horrible discovery. That jay is perched on the topmost bough of the grove; and the man has caught a glimpse of something buff-coloured behind the aspens. It may be a moose, or only a log. The untried hunter would fire. Not so the trapper. Hap-hazard aim means fighting a wounded moose, or letting the creature drag its agony off to inaccessible haunts. The man worms his way round the thicket, sighting the game with the noiseless circling of a hawk before the drop. An ear blinks. But at that instant the jay perks his head to one side with a curious look at this strange object on the ground. In another second it will be off with a call and the moose up.

His rifle is aimed!

A blinding swish of aspen leaves and snow and smoke! The jay is off with a noisy whistle. And the trapper has leather for moccasins, and heavy filling for his snow-shoes, and meat for his larder.

But he must still get the fine filling for heel and toe; and this comes from caribou or deer. The deer, he will still hunt as he has still hunted the moose, with this difference: that the deer runs in circles, jumping back in his own tracks leaving the hunter to follow a cold scent, while it, by a sheer bound—five—eight—twenty feet off at a new angle, makes for the hiding of dense woods. No one but a barbarian would attempt to run down a caribou; for it can only be done by the shameless trick of snaring in crusted snow, or intercepting while swimming, and then—butchery.

The caribou doesn't run. It doesn't bound. It floats away into space.

One moment a sandy-coloured form, with black nose, black feet, and a glory of white statuary above its head, is seen against the far reaches of snow. The next, the form has shrunk—and shrunk—and shrunk, antlers laid back against its neck, till there is a vanishing speck on the horizon. The caribou has not been standing at all. It has skimmed out of sight; and if there is any clear ice across the marshes, it literally glides beyond vision from very speed. But, provided no man-smell crosses its course, the caribou is vulnerable in its habits. Morning and evening, it comes back to the same watering-place; and it returns to the same bed for the night. If the trapper can conceal himself without crossing its trail, he easily obtains the fine filling for his snow-shoes.

Moccasins must now be made.

The trapper shears off the coarse hair with a sharp knife. The hide is soaked; and a blunter blade tears away the remaining hairs till the skin is white and clean. The flesh side is similarly cleaned and the skin rubbed with all the soap and grease it will absorb. A process of beating follows till the hide is limber. Carelessness at this stage makes buckskin soak up water like a sponge and dry to a shapeless board. The skin must be stretched and pulled till it will stretch no more. Frost helps the tanning, drying all moisture out; and the skin becomes as soft as down, without a crease. The smoke of punk from a rotten tree gives the dark yellow colour to the hide and prevents hardening. The skin is now ready for the needle; and all odd bits are hoarded away.

Equipped with moccasins and snow-shoes, the trapper is now the winged messenger of the tragic fates to the forest world.

CHAPTER XI
THE INDIAN TRAPPER

It is dawn when the Indian trapper leaves his lodge.

In midwinter of the Far North, dawn comes late. Stars, which shine with a hard, clear, crystal radiance only seen in northern skies, pale in the gray morning gloom; and the sun comes over the horizon dim through mists of frost-smoke. In an hour the frost-mist, lying thick to the touch like clouds of steam, will have cleared; and there will be nothing from sky-line to sky-line but blinding sunlight and snowglare.

The Indian trapper must be far afield before mid-day. Then the sun casts no man-shadow to scare game from his snares. Black is the flag of betrayal in northern midwinter. It is by the big liquid eye, glistening on the snow like a black marble, that the trapper detects the white hare; and a jet tail-tip streaking over the white wastes in dots and dashes tells him the little ermine, whose coat must line some emperor's coronation robe, is alternately scudding over the drifts and diving below the snow with the forward wriggling of a snake under cover. But the moving man-shadow is bigger and plainer on the snow than the hare's eye or the ermine's jet tip; so the Indian trapper sets out in the gray darkness of morning and must reach his hunting-grounds before high noon.

With long snow-shoes, that carry him over the drifts in swift, coasting strides, he swings out in that easy, ambling, Indian trot, which gives never a jar to the runner, nor rests long enough for the snows to crunch beneath his tread.

The old musket, which he got in trade from the fur post, is over his shoulder, or swinging lightly in one hand. A hunter's knife and short-handled woodman's axe hang through the beaded scarf, belting in his loose, caribou capote. Powder-horn and heavy musk-rat gantlets are attached to the cord about his neck; so without losing either he can fight bare-handed, free and in motion, at a moment's notice. And somewhere, in side pockets or hanging down his back, is his skipertogan—a skin bag with amulet against evil, matches, touchwood, and a scrap of pemmican. As he grows hot, he throws back his hood, running bareheaded and loose about the chest.

Each breath clouds to frost against his face till hair and brows and lashes are fringed with frozen moisture. The white man would hugger his face up with scarf and collar the more for this; but the Indian knows better.

Suddenly chilled breath would soak scarf and collar wet to his skin; and his face would be frozen before he could go five paces. But with dry skin and quickened blood, he can defy the keenest cold; so he loosens his coat and runs the faster.

As the light grows, dim forms shape themselves in the gray haze. Pine groves emerge from the dark, wreathed and festooned in snow. Cones and domes and cornices of snow heap the underbrush and spreading larch boughs. Evergreens are edged with white. Naked trees stand like limned statuary with an antlered crest etched against the white glare. The snow stretches away in a sea of billowed, white drifts that seem to heave and fall to the motions of the runner, mounting and coasting and skimming over the unbroken waste like a bird winging the ocean. And against this endless stretch of drifts billowing away to a boundless circle, of which the man is the centre, his form is dwarfed out of all proportion, till he looks no larger than a bird above the sea.

When the sun rises, strange colour effects are caused by the frost haze. Every shrub takes fire; for the ice drops are a prism, and the result is the same as if there had been a star shower or rainfall of brilliants. Does the Indian trapper see all this? The white man with white man arrogance doubts whether his tawny brother of the wilds sees the beauty about him, because the Indian has no white man's terms of expression. But ask the bronzed trapper the time of day; and he tells you by the length of shadow the sun casts, or the degree of light on the snow. Inquire the season of the year; and he knows by the slant sunlight coming up through the frost smoke of the southern horizon. And get him talking about his Happy Hunting-Grounds; and after he has filled it with the implements and creatures and people of the chase, he will describe it in the metaphor of what he has seen at sunrise and sunset and under the Northern Lights. He does not see these things with the gabbling exclamatories of a tourist. He sees them because they sink into his nature and become part of his mental furniture. The most brilliant description the writer ever heard of the Hereafter was from an old Cree squaw, toothless, wrinkled like leather, belted at the waist like a sack of wool, with hands of dried parchment, and moccasins some five months too odoriferous. Her version ran that Heaven would be full of the music of running waters and south winds; that there would always be warm gold sunlight like a midsummer afternoon, with purple shadows, where tired women could rest; that the trees would be covered with blossoms, and all the pebbles of the shore like dewdrops.

Pushed from the Atlantic seaboard back over the mountains, from the mountains to the Mississippi, west to the Rockies, north to the Great Lakes, all that was to be seen of nature in America the Indian trapper has seen; though he has not understood.

But now he holds only a fringe of hunting-grounds, in the timber lands of the Great Lakes, in the cañons of the Rockies, and across that northern land which converges to Hudson Bay, reaching west to Athabasca, east to Labrador. It is in the basin of Hudson Bay regions that the Indian trapper will find his last hunting-grounds. Here climate excludes the white man, and game is plentiful. Here Indian trappers were snaring before Columbus opened the doors of the New World to the hordes of the Old; and here Indian trappers will hunt as long as the race lasts. When there is no more game, the Indian's doom is sealed; but that day is far distant for the Hudson Bay region.

The Indian trapper has set few large traps. It is midwinter; and by December there is a curious lull in the hunting. All the streams are frozen like rock; but the otter and pekan and mink and marten have not yet begun to forage at random across open field. Some foolish fish always dilly-dally up-stream till the ice shuts them in. Then a strange thing is seen—a kettle of living fish; fish gasping and panting in ice-hemmed water that is gradually lessening as each day's frost freezes another layer to the ice walls of their prison. The banks of such a pond hole are haunted by the otter and his fisher friends. By-and-bye, when the pond is exhausted, these lazy fishers must leave their safe bank and forage across country. Meanwhile, they are quiet.

The bear, too, is still. After much wandering and fastidious choosing—for in trapper vernacular the bear takes a long time to please himself—bruin found an upturned stump. Into the hollow below he clawed grasses. Then he curled up with his nose on his toes and went to sleep under a snow blanket of gathering depth. Deer, moose, and caribou, too, have gone off to their feeding-grounds. Unless they are scattered by a wolf-pack or a hunter's gun, they will not be likely to move till this ground is eaten over. Nor are many beaver seen now. They have long since snuggled into their warm houses, where they will stay till their winter store is all used; and their houses are now hidden under great depths of deepening snow. But the fox and the hare and the ermine are at run; and as long as they are astir, so are their rampant enemies, the lynx and the wolverine and the wolf-pack, all ravenous from the scarcity of other game and greedy as spring crows.

That thought gives wings to the Indian trapper's heels. The pelt of a coyote—or prairie wolf—would scarcely be worth the taking. Even the big, gray timber-wolf would hardly be worth the cost of the shot, except for service as a tepee mat. The white arctic wolf would bring better price. The enormous black or brown arctic wolf would be more valuable; but the value would not repay the risk of the hunt. But all these worthless, ravening rascals are watching the traps as keenly as the trapper does; and would eat up a silver fox, that would be the fortune of any hunter.

The Indian comes to the brush where he has set his rabbit snares across a runway. His dog sniffs the ground, whining. The crust of the snow is broken by a heavy tread. The twigs are all trampled and rabbit fur is fluffed about. The game has been rifled away. The Indian notices several things. The rabbit has been devoured on the spot. That is unlike the wolverine. He would have carried snare, rabbit and all off for a guzzle in his own lair. The footprints have the appearance of having been brushed over; so the thief had a bushy tail. It is not the lynx. There is no trail away from the snare. The marauder has come with a long leap and gone with a long leap. The Indian and his dog make a circuit of the snare till they come on the trail of the intruder; and its size tells the Indian whether his enemy be fox or wolf.

He sets no more snares across that runway, for the rabbits have had their alarm. Going through the brush he finds a fresh runway and sets a new snare.

Then his snow-shoes are winging him over the drifts to the next trap. It is a deadfall. Nothing is in it. The bait is untouched and the trap left undisturbed. A wolverine would have torn the thing to atoms from very wickedness, chewed the bait in two, and spat it out lest there should be poison. The fox would have gone in and had his back broken by the front log. And there is the same brush work over the trampled snow, as if the visitor had tried to sweep out his own trail; and the same long leap away, clearing obstruction of log and drift, to throw a pursuer off the scent. This time the Indian makes two or three circuits; but the snow is so crusted it is impossible to tell whether the scratchings lead out to the open or back to the border of snow-drifted woods. If the animal had followed the line of the traps by running just inside the brush, the Indian would know. But the midwinter day is short, and he has no time to explore the border of the thicket.

Perhaps he has a circle of thirty traps. Of that number he hardly expects game in more than a dozen. If six have a prize, he has done well. Each time he stops to examine a trap he must pause to cover all trace of the man-smell, daubing his own tracks with castoreum, or pomatum, or bears' grease; sweeping the snow over every spot touched by his hand; dragging the flesh side of a fresh pelt across his own trail.

Mid-day comes, the time of the short shadow; and the Indian trapper has found not a thing in his traps. He only knows that some daring enemy has dogged the circle of his snares. That means he must kill the marauder, or find new hunting-grounds. If he had doubt about swift vengeance for the loss of a rabbit, he has none when he comes to the next trap. He sees what is too much for words: what entails as great loss to the poor Indian trapper as an exchange crash to the white man. One of his best steel-traps lies a little distance from the pole to which it was attached. It has been jerked up with a great wrench and pulled as far as the chain would go. The snow is trampled and stained and covered with gray fur as soft and silvery as chinchilla. In the trap is a little paw, fresh cut, scarcely frozen. He had caught a silver fox, the fortune of which hunters dream, as prospectors of gold, and speculators of stocks, and actors of fame. But the wolves, the great, black wolves of the Far North, with eyes full of a treacherous green fire and teeth like tusks, had torn the fur to scraps and devoured the fox not an hour before the trapper came.

He knows now what his enemy is; for he has come so suddenly on their trail he can count four different footprints, and claw-marks of different length. They have fought about the little fox; and some of the smaller wolves have lost fur over it. Then, by the blood-marks, he can tell they have got under cover of the shrub growth to the right.

The Indian says none of the words which the white man might say; but that is nothing to his credit; for just now no words are adequate. But he takes prompt resolution. After the fashion of the old Mosaic law, which somehow is written on the very face of the wilderness as one of its necessities, he decides that only life for life will compensate such loss. The danger of hunting the big, brown wolf—he knows too well to attempt it without help. He will bait his small traps with poison; take out his big, steel wolf traps to-morrow; then with a band of young braves follow the wolf-pack's trail during this lull in the hunting season.

But the animal world knows that old trick of drawing a herring scent across the trail of wise intentions; and of all the animal world, none knows it better than the brown arctic wolf. He carries himself with less of a hang-dog air than his brother wolves, with the same pricking forward of sharp, erect ears, the same crouching trot, the same sneaking, watchful green eyes; but his tail, which is bushy enough to brush out every trace of his tracks, has not the skulking droop of the gray wolf's; and in size he is a giant among wolves.

The trapper shoulders his musket again, and keeping to the open, where he can travel fast on the long snow-shoes, sets out for the next trap. The man-shadow grows longer. It is late in the afternoon. Then all the shadows merge into the purple gloom of early evening; but the Indian travels on; for the circuit of traps leads back to his lodge.

The wolf thief may not be far off; so the man takes his musket from the case. He may chance a shot at the enemy. Where there are woods, wolves run under cover, keeping behind a fringe of brush to windward. The wind carries scent of danger from the open, and the brush forms an ambuscade. Man tracks, where man's dog might scent the trail of a wolf, the wolf clears at a long bound. He leaps over open spaces, if he can; and if he can't, crouches low till he has passed the exposure.

The trapper swings forward in long, straight strides, wasting not an inch of ground, deviating neither to right nor left by as much space as a white man takes to turn on his heels. Suddenly the trapper's dog utters a low whine and stops with ears pricked forward towards the brush. At the same moment the Indian, who has been keeping his eyes on the woods, sees a form rise out of the earth among the shadows. He is not surprised; for he knows the way the wolf travels, and the fox trap could not have been robbed more than an hour ago. The man thinks he has come on the thieves going to the next trap. That is what the wolf means him to think. And the man, too, dissembles; for as he looks the form fades into the gloom, and he decides to run on parallel to the brushwood, with his gun ready. Just ahead is a break in the shrubbery. At the clearing he can see how many wolves there are, and as he is heading home there is little danger.

But at the clearing nothing crosses. The dog dashes off to the woods with wild barking, and the trapper scans the long, white stretch leading back between the bushes to a horizon that is already dim in the steel grays of twilight.

Half a mile down this openway, off the homeward route of his traps, a wolfish figure looms black against the snow—and stands! The dog prances round and round as if he would hold the creature for his master's shot; and the Indian calculates—" After all, there is only one."

What a chance to approach it under cover, as it has approached his traps! The stars are already pricking the blue darkness in cold, steel points; and the Northern Lights are swinging through the gloom like mystic censers to an invisible Spirit, the Spirit of the still, white, wide, northern wastes. It is as clear as day.

One thought of his loss at the fox trap sends the Indian flitting through the underwoods like a hunted partridge. The sharp barkings of the dog increase in fury, and when the trapper emerges in the open, he finds the wolf has straggled a hundred yards farther. That was the meaning of the dog's alarm. Going back to cover, the hunter again advances. But the wolf keeps moving leisurely, and each time the man sights his game it is still out of range for the old-fashioned musket. The man runs faster now, determined to get abreast of the wolf and utterly heedless of the increasing danger, as each step puts greater distance between him and his lodge. He will pass the wolf, come out in front and shoot.

But when he comes to the edge of the woods to get his aim, there is no wolf, and the dog is barking furiously at his own moonlit shadow. The wolf, after the fashion of his kind, has apparently disappeared into the ground, just as he always seems to rise from the earth. The trapper thinks of the "loup-garou," but no wolf-demon of native legend devoured the very real substance of that fox.

The dog stops barking, gives a whine and skulks to his master's feet, while the trapper becomes suddenly aware of low-crouching forms gliding through the underbrush. Eyes look out of the dark in the flash of green lights from a prism. The figures are in hiding, but the moon is shining with a silvery clearness that throws moving wolf shadows on the snow to the trapper's very feet.

Then the man knows that he has been tricked.

The Indian knows the wolf-pack too well to attempt flight from these sleuths of the forest. He knows, too, one thing that wolves of forest and prairie hold in deadly fear—fire. Two or three shots ring into the darkness followed by a yelping howl, which tells him there is one wolf less, and the others will hold off at a safe distance. Contrary to the woodman's traditions of chopping only on a windy day, the Indian whips out his axe and chops with all his might till he has wood enough for a roaring fire. That will keep the rascals away till the pack goes off in full cry, or daylight comes.

Whittling a limber branch from a sapling, the Indian hastily makes a bow, and shoots arrow after arrow with the tip in flame to high mid-air, hoping to signal the far-off lodges. But the night is too clear. The sky is silver with stars, and moonlight and reflected snowglare, and the Northern Lights flicker and wane and fade and flame with a brilliancy that dims the tiny blaze of the arrow signal. The smoke rising from his fire in a straight column falls at the height of the trees, for the frost lies on the land heavy, palpable, impenetrable. And for all the frost is thick to the touch, the night is as clear as burnished steel. That is the peculiarity of northern cold. The air seems to become absolutely compressed with the cold; but that same cold freezes out and precipitates every particle of floating moisture till earth and sky, moon and stars shine with the glistening of polished metal.

A curious crackling, like the rustling of a flag in a gale, comes through the tightening silence. The intelligent half-breed says this is from the Northern Lights. The white man says it is electric activity in compressed air. The Indian says it is a spirit, and he may mutter the words of the braves in death chant:

"If I die, I die valiant,
I go to death fearless.
I die a brave man.
I go to those heroes who died without fear."

Hours pass. The trapper gives over shooting fire arrows into the air. He heaps his fire and watches, musket in hand. The light of the moon is white like statuary. The snow is pure as statuary. The snow-edged trees are chiselled clear like statuary; and the silence is of stone. Only the snap of the blaze, the crackling of the frosted air, the break of a twig back among the brush, where something has moved, and the little, low, smothered barkings of the dog on guard.

By-and-bye the rustling through the brush ceases; and the dog at last lowers his ears and lies quiet. The trapper throws a stick into the woods and sends the dog after it. The dog comes back without any barkings of alarm. The man knows that the wolves have drawn off. Will he wait out that long Northern night? He has had nothing to eat but the piece of pemmican. The heavy frost drowsiness will come presently; and if he falls asleep the fire will go out. An hour's run will carry him home; but to make speed with the snow-shoes he must run in the open, exposed to all watchers.

When an Indian balances motives, the motive of hunger invariably prevails. Pulling up his hood, belting in the caribou coat and kicking up the dog, the trapper strikes out for the open way leading back to the line of his traps, and the hollow where the lodges have been built for shelter against wind. There is another reason for building lodges in a hollow. Sound of the hunter will not carry to the game; but neither will sound of the game carry to the hunter.

And if the game should turn hunter and the man turn hunted! The trapper speeds down the snowy slope, striding, sliding, coasting, vaulting over hummocks of snow, glissading down the drifts, leaping rather than running. The frosty air acts as a conductor to sound, and the frost films come in stings against the face of the man whose eye, ear, and touch are strained for danger. It is the dog that catches the first breath of peril, uttering a smothered "woo! woo!" The trapper tries to persuade himself the alarm was only the far scream of a wolf-hunted lynx; but it comes again, deep and faint, like an echo in a dome. One glance over his shoulder shows him black forms on the snow-crest against the sky.

He has been tricked again, and knows how the fox feels before the dogs in full cry.

The trapper is no longer a man. He is a hunted thing with terror crazing his blood and the sleuth-hounds of the wilds on his trail. Something goes wrong with his snow-shoe. Stooping to right the slip-strings, he sees that the dog's feet have been cut by the snow crust and are bleeding. It is life for life now; the old, hard, inexorable Mosaic law, that has no new dispensation in the northern wilderness, and demands that a beast's life shall not sacrifice a man's.

One blow of his gun and the dog is dead.

The far, faint howl has deepened to a loud, exultant bay. The wolf-pack are in full cry. The man has rounded the open alley between the trees and is speeding down the hillside winged with fear. He hears the pack pause where the dog fell. That gives him respite. The moon is behind, and the man-shadow flits before on the snow like an enemy heading him back. The deep bay comes again, hard, metallic, resonant, nearer! He feels the snow-shoe slipping, but dare not pause. A great drift thrusts across his way and the shadow in front runs slower. They are gaining on him. He hardly knows whether the crunch of snow and pantings for breath are his own or his pursuers'. At the crest of the drift he braces himself and goes to the bottom with the swiftness of a sled on a slide.

The slant moonlight throws another shadow on the snow at his heels.

It is the leader of the pack. The man turns, and tosses up his arms—an Indian trick to stop pursuit. Then he fires. The ravening hunter of man that has been ambushing him half the day rolls over with a piercing howl.

The man is off and away.

If he only had the quick rifle, with which white men and a body-guard of guides hunt down a single quarry, he would be safe enough now. But the old musket is slow loading, and speed will serve him better than another shot.

Then the snow-shoe noose slips completely over his instep to his ankle, throwing the racquet on edge and clogging him back. Before he can right it they are upon him. There is nothing for it now but to face and fight to the last breath. His hood falls back, and he wheels with the moonlight full in his eyes and the Northern Lights waving their mystic flames high overhead. On one side, far away, are the tepee peaks of the lodges; on the other, the solemn, shadowy, snow-wreathed trees, like funeral watchers—watchers of how many brave deaths in a desolate, lonely land where no man raises a cross to him who fought well and died without fear!

The wolf-pack attacks in two ways. In front, by burying the red-gummed fangs in the victim's throat; in the rear, by snapping at sinews of the runner's legs—called hamstringing. Who taught them this devilish ingenuity of attack? The same hard master who teaches the Indian to be as merciless as he is brave—hunger!

Catching the muzzle of his gun, he beats back the snapping red mouths with the butt of his weapon; and the foremost beasts roll under.

They dodge the coming sweep of the uplifted arm.

But the wolves are fighting from zest of the chase now, as much as from hunger. Leaping over their dead fellows, they dodge the coming sweep of the uplifted arm, and crouch to spring. A great brute is reaching for the forward bound; but a mean, small wolf sneaks to the rear of the hunter's fighting shadow. When the man swings his arm and draws back to strike, this miserable cur, that could not have worried the trapper's dog, makes a quick snap at the bend of his knees.

Then the trapper's feet give below him. The wolf has bitten the knee sinews to the bone. The pack leap up, and the man goes down.

And when the spring thaw came, to carry away the heavy snow that fell over the northland that night, the Indians travelling to their summer hunting-grounds found the skeleton of a man. Around it were the bones of three dead wolves; and farther up the hill were the bleaching remains of a fourth.[35]

CHAPTER XII
BA'TISTE, THE BEAR HUNTER

The city man, who goes bear-hunting with a body-guard of armed guides in a field where the hunted have been on the run from the hunter for a century, gets a very tame idea of the natural bear in its natural state. Bears that have had the fear of man inculcated with longe-range repeaters lose confidence in the prowess of an aggressive onset against invisible foes. The city man comes back from the wilds with a legend of how harmless bears have become. In fact, he doesn't believe a wild animal ever attacks unless it is attacked. He doubts whether the bear would go on its life-long career of rapine and death, if hunger did not compel it, or if repeated assault and battery from other animals did not teach the poor bear the art of self-defence.

Grisly old trappers coming down to the frontier towns of the Western States once a year for provisions, or hanging round the forts of the Hudson's Bay Company in Canada for the summer, tell a different tale. Their hunting is done in a field where human presence is still so rare that it is unknown and the bear treats mankind precisely as he treats all other living beings from the moose and the musk-ox to mice and ants—as fair game for his own insatiable maw.

Old hunters may be great spinners of yarns—"liars" the city man calls them—but Montagnais, who squats on his heels round the fur company forts on Peace River, carries ocular evidence in the artificial ridge of a deformed nose that the bear which he slew was a real one with an epicurean relish for that part of Indian anatomy which the Indian considers to be the most choice bit of a moose.[36] And the Kootenay hunter who was sent through the forests of Idaho to follow up the track of a lost brave brought back proof of an actual bear; for he found a dead man lying across a pile of logs with his skull crushed in like an eggshell by something that had risen swift and silent from a lair on the other side of the logs and dealt the climbing brave one quick terrible blow. And little blind Ba'tiste, wizened and old, who spent the last twenty years of his life weaving grass mats and carving curious little wooden animals for the children of the chief factor, could convince you that the bears he slew in his young days were very real bears, altogether different from the clumsy bruins that gambol with boys and girls through fairy books.

That is, he could convince you if he would; for he usually sat weaving and weaving at the grasses—weaving bitter thoughts into the woof of his mat—

without a word. Round his white helmet, such as British soldiers wear in hot lands, he always hung a heavy thick linen thing like the frill of a sun-bonnet, coming over the face as well as the neck—"to keep de sun off," he would mumble out if you asked him why. More than that of the mysterious frill worn on dark days as well as sunny, he would never vouch unless some town-bred man patronizingly pooh-poohed the dangers of bear-hunting. Then the grass strands would tremble with excitement and the little French hunter's body would quiver and he would begin pouring forth a jumble, half habitant half Indian with a mixture of all the oaths from both languages, pointing and pointing at his hidden face and bidding you look what the bear had done to him, but never lifting the thick frill.

It was somewhere between the tributary waters that flow north to the Saskatchewan and the rivers that start near the Saskatchewan to flow south to the Missouri. Ba'tiste and the three trappers who were with him did not know which side of the boundary they were on. By slow travel, stopping one day to trap beaver, pausing on the way to forage for meat, building their canoes where they needed them and abandoning the boats when they made a long overland portage, they were three weeks north of the American fur post on the banks of the Missouri. The hunters were travelling light-handed. That is, they were carrying only a little salt and tea and tobacco. For the rest, they were depending on their muskets. Game had not been plentiful.

Between the prairie and "the Mountains of the Setting Sun"—as the Indians call the Rockies—a long line of tortuous, snaky red crawled sinuously over the crests of the foothills; and all game—bird and beast—will shun a prairie fire. There was no wind. It was the dead hazy calm of Indian summer in the late autumn with the sun swimming in the purplish smoke like a blood-red shield all day and the serpent line of flame flickering and darting little tongues of vermilion against the deep blue horizon all night, days filled with the crisp smell of withered grasses, nights as clear and cold as the echo of a bell. On a windless plain there is no danger from a prairie fire. One may travel for weeks without nearing or distancing the waving tide of fire against a far sky; and the four trappers, running short of rations, decided to try to flank the fire coming around far enough ahead to intercept the game that must be moving away from the fire line.

Nearly all hunters, through some dexterity of natural endowment, unconsciously become specialists. One man sees beaver signs where another sees only deer. For Ba'tiste, the page of nature spelled B-E-A-R! Fifteen bear in a winter is a wonderfully good season's work for any trapper. Ba'tiste's record for one lucky winter was fifty-four. After that he was known as the bear hunter. Such a reputation affects keen hunters differently. The Indian grows cautious almost to cowardice. Ba'tiste grew rash. He would follow a wounded grisly to cover. He would afterward laugh at the episode as a joke if the wounded brute had treed him. "For sure, good t'ing dat was not de prairie dat tam," he would say, flinging down the pelt of his foe. The other trappers with Indian blood in their veins might laugh, but they shook their heads when his back was turned.

Flanking the fire by some of the great gullies that cut the foothills like trenches, the hunters began to find the signs they had been seeking. For Ba'tiste, the many different signs had but one meaning. Where some summer rain pool had dried almost to a soft mud hole, the other trappers saw little cleft foot-marks that meant deer, and prints like a baby's fingers that spelled out the visit of some member of the weasel family, and broad splay-hoof impressions that had spread under the weight as some giant moose had gone shambling over the quaking mud bottom. But Ba'tiste looked only at a long shuffling foot-mark the length of a man's fore-arm with padded ball-like pressures as of monster toes. The French hunter would at once examine which way that great foot had pointed. Were there other impressions dimmer on the dry mud? Did the crushed spear-grass tell any tales of what had passed that mud hole? If it did, Ba'tiste would be seen wandering apparently aimlessly out on the prairie, carrying his uncased rifle carefully that the sunlight should not glint from the barrel, zigzagging up a foothill where perhaps wild plums or shrub berries hung rotting with frost ripeness. Ba'tiste did not stand full height at the top of the hill. He dropped face down, took off his hat, or scarlet "safety" handkerchief, and peered warily over the crest of the hill. If he went on over into the next valley, the other men would say they "guessed he smelt bear." If he came back, they knew he had been on a cold scent that had faded indistinguishably as the grasses thinned.

Southern slopes of prairie and foothill are often matted tangles of a raspberry patch. Here Ba'tiste read many things—stories of many bears, of families, of cubs, of old cross fellows wandering alone. Great slabs of stone had been clawed up by mighty hands. Worms and snails and all the damp clammy things that cling to the cold dark between stone and earth had been gobbled up by some greedy forager. In the trenched ravines crossed by the trappers lay many a hidden forest of cottonwood or poplar or willow. Here was refuge, indeed, for the wandering creatures of the treeless prairie that rolled away from the tops of the cliffs.

Many secrets could be read from the clustered woods of the ravines. The other hunters might look for the fresh nibbled alder bush where a busy beaver had been laying up store for winter, or detect the blink of a russet ear among the seared foliage betraying a deer, or wonder what flesh-eater had caught the poor jack rabbit just outside his shelter of thorny brush.

The hawk soaring and dropping—lilting and falling and lifting again—might mean that a little mink was "playing dead" to induce the bird to swoop down so that the vampire beast could suck the hawk's blood, or that the hawk was watching for an unguarded moment to plunge down with his talons in a poor "fool-hen's" feathers.

These things might interest the others. They did not interest Ba'tiste. Ba'tiste's eyes were for lairs of grass crushed so recently that the spear leaves were even now rising; for holes in the black mould where great ripping claws had been tearing up roots; for hollow logs and rotted stumps where a black bear might have crawled to take his afternoon siesta; for punky trees which a grisly might have torn open to gobble ants' eggs; for scratchings down the bole of poplar or cottonwood where some languid bear had been sharpening his claws in midsummer as a cat will scratch chair-legs; for great pits deep in the clay banks, where some silly badger or gopher ran down to the depths of his burrow in sheer terror only to have old bruin come ripping and tearing to the innermost recesses, with scattered fur left that told what had happened.

Some soft oozy moss-padded lair, deep in the marsh with the reeds of the brittle cat-tails lifting as if a sleeper had just risen, sets Ba'tiste's pulse hopping—jumping—marking time in thrills like the lithe bounds of a pouncing mountain-cat. With tread soft as the velvet paw of a panther, he steals through the cane-brake parting the reeds before each pace, brushing aside softly—silently what might crush!—snap!—sound ever so slight an alarm to the little pricked ears of a shaggy head tossing from side to side—jerk—jerk—from right to left—from left to right—always on the listen!—on the listen!—for prey!—for prey!

"Oh, for sure, that Ba'tiste, he was but a fool-hunter," as his comrades afterward said (it is always so very plain afterward); "that Ba'tiste, he was a fool! What man else go step—step—into the marsh after a bear!"

But the truth was that Ba'tiste, the cunning rascal, always succeeded in coming out of the marsh, out of the bush, out of the windfall, sound as a top, safe and unscratched, with a bear-skin over his shoulder, the head swinging pendant to show what sort of fellow he had mastered.

"Dat wan!—ah!—diable!—he has long sharp nose—he was thin—thin as a barrel all gone but de hoops—ah!—voilà!—he was wan ugly garçon, was dat bear!"

Where the hunters found tufts of fur on the sage brush, bits of skin on the spined cactus, the others might vow coyotes had worried a badger. Ba'tiste would have it that the badger had been slain by a bear. The cached carcass of fawn or doe, of course, meant bear; for the bear is an epicure that would have meat gamey. To that the others would agree.

And so the shortening autumn days with the shimmering heat of a crisp noon and the noiseless chill of starry twilights found the trappers canoeing leisurely up-stream from the northern tributaries of the Missouri nearing the long overland trail that led to the hunting-fields in Canada.

One evening they came to a place bounded by high cliff banks with the flats heavily wooded by poplar and willow. Ba'tiste had found signs that were hot—oh! so hot! The mould of an uprooted gopher hole was so fresh that it had not yet dried. This was not a region of timber-wolves. What had dug that hole? Not the small, skulking coyote—the vagrant of prairie life! Oh!—no!—the coyote like other vagrants earns his living without work, by skulking in the wake of the business-like badger; and when the badger goes down in the gopher hole, Master Coyote stands nearby and gobbles up all the stray gophers that bolt to escape the invading badger.[37] What had dug the hole? Ba'tiste thinks that he knows.

That was on open prairie. Just below the cliff is another kind of hole—a roundish pit dug between moss-covered logs and earth wall, a pit with grass clawed down into it, snug and hidden and sheltered as a bird's nest. If the pit is what Ba'tiste thinks, somewhere on the banks of the stream should be a watering-place. He proposes that they beach the canoes and camp here. Twilight is not a good time to still hunt an unseen bear. Twilight is the time when the bear himself goes still hunting. Ba'tiste will go out in the early morning. Meantime if he stumbles on what looks like a trail to the watering-place, he will set a trap.

Camp is not for the regular trapper what it is for the amateur hunter—a time of rest and waiting while others skin the game and prepare supper.

One hunter whittles the willow sticks that are to make the camp fire. Another gathers moss or boughs for a bed. If fish can be got, some one has out a line. The kettle hisses from the cross-bar between notched sticks above the fire, and the meat sizzling at the end of a forked twig sends up a flavour that whets every appetite. Over the upturned canoes bend a couple of men gumming afresh all the splits and seams against to-morrow's voyage. Then with a flip-flop that tells of the other side of the flap-jacks being browned, the cook yodels in crescendo that "Sup—per!—'s—read—ee!"

Supper over, a trap or two may be set in likely places. The men may take a plunge; for in spite of their tawny skins, these earth-coloured fellows have closer acquaintance with water than their appearance would indicate. The man-smell is as acute to the beast's nose as the rank fur-animal-smell is to the man's nose; and the first thing that an Indian who has had a long run of ill-luck does is to get a native "sweating-bath" and make himself clean.

On the ripple of the flowing river are the red bars of the camp fire. Among the willows, perhaps, the bole of some birch stands out white and spectral. Though there is no wind, the poplars shiver with a fall of wan, faded leaves like snow-flakes on the grave of summer. Red bills and whisky-jacks and lonely phoebe-birds came fluttering and pecking at the crumbs. Out from the gray thicket bounds a cottontail to jerk up on his hind legs with surprise at the camp fire. A blink of his long ear, and he has bounded back to tell the news to his rabbit family. Overhead, with shrill clangour, single file and in long wavering V lines, wing geese migrating southward for the season. The children's hour, has a great poet called a certain time of day? Then this is the hour of the wilderness hunter, the hour when "the Mountains of the Setting Sun" are flooded in fiery lights from zone to zenith with the snowy heights overtopping the far rolling prairie like clouds of opal at poise in mid-heaven, the hour when the camp fire lies on the russet autumn-tinged earth like a red jewel, and the far line of the prairie fire billows against the darkening east in a tide of vermilion flame.

Unless it is raining, the voyageurs do not erect their tent; for they will sleep in the open, feet to the fire, or under the canoes, close to the great earth, into whose very fibre their beings seem to be rooted. And now is the time when the hunters spin their yarns and exchange notes of all they have seen in the long silent day. There was the prairie chicken with a late brood of half-grown clumsy clucking chicks amply able to take care of themselves, but still clinging to the old mother's care. When the hunter came suddenly on them, over the old hen went, flopping broken-winged to decoy the trapper till her children could run for shelter—when—lo!—of a sudden, the broken wing is mended and away she darts on both wings before he has uncased his gun! There are the stories of bear hunters like Ba'tiste sitting on the other side of the fire there, who have been caught in their own bear traps and held till they died of starvation and their bones bleached in the rusted steel.

That story has such small relish for Ba'tiste that he hitches farther away from the others and lies back flat on the ground close to the willow under-tangle with his head on his hand.

"For sure," says Ba'tiste contemptuously, "nobody doesn't need no tree to climb here! Sacré!—cry wolf!—wolf!—and for sure!—diable!—de beeg loup-garou will eat you yet!"

Down somewhere from those stars overhead drops a call silvery as a flute, clear as a piccolo—some night bird lifting like a mote on the far oceans of air. The trappers look up with a movement that in other men would be a nervous start; for any shrill cry pierces the silence of the prairie in almost a stab. Then the men go on with their yarn telling of how the Blackfeet murdered some traders on this very ground not long ago till the gloom gathering over willow thicket and encircling cliffs seems peopled with those marauding warriors. One man rises, saying that he is "goin' to turn in" and is taking a step through the dark to his canoe when there is a dull pouncing thud. For an instant the trappers thought that their comrade had stumbled over his boat. But a heavy groan—a low guttural cry—a shout of "Help—help—help Ba'tiste!" and the man who had risen plunged into the crashing cane-brake, calling out incoherently for them to "help—help Ba'tiste!"

In the confusion of cries and darkness, it was impossible for the other two trappers to know what had happened. Their first thought was of the Indians whose crimes they had been telling. Their second was for their rifles—and they had both sprung over the fire where they saw the third man striking—striking—striking wildly at something in the dark. A low worrying growl—and they descried the Frenchman rolling over and over, clutched by or clutching a huge furry form—hitting—plunging with his knife—struggling—screaming with agony.

"It's Ba'tiste! It's a bear!" shouted the third man, who was attempting to drive the brute off by raining blows on its head.

Man and bear were an indistinguishable struggling mass. Should they shoot in the half-dark? Then the Frenchman uttered the scream of one in death-throes: "Shoot!—shoot!—shoot quick! She's striking my face!—she's striking my face——"

And before the words had died, sharp flashes of light cleft the dark—the great beast rolled over with a coughing growl, and the trappers raised their comrade from the ground.

The bear had had him on his back between her teeth by the thick chest piece of his double-breasted buckskin. Except for his face, he seemed uninjured; but down that face the great brute had drawn the claws of her fore paw.

Ba'tiste raised his hands to his face.

"Mon dieu!" he asked thickly, fumbling with both hands, "what is done to my eyes? Is the fire out? I cannot see!"

Then the man who had fought like a demon armed with only a hunting-knife fainted because of what his hands felt.

Traitors there are among trappers as among all other classes, men like those who deserted Glass on the Missouri, and Scott on the Platte, and how many others whose treachery will never be known.

But Ba'tiste's comrades stayed with him on the banks of the river that flows into the Missouri. One cared for the blind man. The other two foraged for game. When the wounded hunter could be moved, they put him in a canoe and hurried down-stream to the fur post before the freezing of the rivers. At the fur post, the doctor did what he could; but a doctor cannot restore what has been torn away. The next spring, Ba'tiste was put on a pack horse and sent to his relatives at the Canadian fur post. Here his sisters made him the curtain to hang round his helmet and set him to weaving grass mats that the days might not drag so wearily.

Ask Ba'tiste whether he agrees with the amateur hunter that bears never attack unless they are attacked, that they would never become ravening creatures of prey unless the assaults of other creatures taught them ferocity, ask Ba'tiste this and something resembling the snarl of a baited beast breaks from the lipless face under the veil:

"S—s—sz!—" with a quiver of inexpressible rage. "The bear—it is an animal!—the bear!—it is a beast!—toujours!—the bear!—it is a beast!—always—always!" And his hands clinch.

Then he falls to carving of the little wooden animals and weaving of sad, sad, bitter thoughts into the warp of the Indian mat.

Are such onslaughts common among bears, or are they the mad freaks of the bear's nature? President Roosevelt tells of two soldiers bitten to death in the South-West; and M. L'Abbé Dugast, of St. Boniface, Manitoba, incidentally relates an experience almost similar to that of Ba'tiste which occurred in the North-West. Lest Ba'tiste's case seem overdrawn, I quote the Abbé's words:

"At a little distance Madame Lajimoniere and the other women were preparing the tents for the night, when all at once Bouvier gave a cry of distress and called to his companions to help him. At the first shout, each hunter seized his gun and prepared to defend himself against the attack of an enemy; they hurried to the other side of the ditch to see what was the matter with Bouvier, and what he was struggling with. They had no idea that a wild animal would come near the fire to attack a man even under cover of night; for fire usually has the effect of frightening wild beasts. However, almost before the four hunters knew what had happened, they saw their unfortunate companion dragged into the woods by a bear followed by her two cubs. She held Bouvier in her claws and struck him savagely in the face to stun him. As soon as she saw the four men in pursuit, she redoubled her fury against her prey, tearing his face with her claws. M. Lajimoniere, who was an intrepid hunter, baited her with the butt end of his gun to make her let go her hold, as he dared not shoot for fear of killing the man while trying to save him, but Bouvier, who felt himself being choked, cried with all his strength: 'Shoot; I would rather be shot than eaten alive!' M. Lajimoniere pulled the trigger as close to the bear as possible, wounding her mortally. She let go Bouvier and before her strength was exhausted made a wild attack upon M. Lajimoniere, who expected this and as his gun had only one barrel loaded, he ran towards the canoe, where he had a second gun fully charged. He had hardly seized it before the bear reached the shore and tried to climb into the canoe, but fearing no longer to wound his friend, M. Lajimoniere aimed full at her breast and this time she was killed instantly. As soon as the bear was no longer to be feared, Madame Lajimoniere, who had been trembling with fear during the tumult, went to raise the unfortunate Bouvier, who was covered with wounds and nearly dead. The bear had torn the skin from his face with her nails from the roots of his hair to the lower part of his chin. His eyes and nose were gone—in fact his features were indiscernible—but he was not mortally injured. His wounds were dressed as well as the circumstances would permit, and thus crippled he was carried to the Fort of the Prairies, Madame Lajimoniere taking care of him all through the journey. In time his wounds were successfully healed, but he was blind and infirm to the end of his life. He dwelt at the Fort of the Prairies for many years, but when the first missionaries reached Red River in 1818, he persuaded his friends to send him to St. Boniface to meet the priests and ended his days in M. Provencher's house. He employed his time during the last years of his life in making crosses and crucifixes blind as he was, but he never made any chefs d'[oe]uvre."

Such is bear-hunting and such is the nature of the bear. And these things are not of the past. Wherever long-range repeaters have not put the fear of man in the animal heart, the bear is the aggressor. Even as I write comes word from a little frontier fur post which I visited in 1901, of a seven-year-old boy being waylaid and devoured by a grisly only four miles back from a transcontinental railway. This is the second death from the unprovoked attacks of bears within a month in that country—and that month, the month of August, 1902, when sentimental ladies and gentlemen many miles away from danger are sagely discussing whether the bear is naturally ferocious or not—whether, in a word, it is altogether humane to hunt bears.

CHAPTER XIII
JOHN COLTER—FREE TRAPPER

Long before sunrise hunters were astir in the mountains.

The Crows were robbers, the Blackfeet murderers; and scouts of both tribes haunted every mountain defile where a white hunter might pass with provisions and peltries which these rascals could plunder.

The trappers circumvented their foes by setting the traps after nightfall and lifting the game before daybreak.

Night in the mountains was full of a mystery that the imagination of the Indians peopled with terrors enough to frighten them away. The sudden stilling of mountain torrent and noisy leaping cataract at sundown when the thaw of the upper snows ceased, the smothered roar of rivers under ice, the rush of whirlpools through the blackness of some far cañon, the crashing of rocks thrown down by unknown forces, the shivering echo that multiplied itself a thousandfold and ran "rocketing" from peak to peak startling the silences—these things filled the Indian with superstitious fears.

The gnomes, called in trapper's vernacular "hoodoos"—great pillars of sandstone higher than a house, left standing in valleys by prehistoric floods—were to the Crows and Blackfeet petrified giants that only awakened at night to hurl down rocks on intruding mortals. And often the quiver of a shadow in the night wind gave reality to the Indian's fears. The purr of streams over rocky bed was whispering, the queer quaking echoes of falling rocks were giants at war, and the mists rising from swaying waterfalls, spirit-forms portending death.

Morning came more ghostly among the peaks.

Thick white clouds banked the mountains from peak to base, blotting out every scar and tor as a sponge might wash a slate. Valleys lay blanketed in smoking mist. As the sun came gradually up to the horizon far away east behind the mountains, scarp and pinnacle butted through the fog, stood out bodily from the mist, seemed to move like living giants from the cloud banks. "How could they do that if they were not alive?" asked the Indian. Elsewhere, shadows came from sun, moon, starlight, or camp-fire. But in these valleys were pencilled shadows of peaks upside down, shadows all the colours of the rainbow pointing to the bottom of the green Alpine lakes, hours and hours before any sun had risen to cause the shadows. All this meant "bad medicine" to the Indian, or, in white man's language, mystery.

Unless they were foraging in large bands, Crows and Blackfeet shunned the mountains after nightfall. That gave the white man a chance to trap in safety.

Early one morning two white men slipped out of their sequestered cabin built in hiding of the hills at the head waters of the Missouri. Under covert of brushwood lay a long odd-shaped canoe, sharp enough at the prow to cleave the narrowest waters between rocks, so sharp that French voyageurs gave this queer craft the name "canot à bec d'esturgeon"—that is, a canoe like the nose of a sturgeon. This American adaptation of the Frenchman's craft was not of birch-bark. That would be too frail to essay the rock-ribbed cañons of the mountain streams. It was usually a common dugout, hollowed from a cottonwood or other light timber, with such an angular narrow prow that it could take the sheerest dip and mount the steepest wave-crest where a rounder boat would fill and swamp. Dragging this from cover, the two white men pushed out on the Jefferson Fork, dipping now on this side, now on that, using the reversible double-bladed paddles which only an amphibious boatman can manage. The two men shot out in midstream, where the mists would hide them from each shore; a moment later the white fog had enfolded them, and there was no trace of human presence but the trail of dimpling ripples in the wake of the canoe.

No talking, no whistling, not a sound to betray them. And there were good reasons why these men did not wish their presence known. One was Potts, the other John Colter. Both had been with the Lewis and Clark exploring party of 1804-'05, when a Blackfoot brave had been slain for horse-thieving by the first white men to cross the Upper Missouri. Besides, the year before coming to the Jefferson, Colter had been with the Missouri Company's fur brigade under Manuel Lisa, and had gone to the Crows as an emissary from the fur company. While with the Crows, a battle had taken place against the Blackfeet, in which they suffered heavy loss owing to Colter's prowess. That made the Blackfeet sworn enemies to Colter.

Turning off the Jefferson, the trappers headed their canoe up a side stream, probably one of those marshy reaches where beavers have formed a swamp by damming up the current of a sluggish stream. Such quiet waters are favourite resorts for beaver and mink and marten and pekan. Setting their traps only after nightfall, the two men could not possibly have put out more than forty or fifty. Thirty traps are a heavy day's work for one man. Six prizes out of thirty are considered a wonderful run of luck; but the empty traps must be examined as carefully as the successful ones. Many that have been mauled, "scented" by a beaver scout and left, must be replaced. Others must have fresh bait; others, again, carried to better grounds where there are more game signs.

Either this was a very lucky morning and the men were detained taking fresh pelts, or it was a very unlucky morning and the men had decided to trap farther up-stream; for when the mists began to rise, the hunters were still in their canoe. Leaving the beaver meadow, they continued paddling up-stream away from the Jefferson. A more hidden water-course they could hardly have found. The swampy beaver-runs narrowed, the shores rose higher and higher into rampart walls, and the dark-shadowed waters came leaping down in the lumpy, uneven runnels of a small cañon. You can always tell whether the waters of a cañon are compressed or not, whether they come from broad, swampy meadows or clear snow streams smaller than the cañon. The marsh waters roll down swift and black and turbid, raging against the crowding walls; the snow streams leap clear and foaming as champagne, and are in too great a hurry to stop and quarrel with the rocks. It is altogether likely these men recognised swampy water, and were ascending the cañon in search of a fresh beaver-marsh; or they would not have continued paddling six miles above the Jefferson with daylight growing plainer at every mile. First the mist rose like a smoky exhalation from the river; then it flaunted across the rampart walls in banners; then the far mountain peaks took form against the sky, islands in a sea of fog; then the cloud banks were floating in mid-heaven blindingly white from a sun that painted each cañon wall in the depths of the water.

How much farther would the cañon lead? Should they go higher up or not? Was it wooded or clear plain above the walls? The man paused. What was that noise?

"Like buffalo," said Potts.

"Might be Blackfeet," answered Colter.

No. What would Blackfeet be doing, riding at a pace to make such thunder so close to a cañon? It was only a buffalo herd stampeding on the annual southern run. Again Colter urged that the noise might be from Indians. It would be safer for them to retreat at once. At which Potts wanted to know if Colter were afraid, using a stronger word—"coward."

Afraid? Colter afraid? Colter who had remained behind Lewis and Clark's men to trap alone in the wilds for nearly two years, who had left Manuel Lisa's brigade to go alone among the thieving Crows, whose leadership had helped the Crows to defeat the Blackfeet?

Anyway, it would now be as dangerous to go back as forward. They plainly couldn't land here. Let them go ahead where the walls seemed to slope down to shore. Two or three strokes sent the canoe round an elbow of rock into the narrow course of a creek. Instantly out sprang five or six hundred Blackfeet warriors with weapons levelled guarding both sides of the stream.

An Indian scout had discovered the trail of the white men and sent the whole band scouring ahead to intercept them at this narrow pass. The chief stepped forward, and with signals that were a command beckoned the hunters ashore.

As is nearly always the case, the rash man was the one to lose his head, the cautious man the one to keep his presence of mind. Potts was for an attempt at flight, when every bow on both sides of the river would have let fly a shot. Colter was for accepting the situation, trusting to his own wit for subsequent escape.

Colter, who was acting as steersman, sent the canoe ashore. Bottom had not grated before a savage snatched Potts's rifle from his hands. Springing ashore, Colter forcibly wrested the weapon back and coolly handed it to Potts.

But Potts had lost all the rash courage of a moment before, and with one push sent the canoe into mid-stream. Colter shouted at him to come back—come back! Indians have more effective arguments. A bow-string twanged, and Potts screamed out, "Colter, I am wounded!"

Again Colter urged him to land. The wound turned Pott's momentary fright to a paroxysm of rage. Aiming his rifle, he shot his Indian assailant dead. If it was torture that he feared, that act assured him at least a quick death; for, in Colter's language, man and boat were instantaneously "made a riddle of."

No man admires courage more than the Indian; and the Blackfeet recognised in their captive one who had been ready to defend his comrade against them all, and who had led the Crows to victory against their own band.

The prisoner surrendered his weapons. He was stripped naked, but neither showed sign of fear nor made a move to escape. Evidently the Blackfeet could have rare sport with this game white man. His life in the Indian country had taught him a few words of the Blackfoot language. He heard them conferring as to how he should be tortured to atone for all that the Blackfeet had suffered at white men's hands. One warrior suggested that the hunter be set up as a target and shot at. Would he then be so brave?

But the chief shook his head. That was not game enough sport for Blackfeet warriors. That would be letting a man die passively. And how this man could fight if he had an opportunity! How he could resist torture if he had any chance of escaping the torture!

But Colter stood impassive and listened. Doubtless he regretted having left the well-defended brigades of the fur companies to hunt alone in the wilderness. But the fascination of the wild life is as a gambler's vice—the more a man has, the more he wants. Had not Colter crossed the Rockies with Lewis and Clark and spent two years in the mountain fastnesses? Yet when he reached the Mandans on the way home, the revulsion against all the trammels of civilization moved him so strongly that he asked permission to return to the wilderness, where he spent two more years. Had he not set out for St. Louis a second time, met Lisa coming up the Missouri with a brigade of hunters, and for the third time turned his face to the wilderness? Had he not wandered with the Crows, fought the Blackfeet, gone down to St. Louis, and been impelled by that strange impulse of adventure which was to the hunter what the instinct of migration is to bird and fish and buffalo and all wild things—to go yet again to the wilderness? Such was the passion for the wilds that ruled the life of all free trappers.

The free trappers formed a class by themselves.

Other trappers either hunted on a salary of $200, $300, $400 a year, or on shares, like fishermen of the Grand Banks outfitted by "planters," or like western prospectors outfitted by companies that supply provisions, boats, and horses, expecting in return the major share of profits. The free trappers fitted themselves out, owed allegiance to no man, hunted where and how they chose, and refused to carry their furs to any fort but the one that paid the highest prices. For the mangeurs de lard, as they called the fur company raftsmen, they had a supreme contempt. For the methods of the fur companies, putting rivals to sleep with laudanum or bullet and ever stirring the savages up to warfare, the free trappers had a rough and emphatically expressed loathing.

The crime of corrupting natives can never be laid to the free trapper. He carried neither poison, nor what was worse than poison to the Indian—whisky—among the native tribes. The free trapper lived on good terms with the Indian, because his safety depended on the Indian. Renegades like Bird, the deserter from the Hudson's Bay Company, or Rose, who abandoned the Astorians, or Beckwourth of apocryphal fame, might cast off civilization and become Indian chiefs; but, after all, these men were not guilty of half so hideous crimes as the great fur companies of boasted respectability. Wyeth of Boston, and Captain Bonneville of the army, whose underlings caused such murderous slaughter among the Root Diggers, were not free trappers in the true sense of the term. Wyeth was an enthusiast who caught the fever of the wilds; and Captain Bonneville, a gay adventurer, whose men shot down more Indians in one trip than all the free trappers of America shot in a century. As for the desperado Harvey, whom Larpenteur reports shooting Indians like dogs, his crimes were committed under the walls of the American Fur Company's fort. MacLellan and Crooks and John Day—before they joined the Astorians—and Boone and Carson and Colter, are names that stand for the true type of free trapper.

The free trapper went among the Indians with no defence but good behaviour and the keenness of his wit. Whatever crimes the free trapper might be guilty of towards white men, he was guilty of few towards the Indians. Consequently, free trappers were all through Minnesota and the region westward of the Mississippi forty years before the fur companies dared to venture among the Sioux. Fisher and Fraser and Woods knew the Upper Missouri before 1806; and Brugiere had been on the Columbia many years before the Astorians came in 1811.

One crime the free trappers may be charged with—a reckless waste of precious furs. The great companies always encouraged the Indians not to hunt more game than they needed for the season's support. And no Indian hunter, uncorrupted by white men, would molest game while the mothers were with their young. Famine had taught them the punishment that follows reckless hunting. But the free trappers were here to-day and away to-morrow, like a Chinaman, to take all they could get regardless of results; and the results were the rapid extinction of fur-bearing game.

Always there were more free trappers in the United States than in Canada. Before the union of Hudson's Bay and Nor' Wester in Canada, all classes of trappers were absorbed by one of the two great companies. After the union, when the monopoly enjoyed by the Hudson's Bay did not permit it literally to drive a free trapper out, it could always "freeze" him out by withholding supplies in its great white northern wildernesses, or by refusing to give him transport. When the monopoly passed away in 1871, free trappers pressed north from the Missouri, where their methods had exterminated game, and carried on the same ruthless warfare on the Saskatchewan. North of the Saskatchewan, where very remoteness barred strangers out, the Hudson's Bay Company still held undisputed sway; and Lord Strathcona, the governor of the company, was able to say only two years ago, "the fur trade is quite as large as ever it was."

Among free hunters, Canada had only one commanding figure—John Johnston of the Soo, who settled at La Pointe on Lake Superior in 1792, formed league with Wabogish, "the White Fisher," and became the most famous trader of the Lakes. His life, too, was almost as eventful as Colter's. A member of the Irish nobility, some secret which he never chose to reveal drove him to the wilds. Wabogish, the "White Fisher," had a daughter who refused the wooings of all her tribe's warriors. In vain Johnston sued for her hand. Old Wabogish bade the white man go sell his Irish estates and prove his devotion by buying as vast estates in America. Johnston took the old chief at his word, and married the haughty princess of the Lake. When the War of 1812 set all the tribes by the ears, Johnston and his wife had as thrilling adventures as ever Colter knew among the Blackfeet.

Many a free trapper, and partner of the fur companies as well, secured his own safety by marrying the daughter of a chief, as Johnston had. These were not the lightly-come, lightly-go affairs of the vagrant adventurer. If the husband had not cast off civilization like a garment, the wife had to put it on like a garment; and not an ill-fitting garment either, when one considers that the convents of the quiet nuns dotted the wilderness like oases in a desert almost contemporaneous with the fur trade. If the trapper had not sunk to the level of the savages, the little daughter of the chief was educated by the nuns for her new position. I recall several cases where the child was sent across the Atlantic to an English governess so that the equality would be literal and not a sentimental fiction. And yet, on no subject has the western fur trader received more persistent and unjust condemnation. The heroism that culminated in the union of Pocahontas with a noted Virginian won applause, and almost similar circumstances dictated the union of fur traders with the daughters of Indian chiefs; but because the fur trader has not posed as a sentimentalist, he has become more or less of a target for the index finger of the Pharisee.[38]

North of the boundary the free trapper had small chance against the Hudson's Bay Company. As long as the slow-going Mackinaw Company, itself chiefly recruited from free trappers, ruled at the junction of the Lakes, the free trappers held the hunting-grounds of the Mississippi; but after the Mackinaw was absorbed by the aggressive American Fur Company, the free hunters were pushed westward. On the Lower Missouri competition raged from 1810, so that circumstances drove the free trapper westward to the mountains, where he is hunting in the twentieth century as his prototype hunted two hundred years ago.

In Canada—of course after 1870—he entered the mountains chiefly by three passes: (1) Yellow Head Pass southward of the Athabasca; (2) the narrow gap where the Bow emerges to the plains—that is, the river where the Indians found the best wood for the making of bows; (3) north of the boundary, through that narrow defile overtowered by the lonely flat-crowned peak called Crows Nest Mountain—that is, where the fugitive Crows took refuge from the pursuing Blackfeet.

In the United States, the free hunters also approached the mountains by three main routes: (1) Up the Platte; (2) westward from the Missouri across the plains; (3) by the Three Forks of the Missouri. For instance, it was coming down the Platte that poor Scott's canoe was overturned, his powder lost, and his rifles rendered useless. Game had retreated to the mountains with spring's advance. Berries were not ripe by the time trappers were descending with their winter's hunt. Scott and his famishing men could not find edible roots. Each day Scott weakened. There was no food. Finally, Scott had strength to go no farther. His men had found tracks of some other hunting party far to the fore. They thought that, in any case, he could not live. What ought they to do? Hang back and starve with him, or hasten forward while they had strength, to the party whose track they had espied? On pretence of seeking roots, they deserted the helpless man. Perhaps they did not come up with the advance party till they were sure that Scott must have died; for they did not go back to his aid. The next spring when these same hunters went up the Platte, they found the skeleton of poor Scott sixty miles from the place where they had left him. The terror that spurred the emaciated man to drag himself all this weary distance can barely be conceived; but such were the fearful odds taken by every free trapper who went up the Platte, across the parched plains, or to the head waters of the Missouri.

The time for the free trappers to go out was, in Indian language, "when the leaves began to fall." If a mighty hunter like Colter, the trapper was to the savage "big Indian me"; if only an ordinary vagrant of woods and streams, the white man was "big knife you," in distinction to the red man carrying only primitive weapons. Very often the free trapper slipped away from the fur post secretly, or at night; for there were questions of licenses which he disregarded, knowing well that the buyer of his furs would not inform for fear of losing the pelts. Also and more important in counseling caution, the powerful fur companies had spies on the watch to dog the free trapper to his hunting-grounds; and rival hunters would not hesitate to bribe the natives with a keg of rum for all the peltries which the free trapper had already bought by advancing provisions to Indian hunters. Indeed, rival hunters have not hesitated to bribe the savages to pillage and murder the free trapper; for there was no law in the fur trading country, and no one to ask what became of the free hunter who went alone into the wilderness and never returned.

Going out alone, or with only one partner, the free hunter encumbered himself with few provisions. Two dollars worth of tobacco would buy a thousand pounds of "jerked" buffalo meat, and a few gaudy trinkets for a squaw all the pemmican white men could use.

Going by the river routes, four days out from St. Louis brought the trapper into regions of danger. Indian scouts hung on the watch among the sedge of the river bank. One thin line of upcurling smoke, or a piece of string—

babiche (leather cord, called by the Indians assapapish)—fluttering from a shrub, or little sticks casually dropped on the river bank pointing one way, all were signs that told of marauding bands. Some birch tree was notched with an Indian cipher—a hunter had passed that way and claimed the bark for his next year's canoe. Or the mark might be on a cottonwood—some man wanted this tree for a dugout. Perhaps a stake stood with a mark at the entrance to a beaver-marsh—some hunter had found this ground first and warned all other trappers off by the code of wilderness honour. Notched tree-trunks told of some runner gone across country, blazing a trail by which he could return. Had a piece of fungus been torn from a hemlock log? There were Indians near, and the squaw had taken the thing to whiten leather. If a sudden puff of black smoke spread out in a cone above some distant tree, it was an ominous sign to the trapper. The Indians had set fire to the inside of a punky trunk and the shooting flames were a rallying call.

In the most perilous regions the trapper travelled only after nightfall with muffled paddles—that is, muffled where the handle might strike the gunwale. Camp-fires warned him which side of the river to avoid; and often a trapper slipping past under the shadow of one bank saw hobgoblin figures dancing round the flames of the other bank—Indians celebrating their scalp dance. In these places the white hunter ate cold meals to avoid lighting a fire; or if he lighted a fire, after cooking his meal he withdrew at once and slept at a distance from the light that might betray him.

The greatest risk of travelling after dark during the spring floods arose from what the voyageurs called embarras—trees torn from the banks sticking in the soft bottom like derelicts with branches to entangle the trapper's craft; but the embarras often befriended the solitary white man. Usually he slept on shore rolled in a buffalo-robe; but if Indian signs were fresh, he moored his canoe in mid-current and slept under hiding of the driftwood. Friendly Indians did not conceal themselves, but came to the river bank waving a buffalo-robe and spreading it out to signal a welcome to the white man; when the trapper would go ashore, whiff pipes with the chiefs and perhaps spend the night listening to the tales of exploits which each notch on the calumet typified. Incidents that meant nothing to other men were full of significance to the lone voyageur through hostile lands. Always the spring floods drifted down numbers of dead buffalo; and the carrion birds sat on the trees of the shore with their wings spread out to dry in the sun. The sudden flacker of a rising flock betrayed something prowling in ambush on the bank; so did the splash of a snake from overhanging branches into the water.

Different sorts of dangers beset the free trapper crossing the plains to the mountains. The fur company brigades always had escort of armed guard and provision packers. The free trappers went alone or in pairs, picketing horses to the saddle overlaid with a buffalo-robe for a pillow, cooking meals on chip fires, using a slow-burning wormwood bark for matches, and trusting their horses or dog to give the alarm if the bands of coyotes hovering through the night dusk approached too near. On the high rolling plains, hostiles could be descried at a distance, coming over the horizon head and top first like the peak of a sail, or emerging from the "coolies"—dried sloughs—like wolves from the earth. Enemies could be seen soon enough; but where could the trapper hide on bare prairie? He didn't attempt to hide. He simply set fire to the prairie and took refuge on the lee side. That device failing, he was at his enemies' mercy.

On the plains, the greatest danger was from lack of water. At one season the trapper might know where to find good camping streams. The next year when he came to those streams they were dry.

> "After leaving the buffalo meadows a dreadful scarcity of water ensued," wrote Charles MacKenzie, of the famous MacKenzie clan. He was journeying north from the Missouri. "We had to alter our course and steer to a distant lake. When we got there we found the lake dry. However, we dug a pit which produced a kind of stinking liquid which we all drank. It was salt and bitter, caused an inflammation of the mouth, left a disagreeable roughness of the throat, and seemed to increase our thirst.... We passed the night under great uneasiness. Next day we continued our journey, but not a drop of water was to be found, ... and our distress became insupportable.... All at once our horses became so unruly that we could not manage them. We observed that they showed an inclination towards a hill which was close by. It struck me that they might have scented water.... I ascended to the top, where, to my great joy, I discovered a small pool.... My horse plunged in before I could prevent him, ... and all the horses drank to excess."

"The plains across"—which was a western expression meaning the end of that part of the trip—there rose on the west rolling foothills and dark peaked profiles against the sky scarcely to be distinguished from gray cloud banks. These were the mountains; and the real hazards of free trapping began. No use to follow the easiest passes to the most frequented valleys. The fur company brigades marched through these, sweeping up game like a forest fire; so the free trappers sought out the hidden, inaccessible valleys, going where neither pack horse nor canot à bec d'esturgeon could follow. How did they do it? Very much the way Simon Fraser's hunters crawled down the river-course named after him. "Our shoes," said one trapper, "did not last a single day."

> "We had to plunge our daggers into the ground, ... otherwise we would slide into the river," wrote Fraser. "We cut steps into the declivity, fastened a line to the front of the canoe, with which some of the men ascended in order to haul it up. .. Our lives hung, as it were, upon a thread, as the failure of the line or the false step of the man might have hurled us into eternity.... We had to pass where no human being should venture.... Steps were formed like a ladder on the shrouds of a ship, by poles hanging to one another and crossed at certain distances with twigs, the whole suspended from the top to the foot of immense precipices, and fastened at both extremities to stones and trees."

He speaks of the worst places being where these frail swaying ladders led up to the overhanging ledge of a shelving precipice.

Such were the very real adventures of the trapper's life, a life whose fascinations lured John Colter from civilization to the wilds again and again till he came back once too often and found himself stripped, helpless, captive, in the hands of the Blackfeet.

It would be poor sport torturing a prisoner who showed no more fear than this impassive white man coolly listening and waiting for them to compass his death. So the chief dismissed the suggestion to shoot at their captive as a target. Suddenly the Blackfoot leader turned to Colter. "Could the white man run fast?" he asked. In a flash Colter guessed what was to be his fate. He, the hunter, was to be hunted. No, he cunningly signalled, he was only a poor runner.

Bidding his warriors stand still, the chief roughly led Colter out three hundred yards. Then he set his captive free, and the exultant shriek of the running warriors told what manner of sport this was to be. It was a race for life.

The white man shot out with all the power of muscles hard as iron-wood and tense as a bent bow. Fear winged the man running for his life to outrace the winged arrows coming from the shouting warriors three hundred yards behind. Before him stretched a plain six miles wide, the distance he had so thoughtlessly paddled between the rampart walls of the cañon but a few hours ago. At the Jefferson was a thick forest growth where a fugitive might escape. Somewhere along the Jefferson was his own hidden cabin.

Across this plain sped Colter, pursued by a band of six hundred shrieking demons. Not one breath did he waste looking back over his shoulder till he was more than half-way across the plain, and could tell from the fading uproar that he was outdistancing his hunters. Perhaps it was the last look of despair; but it spurred the jaded racer to redoubled efforts. All the Indians had been left to the rear but one, who was only a hundred yards behind.

There was, then, a racing chance of escape! Colter let out in a burst of renewed speed that brought blood gushing over his face, while the cactus spines cut his naked feet like knives. The river was in sight. A mile more, he would be in the wood! But the Indian behind was gaining at every step. Another backward look! The savage was not thirty yards away! He had poised his spear to launch it in Colter's back, when the white man turned fagged and beaten, threw up his arms and stopped!

This is an Indian ruse to arrest the pursuit of a wild beast. By force of habit it stopped the Indian too, and disconcerted him so that instead of launching his spear, he fell flat on his face, breaking the shaft in his hand. With a leap, Colter had snatched up the broken point and pinned the savage through the body to the earth.

That intercepted the foremost of the other warriors, who stopped to rescue their brave and gave Colter time to reach the river.

In he plunged, fainting and dazed, swimming for an island in mid-current where driftwood had formed a sheltered raft. Under this he dived, coming up with his head among branches of trees.

All that day the Blackfeet searched the island for Colter, running from log to log of the drift; but the close-grown brushwood hid the white man. At night he swam down-stream like any other hunted animal that wants to throw pursuers off the trail, went ashore and struck across country, seven days' journey for the Missouri Company's fort on the Bighorn River.

Naked and unarmed, he succeeded in reaching the distant fur post, having subsisted entirely on roots and berries.

Chittenden says that poor Colter's adventure only won for him in St. Louis the reputation of a colossal liar. But traditions of his escape were current among all hunters and Indian tribes on the Missouri, so that when Bradbury, the English scientist, went west with the Astorians in 1811, he sifted the matter, accepted it as truth, and preserved the episode for history in a small-type foot-note to his book published in London in 1817.

Two other adventures are on record similar to Colter's: one of Oskononton's escape by diving under a raft, told in Ross's Fur Hunters; the other of a poor Indian fleeing up the Ottawa from pursuing Iroquois of the Five Nations and diving under the broken bottom of an old beaver-dam, told in the original Jesuit Relations.

And yet when the Astorians went up the Missouri a few years later, Colter could scarcely resist the impulse to go a fourth time to the wilds. But fascinations stronger than the wooings of the wilds had come to his life—he had taken to himself a bride.

CHAPTER XIV
THE GREATEST FUR COMPANY OF THE WORLD

In the history of the world only one corporate company has maintained empire over an area as large as Europe. Only one corporate company has lived up to its constitution for nearly three centuries. Only one corporate company's sway has been so beneficent that its profits have stood in exact proportion to the well-being of its subjects. Indeed, few armies can boast a rank and file of men who never once retreated in three hundred years, whose lives, generation after generation, were one long bivouac of hardship, of danger, of ambushed death, of grim purpose, of silent achievement.

Such was the company of "Adventurers of England Trading into Hudson's Bay," as the charter of 1670 designated them.[39] Such is the Hudson's Bay Company to-day still trading with savages in the white wilderness of the north as it was when Charles II granted a royal charter for the fur trade to his cousin Prince Rupert.

Governors and chief factors have changed with the changing centuries; but the character of the company's personnel has never changed. Prince Rupert, the first governor, was succeeded by the Duke of York (James II); and the royal governor by a long line of distinguished public men down to Lord Strathcona, the present governor, and C. C. Chipman, the chief commissioner or executive officer. All have been men of noted achievement, often in touch with the Crown, always with that passion for executive and mastery of difficulty which exults most when the conflict is keenest.

Pioneers face the unknown when circumstances push them into it. Adventurers rush into the unknown for the zest of conquering it. It has been to the adventuring class that fur traders have belonged.

Radisson and Groseillers, the two Frenchmen who first brought back word of the great wealth in furs round the far northern sea, had been gentlemen adventurers—"rascals" their enemies called them. Prince Rupert, who leagued himself with the Frenchmen to obtain a charter for his fur trade, had been an adventurer of the high seas—"pirate" we would say—long before he became first governor of the Hudson's Bay Company. And the Duke of Marlborough, the company's third governor, was as great an adventurer as he was a general.

Latterly the word "adventurer" has fallen in such evil repute, it may scarcely be applied to living actors. But using it in the old-time sense of militant hero, what cavalier of gold braid and spurs could be more of an adventurer than young Donald Smith who traded in the desolate wastes of Labrador, spending seventeen years in the hardest field of the fur company, tramping on snow-shoes half the width of a continent, camping where night overtook him under blanketing of snow-drifts, who rose step by step from trader on the east coast to commissioner in the west? And this Donald Smith became Lord Strathcona, the governor of the Hudson's Bay Company.

Men bold in action and conservative in traditions have ruled the company. The governor resident in England is now represented by the chief commissioner, who in turn is represented at each of the many inland forts by a chief factor of the district. Nominally, the fur-trader's northern realm is governed by the Parliament of Canada. Virtually, the chief factor rules as autocratically to-day as he did before the Canadian Government took over the proprietary rights of the fur company.

How did these rulers of the wilds, these princes of the fur trade, live in lonely forts and mountain fastnesses? Visit one of the northern forts as it exists to-day.

The colder the climate, the finer the fur. The farther north the fort, the more typical it is of the fur-trader's realm.

For six, seven, eight months of the year, the fur-trader's world is a white wilderness of snow; snow water-waved by winds that sweep from the pole; snow drifted into ramparts round the fort stockades till the highest picket sinks beneath the white flood and the corner bastions are almost submerged and the entrance to the central gate resembles the cutting of a railway tunnel; snow that billows to the unbroken reaches of the circling sky-line like a white sea. East, frost-mist hides the low horizon in clouds of smoke, for the sun which rises from the east in other climes rises from the south-east here; and until the spring equinox, bringing summer with a flood-tide of thaw, gray darkness hangs in the east like a fog. South, the sun moves across the snowy levels in a wheel of fire, for it has scarcely risen full sphered above the sky-line before it sinks again etching drift and tip of half-buried brush in long lonely fading shadows. The west shimmers in warm purplish grays, for the moist Chinook winds come over the mountains melting the snow by magic. North, is the cold steel of ice by day; and at night Northern Lights darting through the polar dark like burnished spears.

Christmas day is welcomed at the northern fur posts by a firing of cannon from the snow-muffled bastions. Before the stars have faded, chapel services begin. Frequently on either Christmas or New Year's day, a grand feast is given the tawny-skinned habitués of the fort, who come shuffling to the main mess-room with no other announcement than the lifting of the latch, and billet themselves on the hospitality of a host that has never turned hungry Indians from its doors.

For reasons well-known to the woodcraftsman, a sudden lull falls on winter hunting in December, and all the trappers within a week's journey from the fort, all the half-breed guides who add to the instinct of native craft the reasoning of the white, all the Indian hunters ranging river-course and mountain have come by snow-shoes and dog train to spend festive days at the fort. A great jangling of bells announces the huskies (dog trains) scampering over the crusted snow-drifts. A babel of barks and curses follows, for the huskies celebrate their arrival by tangling themselves up in their harness and enjoying a free fight.

Dogs unharnessed, in troop the trappers to the banquet-hall, flinging packs of tightly roped peltries down promiscuously, to be sorted next day. One Indian enters just as he has left the hunting-field, clad from head to heel in white caribou with the antlers left on the capote as a decoy. His squaw has togged out for the occasion in a comical medley of brass bracelets and finger-rings, with a bear's claw necklace and ermine ruff which no city connoisseur could possibly mistake for rabbit. If a daughter yet remain unappropriated she will display the gayest attire—red flannel galore, red shawl, red scarf, with perhaps an apron of white fox-skin and moccasins garnished in coloured grasses. The braves outdo even a vain young squaw. Whole fox, mink, or otter skins have been braided to the end of their hair, and hang down in two plaits to the floor. Whitest of buckskin has been ornamented with brightest of beads, and over all hangs the gaudiest of blankets, it may be a musk-ox-skin with the feats of the warrior set forth in rude drawings on the smooth side.

Children and old people, too, come to the feast, for the Indian's stomach is the magnet that draws his soul. Grotesque little figures the children are, with men's trousers shambling past their heels, rabbit-skin coats with the fur turned in, and on top of all some old stovepipe hat or discarded busby coming half-way down to the urchin's neck. The old people have more resemblance to parchment on gnarled sticks than to human beings. They shiver under dirty blankets with every sort of cast-off rag tied about their limbs, hobbling lame from frozen feet or rheumatism, mumbling toothless requests for something to eat or something to wear, for tobacco, the solace of Indian woes, or what is next best—tea.

Among so many guests are many needs. One half-breed from a far wintering outpost, where perhaps a white man and this guide are living in a chinked shack awaiting a hunting party's return, arrives at the fort with frozen feet. Little Labree's feet must be thawed out, and sometimes little Labree dies under the process, leaving as a legacy to the chief factor the death-bed pledge that the corpse be taken to a distant tribal burying-ground. And no matter how inclement the winter, the chief factor keeps his pledge, for the integrity of a promise is the only law in the fur-trader's realm. Special attentions, too, must be paid those old retainers who have acted as mentors of the fort in times of trouble.

A few years ago it would not have been safe to give this treat inside the fort walls. Rations would have been served through loop-holes and the feast held outside the gates; but so faithfully have the Indians become bound to the Hudson's Bay Company there are not three forts in the fur territory where Indians must be excluded.

Of the feast little need be said. Like the camel, the Indian lays up store for the morrow, judging from his capacity for weeks of morrows. His benefactor no more dines with him than a plantation master of the South would have dined with feasting slaves. Elsewhere a bell calls the company officers to breakfast at 7.30, dinner at 1, supper at 7. Officers dine first, white hunters and trappers second, that difference between master and servant being maintained which is part of the company's almost military discipline. In the large forts are libraries, whither resort the officers for the long winter nights. But over the feast wild hilarity reigns.

A French-Canadian fiddler strikes up a tuneless jig that sets the Indians pounding the floor in figureless dances with moccasined heels till midday glides into midnight and midnight to morning. I remember hearing of one such midday feast in Red River settlement that prolonged itself past four of the second morning. Against the walls sit old folks spinning yarns of the past. There is a print of Sir George Simpson behind one raconteur's head. Ah! yes, the oldest guides all remember Sir George, though half a century has passed since his day. He was the governor who travelled with flags flying from every prow, and cannon firing when he left the forts, and men drawn up in procession like soldiers guarding an emperor when he entered the fur posts with coureurs and all the flourish of royal state. Then some story-teller recalls how he has heard the old guides tell of the imperious governor once provoking personal conflict with an equally imperious steersman, who first ducked the governor into a lake they were traversing and then ducked into the lake himself to rescue the governor.

And there is a crucifix high on the wall left by Père Lacomb the last time the famous missionary to the red men of the Far North passed this way; and every Indian calls up some kindness done, some sacrifice by Father Lacomb. On the gun-rack are old muskets and Indian masks and scalp-locks, bringing back the days when Russian traders instigated a massacre at this fort and when white traders flew at each other's throats as Nor' Westers struggled with Hudson's Bay for supremacy in the fur trade.

"Ah, oui, those white men, they were brave fighters, they did not know how to stop. Mais, sacré, they were fools, those white men after all! Instead of hiding in ambush to catch the foe, those white men measured off paces, stood up face to face and fired blank—oui—fired blank! Ugh! Of course, one fool he was kill' and the other fool, most like, he was wound'! Ugh, by Gar! What Indian would have so little sense?"[40]

Of hunting tales, the Indian store is exhaustless. That enormous bear-skin stretched to four pegs on the wall brings up Montagnais, the Noseless One, who still lives on Peace River and once slew the largest bear ever killed in the Rockies, returning to this very fort with one hand dragging the enormous skin and the other holding the place which his nose no longer graced.

"Montagnais? Ah, bien messieur! Montagnais, he brave man! Venez ici—bien—so—I tole you 'bout heem," begins some French-Canadian trapper with a strong tinge of Indian blood in his swarthy skin. "Bigosh! He brave man! I tole you 'bout dat happen! Montagnais, he go stumble t'rough snow—how you call dat?—hill, steep—steep! Oui, by Gar! dat vas steep hill! de snow, she go slide, slide, lak' de—de gran' rapeed, see?" emphasizing the snow-slide with illustrative gesture. "Bien, donc! Mais, Montagnais, he stick gun-stock in de snow stop heem fall—so—see? Tonnerre! Bigosh! for sure she go off wan beeg bang! Sacré! She make so much noise she wake wan beeg ol' bear sleep in snow. Montagnais, he tumble on hees back! Mais, messieur, de bear—diable! 'fore Montagnais wink hees eye de bear jump on top lak' wan beeg loup-garou! Montagnais, he brave man—he not scare—he say wan leetle prayer, wan han' he cover his eyes! Odder han'—sacré—dat grab hees knife out hees belt—sz-sz-sz, messieur. For sure he feel her breat'—diable!—for sure he fin' de place her heart beat—Tonnerre! Vite! he stick dat knife in straight up hees wrist, into de heart dat bear! Dat bes' t'ing do—for sure de leetle prayer dat tole him best t'ing do! De bear she roll over—over—dead's wan stone—c'est vrai! she no mor' jump top Montagnais! Bien, ma frien'! Montagnais, he roll over too—leetle bit scare! Mais, hees nose! Ah! bigosh! de bear she got dat; dat all nose he ever haf no mor'! C'est vrai messieur, bien!"

And with a finishing flourish the story-teller takes to himself all the credit of Montagnais's heroism.

But in all the feasting, trade has not been forgotten; and as soon as the Indians recover from post-prandial torpor bartering begins. In one of the warehouses stands a trader. An Indian approaches with a pack of peltries weighing from eighty to a hundred pounds. Throwing it down, he spreads out the contents. Of otter and mink and pekan there will be plenty, for these fish-eaters are most easily taken before midwinter frost has frozen the streams solid. In recent years there have been few beaver-skins, a closed season of several years giving the little rodents a chance to multiply. By treaty the Indian may hunt all creatures of the chase as long as "the sun rises and the rivers flow"; but the fur-trader can enforce a closed season by refusing to barter for the pelts. Of musk-rat-skins, hundreds of thousands are carried to the forts every season. The little haycock houses of musk-rats offer the trapper easy prey when frost freezes the sloughs, shutting off retreat below, and heavy snow-fall has not yet hidden the little creatures' winter home.

The trading is done in several ways. Among the Eskimo, whose arithmetical powers seldom exceed a few units, the trader holds up his hand with one, two, three fingers raised, signifying that he offers for the skin before him equivalents in value to one, two, three prime beaver. If satisfied, the Indian passes over the furs and the trader gives flannel, beads, powder, knives, tea, or tobacco to the value of the beaver-skins indicated by the raised fingers. If the Indian demands more, hunter and trader wrangle in pantomime till compromise is effected.

But always beaver-skin is the unit of coin. Beaver are the Indian's dollars and cents, his shillings and pence, his tokens of currency.

South of the Arctics, where native intelligence is of higher grade, the beaver values are represented by goose-quills, small sticks, bits of shell, or, most common of all, disks of lead, tea-chests melted down, stamped on one side with the company arms, on the other with the figures 1, 2, 1/2, 1/4, representing so much value in beaver.

First of all, then, furs in the pack must be sorted, silver fox worth five hundred dollars separated from cross fox and blue and white worth from ten dollars down, according to quality, and from common red fox worth less. Twenty years ago it was no unusual thing for the Hudson's Bay Company to send to England yearly 10,000 cross fox-skins, 7,000 blue, 100,000 red, half a dozen silver. Few wolf-skins are in the trapper's pack unless particularly fine specimens of brown arctic and white arctic, bought as a curiosity and not for value as skins. Against the wolf, the trapper wages war as against a pest that destroys other game, and not for its skin. Next to musk-rat the most plentiful fur taken by the Indian, though not highly esteemed by the trader, will be that of the rabbit or varying hare. Buffalo was once the staple of the hunter. What the buffalo was the white rabbit is to-day. From it the Indian gets clothing, tepee, covers, blankets, thongs, food. From it the white man who is a manufacturer of furs gets gray fox and chinchilla and seal in imitation. Except one year in seven, when a rabbit plague spares the land by cutting down their prolific numbers, the varying hare is plentiful enough to sustain the Indian.

Having received so many bits of lead for his furs, the Indian goes to the store counter where begins interminable dickering. Montagnais's squaw has only fifty "beaver" coin, and her desires are a hundredfold what those will buy. Besides, the copper-skinned lady enjoys beating down prices and driving a bargain so well that she would think the clerk a cheat if he asked a fixed price from the first. She expects him to have a sliding scale of prices for his goods as she has for her furs. At the termination of each bargain, so many coins pass across the counter. Frequently an Indian presents himself at the counter without beaver enough to buy necessaries. What then? I doubt if in all the years of Hudson's Bay Company rule one needy Indian has ever been turned away. The trader advances what the Indian needs and chalks up so many "beaver" against the trapper's next hunt.

Long ago, when rival traders strove for the furs, whisky played a disgracefully prominent part in all bartering, the drunk Indian being an easier victim than the sober, and the Indian mad with thirst for liquor the most easily cajoled of all. But to-day when there is no competition, whisky plays no part whatever. Whisky is in the fort, so is pain killer, for which the Indian has as keen an appetite, both for the exigencies of hazardous life in an unsparing climate beyond medical aid; but the first thing Hudson's Bay traders did in 1885, when rebel Indians surrounded the Saskatchewan forts, was to split the casks and spill all alcohol. The second thing was to bury ammunition—showing which influence they considered the more dangerous.

Ermine is at its best when the cold is most intense, the tawny weasel coat turning from fawn to yellow, from yellow to cream and snow-white, according to the latitude north and the season. Unless it is the pelt of the baby ermine, soft as swan's down, tail-tip jet as onyx, the best ermine is not likely to be in a pack brought to the fort as early as Christmas.

Fox, lynx, mink, marten, otter, and bear, the trapper can take with steel-traps of a size varying with the game, or even with the clumsily constructed deadfall, the log suspended above the bait being heavy or light, according to the hunter's expectation of large or small intruder; but the ermine with fur as easily damaged as finest gauze must be handled differently.

Going the rounds of his traps, the hunter has noted curious tiny tracks like the dots and dashes of a telegraphic code. Here are little prints slurring into one another in a dash; there, a dead stop, where the quick-eared stoat has paused with beady eyes alert for snowbird or rabbit. Here, again, a clear blank on the snow where the crafty little forager has dived below the light surface and wriggled forward like a snake to dart up with a plunge of fangs into the heart-blood of the unwary snow-bunting. From the length of the leaps, the trapper judges the age of the ermine; fourteen inches from nose to tail-tip means a full-grown ermine with hair too coarse to be damaged by a snare. The man suspends the noose of a looped twine across the runway from a twig bent down so that the weight of the ermine on the string sends the twig springing back with a jerk that lifts the ermine off the ground, strangling it instantly. Perhaps on one side of the twine he has left bait—smeared grease, or a bit of meat.

If the tracks are like the prints of a baby's fingers, close and small, the trapper hopes to capture a pelt fit for a throne cloak, the skin for which the Louis of France used to pay, in modern money, from a hundred dollars to a hundred and fifty dollars. The full-grown ermines will be worth only some few "beaver" at the fort. Perfect fur would be marred by the twine snare, so the trapper devises as cunning a death for the ermine as the ermine devises when it darts up through the snow with its spear-teeth clutched in the throat of a poor rabbit. Smearing his hunting-knife with grease, he lays it across the track. The little ermine comes trotting in dots and dashes and gallops and dives to the knife. It smells the grease, and all the curiosity which has been teaching it to forage for food since it was born urges it to put out its tongue and taste. That greasy smell of meat it knows; but that frost-silvered bit of steel is something new. The knife is frosted like ice. Ice the ermine has licked, so he licks the knife. But alas for the resemblance between ice and steel! Ice turns to water under the warm tongue; steel turns to fire that blisters and holds the foolish little stoat by his inquisitive tongue a hopeless prisoner till the trapper comes. And lest marauding wolverine or lynx should come first and gobble up priceless ermine, the trapper comes soon. And that is the end for the ermine.

Before settlers invaded the valley of the Saskatchewan the furs taken at a leading fort would amount to:

Bear of all varieties	400
Ermine, medium	200
Blue fox	4
Red fox	91
Silver fox	3
Marten	2,000

Musk-rat	200,000
Mink	8,000
Otter	500
Skunk	6
Wolf	100
Beaver	5,000
Pekan (fisher)	50
Cross fox	30
White fox	400
Lynx	400
Wolverine	200

The value of these furs in "beaver" currency varied with the fashions of the civilized world, with the scarcity or plenty of the furs, with the locality of the fort. Before beaver became so scarce, 100 beaver equalled 40 marten or 10 otter or 300 musk-rat; 25 beaver equalled 500 rabbit; 1 beaver equalled 2 white fox; and so on down the scale. But no set table of values can be given other than the prices realized at the annual sale of Hudson's Bay furs, held publicly in London.

To understand the values of these furs to the Indian, "beaver" currency must be compared to merchandise, one beaver buying such a red handkerchief as trappers wear around their brows to notify other hunters not to shoot; one beaver buys a hunting-knife, two an axe, from eight to twenty a gun or rifle, according to its quality. And in one old trading list I found—vanity of vanities—"one beaver equals looking-glass."

Trading over, the trappers disperse to their winter hunting-grounds, which the main body of hunters never leaves from October, when they go on the fall hunt, to June, when the long straggling brigades of canoes and keel boats and pack horses and jolting ox-carts come back to the fort with the harvest of winter furs.

Signs unnoted by the denizens of city serve to guide the trappers over trackless wastes of illimitable snow. A whitish haze of frost may hide the sun, or continuous snow-fall-blur every land-mark. What heeds the trapper?

The slope of the rolling hills, the lie of the frozen river-beds, the branches of underbrush protruding through billowed drifts are hands that point the trapper's compass. For those hunters who have gone westward to the mountains, the task of threading pathless forest stillness is more difficult. At a certain altitude in the mountains, much frequented by game because undisturbed by storms, snow falls—falls—falls, without ceasing, heaping the pines with snow mushrooms, blotting out the sun, cloaking in heavy white flakes the notched bark blazed as a trail, transforming the rustling green forests to a silent spectral world without a mark to direct the hunter. Here the woodcraftsman's lore comes to his aid. He looks to the snow-coned tops of the pine trees. The tops of pine trees lean ever so slightly towards the rising sun. With his snow-shoes he digs away the snow at the roots of trees to get down to the moss. Moss grows from the roots of trees on the shady side—that is, the north. And simplest of all, demanding only that a wanderer use his eyes—which the white man seldom does—the limbs of the northern trees are most numerous on the south. The trapper may be waylaid by storms, or starved by sudden migration of game from the grounds to which he has come, or run to earth by the ravenous timber-wolves that pursue the dog teams for leagues; but the trapper with Indian blood in his veins will not be lost.

One imminent danger is of accident beyond aid. A young Indian hunter of Moose Factory set out with his wife and two children for the winter hunting-grounds in the forest south of James Bay. To save the daily allowance of a fish for each dog, they did not take the dog teams. When chopping, the hunter injured his leg. The wound proved stubborn. Game was scarce, and they had not enough food to remain in the lodge. Wrapping her husband in robes on the long toboggan sleigh, the squaw placed the younger child beside him and with the other began tramping through the forest drawing the sleigh behind. The drifts were not deep enough for swift snow-shoeing over underbrush, and their speed was not half so speedy as the hunger that pursues northern hunters like the Fenris Wolf of Norse myth. The woman sank exhausted on the snow and the older boy, nerved with fear, pushed on to Moose Factory for help. Guided by the boy back through the forests, the fort people found the hunter dead in the sleigh, the mother crouched forward unconscious from cold, stripped of the clothing which she had wrapped round the child taken in her arms to warm with her own body. The child was alive and well. The fur traders nursed the woman back to life, though she looked more like a withered creature of eighty than a woman barely in her twenties. She explained with a simple unconsciousness of heroism that the ground had been too hard for her to bury her husband, and she was afraid to leave the body and go on to the fort lest the wolves should molest the dead.[41]

The arrival of the mail packet is one of the most welcome breaks in the monotony of life at the fur post. When the mail comes, all white habitants of the fort take a week's holidays to read letters and news of the outside world.

Railways run from Lake Superior to the Pacific; but off the line of railways mail is carried as of old. In summer-time overland runners, canoe, and company steamers bear the mail to the forts of Hudson Bay, of the Saskatchewan, of the Rockies, and the MacKenzie. In winter, scampering huskies with a running postman winged with snow-shoes dash across the snowy wastes through silent forests to the lonely forts of the bay, or slide over the prairie drifts with the music of tinkling bells and soft crunch-crunch of sleigh runners through the snow crust to the leagueless world of the Far North.

Forty miles a day, a couch of spruce boughs where the racquets have dug a hole in the snow, sleighs placed on edge as a wind break, dogs crouched on the buffalo-robes snarling over the frozen fish, deep bayings from the running wolf-pack, and before the stars have faded from the frosty sky, the mail-carrier has risen and is coasting away fast as the huskies can gallop.

Another picturesque feature of the fur trade was the long caravan of ox-carts that used to screech and creak and jolt over the rutted prairie roads between Winnipeg and St. Paul. More than 1,500 Hudson's Bay Company carts manned by 500 traders with tawny spouses and black-eyed impish children, squatted on top of the load, left Canada for St. Paul in August and returned in October. The carts were made without a rivet of iron. Bent wood formed the tires of the two wheels. Hardwood axles told their woes to the world in the scream of shrill bagpipes. Wooden racks took the place of cart box. In the shafts trod a staid old ox guided from the horns or with a halter, drawing the load with collar instead of a yoke. The harness was of skin thongs. In place of the ox sometimes was a "shagganippy" pony, raw and unkempt, which the imps lashed without mercy or the slightest inconvenience to the horse.

Carrying goods over long portage in MacKenzie River region with the old-fashioned Red River ox-carts.

A red flag with the letters H. B. C. in white decorated the leading cart. During the Sioux massacres the fur caravans were unmolested, for the Indians recognised the flags and wished to remain on good terms with the fur traders.

Ox-carts still bring furs to Hudson's Bay Company posts, and screech over the corduroyed swamps of the MacKenzie; but the railway has replaced the caravan as a carrier of freight.

Hudson's Bay Company steamers now ply on the largest of the inland rivers with long lines of fur-laden barges in tow; but the canoe brigades still bring the winter's hunt to the forts in spring. Five to eight craft make a brigade, each manned by eight paddlers with an experienced steersman, who is usually also guide. But the one ranking first in importance is the bowman, whose quick eye must detect signs of nearing rapids, whose steel-shod pole gives the cue to the other paddlers and steers the craft past foamy reefs. The bowman it is who leaps out first when there is "tracking"—pulling the craft up-stream by tow-line—who stands waist high in ice water steadying the rocking bark lest a sudden swirl spill furs to the bottom, who hands out the packs to the others when the waters are too turbulent for "tracking" and there must be a "portage," and who leads the brigade on a run—half trot, half amble—overland to the calmer currents. "Pipes" are the measure of a portage—that is, the pipes smoked while the voyageurs are on the run. The bowman it is who can thread a network of water-ways by day or dark, past rapids or whirlpools, with the certainty of an arrow to the mark. On all long trips by dog train or canoe, pemmican made of buffalo meat and marrow put in air-tight bags was the standard food. The pemmican now used is of moose or caribou beef.

The only way to get an accurate idea of the size of the kingdom ruled by these monarchs of the lonely wastes is by comparison.

Take a map of North America. On the east is Labrador, a peninsula as vast as Germany and Holland and Belgium and half of France. On the coast and across the unknown interior are the magical letters H. B. C., meaning Hudson's Bay Company fort (past or present), a little whitewashed square with eighteen-foot posts planted picket-wise for a wall, match-box bastions loopholed for musketry, a barracks-like structure across the court-yard with a high lookout of some sort near the gate. Here some trader with wife and children and staff of Indian servants has held his own against savagery and desolating loneliness. In one of these forts Lord Strathcona passed his youth.

Once more to the map. With one prong of a compass in the centre of Hudson Bay, describe a circle. The northern half embraces the baffling arctics; but on the line of the southern circumference like beads on a string are Churchill high on the left, York below in black capitals as befits the importance of the great fur emporium of the bay, Severn and Albany and Moose and Rupert and Fort George round the south, and to the right, larger and more strongly built forts than in Labrador, with the ruins of stone walls at Churchill that have a depth of fifteen feet. Six-pounders once mounted these bastions. The remnants of galleries for soldiery run round the inside walls. A flag floats over each fort with the letters H. B. C.[42] Officers' dwellings occupy the centre of the court-yard. Banked against the walls are the men's quarters, fur presses, stables, storerooms. Always there is a chapel, at one fort a hospital, at others the relics of stoutly built old powder magazines made to withstand the siege of hand grenades tossed in by French assailants from the bay, who knew that the loot of a fur post was better harvest than a treasure ship. Elsewhere two small bastions situated diagonally across from each other were sufficient to protect the fur post by sending a raking fire along the walls; but here there was danger of the French fleet, and the walls were built with bastion and trench and rampart.

Again to the map. Between Hudson Bay and the Rocky Mountains stretches an American Siberia—the Barren Lands. Here, too, on every important waterway, Athabasca and the Liard and the MacKenzie into the land of winter night and midnight sun, extend Hudson's Bay Company posts. We think of these northern streams as ice-jammed, sluggish currents, with mean log villages on their banks. The fur posts of the sub-arctics are not imposing with picket fences in place of stockades, for no French foe was feared here. But the MacKenzie River is one of the longest in the world, with two tributaries each more than 1,000 miles in length. It has a width of a mile, and a succession of rapids that rival the St. Lawrence, and palisaded banks higher than the Hudson River's, and half a dozen lakes into one of which you could drop two New England States without raising a sand bar.

The map again. Between the prairie and the Pacific Ocean is a wilderness of peaks, a Switzerland stretched into half the length of a continent. Here, too, like eagle nests in rocky fastnesses are fur posts.

Such is the realm of the Hudson's Bay Company to-day.

Before 1812 there was no international boundary in the fur trade. But after the war Congress barred out Canadian companies. The next curtailment of hunting-ground came in 1869-'70, when the company surrendered proprietary rights to the Canadian Government, retaining only the right to trade in the vast north land. The formation of new Canadian provinces took place south of the Saskatchewan; but north the company barters pelts undisturbed as of old. Yearly the staffs are shifted from post to post as the fortunes of the hunt vary; but the principal posts not including winter quarters for a special hunt have probably not exceeded two hundred in number, nor fallen below one hundred for the last century. Of these the greater numbers are of course in the Far North. When the Hudson's Bay Company was fighting rivals, Nor' Westers from Montreal, Americans from St. Louis, it must have employed as traders, packers, coureurs, canoe men, hunters, and guides, at least 5,000 men; for its rival employed that number, and "The Old Lady," as the enemy called it, always held her own. Over this wilderness army were from 250 to 300 officers, each with the power of life and death in his hands. To the honour of the company, be it said, this power was seldom abused.[43] Occasionally a brutal sea-captain might use lash and triangle and branding along the northern coast; but officers defenceless among savage hordes must of necessity have lived on terms of justice with their men.

The Canadian Government now exercises judicial functions; but where less than 700 mounted police patrol a territory as large as Siberia, the company's factor is still the chief representative of the law's power. Times without number under the old régime has a Hudson's Bay officer set out alone and tracked an Indian murderer to hidden fastness, there to arrest him or shoot him dead on the spot; because if murder went unpunished that mysterious impulse to kill which is as rife in the savage heart as in the wolf's would work its havoc unchecked.

Just as surely as "the sun rises and the rivers flow" the savage knows when the hunt fails he will receive help from the Hudson's Bay officer. But just as surely he knows if he commits any crime that same unbending, fearless white man will pursue—and pursue—and pursue guilt to the death. One case is on record of a trader thrashing an Indian within an inch of his life for impudence to officers two or three years before. Of course, the vendetta may cut both ways, the Indian treasuring vengeance in his heart till he can wreak it. That is an added reason why the white man's justice must be unimpeachable. "Pro pelle cutem," says the motto of the company arms. Without flippancy it might be said "An eye for an eye and a tooth for a tooth," as well as "A skin for a skin"—which explains the freedom from crime among northern Indians.

And who are the subjects living under this Mosaic paternalism?

Stunted Eskimo of the Far North, creatures as amphibious as the seals whose coats they wear, with the lustreless eyes of dwarfed intelligence and the agility of seal flippers as they whisk double-bladed paddles from side to side of the darting kyacks; wandering Montagnais from the domed hills of Labrador, lonely and sad and silent as the naked desolation of their rugged land; Ojibways soft-voiced as the forest glooms in that vast land of spruce tangle north of the Great Lakes; Crees and Sioux from the plains, cunning with the stealth of creatures that have hunted and been hunted on the shelterless prairie; Blackfeet and Crows, game birds of the foothills that have harried all other tribes for tribute, keen-eyed as the eagles on the mountains behind them, glorying in war as the finest kind of hunting; mountain tribes—Stonies, Kootenais, Shoshonies—splendid types of manhood because only the fittest can survive the hardships of the mountains; coast Indians, Chinook and Chilcoot—low and lazy because the great rivers feed them with salmon and they have no need to work.

Over these lawless Arabs of the New World wilderness the Hudson's Bay Company has ruled for two and a half centuries with smaller loss of life in the aggregate than the railways of the United States cause in a single year.

Hunters have been lost in the wilds. White trappers have been assassinated by Indians. Forts have been wiped out of existence. Ten, twenty, thirty traders have been massacred at different times. But, then, the loss of life on railways totals up to thousands in a single year.

When fighting rivals long ago, it is true that the Hudson's Bay Company recognised neither human nor divine law. Grant the charge and weigh it against the benefits of the company's rule. When Hearne visited Chippewyans two centuries ago he found the Indians in a state uncontaminated by the trader; and that state will give the ordinary reader cold shivers of horror at the details of massacre and degradation. Every visitor since has reported the same tribe improved in standard of living under Hudson's Bay rule. Recently a well-known Canadian governor making an itinerary of the territory round the bay found the Indians such devout Christians that they put his white retinue to shame. Returning to civilization, the governor was observed attending the services of his own denomination with a greater fury than was his wont. Asked the reason, he confided to a club friend that he would be blanked if he could allow heathen Indians to be better Christians than he was.

Some of the shiftless Indians may be hopelessly in debt to the company for advanced provisions, but if the company had not made these advances the Indians would have starved, and the debt is never exacted by seizure of the hunt that should go to feed a family.

Of how many other creditors may that be said? Of how many companies that it has cared for the sick, sought the lost, fed the starving, housed the homeless? With all its faults, that is the record of the Hudson's Bay Company.

CHAPTER XV
KOOT AND THE BOB-CAT

Old whaling ships, that tumble round the world and back again from coast to coast over strange seas, hardly ever suffer any of the terrible disasters that are always overtaking the proud men-of-war and swift liners equipped with all that science can do for them against misfortune. Ask an old salt why this is, and he will probably tell you that he feels his way forward or else that he steers by the same chart as that—jerking his thumb sideways from the wheel towards some sea gull careening over the billows. A something, that is akin to the instinct of wild creatures warning them when to go north for the summer, when to go south for the winter, when to scud for shelter from coming storm, guides the old whaler across chartless seas.

So it is with the trapper. He may be caught in one of his great steel-traps and perish on the prairie. He may run short of water and die of thirst on the desert. He may get his pack horses tangled up in a valley where there is no game and be reduced to the alternative of destroying what will carry him back to safety or starving with a horse still under him, before he can get over the mountains into another valley—but the true trapper will literally never lose himself. Lewis and Clark rightly merit the fame of having first explored the Missouri-Columbia route; but years before the Louisiana purchase, free trappers were already on the Columbia. David Thompson of the North-West Company was the first Canadian to explore the lower Columbia; but before Thompson had crossed the Rockies, French hunters were already ranging the forests of the Pacific slope. How did these coasters of the wilds guide themselves over prairies that were a chartless sea and mountains that were a wilderness? How does the wavey know where to find the rush-grown inland pools? Who tells the caribou mother to seek refuge on islands where the water will cut off the wolves that would prey on her young?

Something, which may be the result of generations of accumulated observation, guides the wavey and the caribou. Something, which may be the result of unconscious inference from a life-time of observation, guides the man. In the animal we call it instinct, in the man, reason; and in the case of the trapper tracking pathless wilds, the conscious reason of the man seems almost merged in the automatic instinct of the brute. It is not sharp-sightedness—though no man is sharper of sight than the trapper. It is not acuteness of hearing—though the trapper learns to listen with the noiseless stealth of the pencil-eared lynx. It is not touch—in the sense of tactile contact—any more than it is touch that tells a suddenly awakened sleeper of an unexpected noiseless presence in a dark room. It is something deeper than the tabulated five senses, a sixth sense—a sense of feel, without contact—a sense on which the whole sensate world writes its records as on a palimpsest. This palimpsest is the trapper's chart, this sense of feel, his weapon against the instinct of the brute. What part it plays in the life of every ranger of the wilds can best be illustrated by telling how Koot found his way to the fur post after the rabbit-hunt.

When the midwinter lull falls on the hunt, there is little use in the trapper going far afield. Moose have "yarded up." Bear have "holed up" and the beaver are housed till dwindling stores compel them to come out from their snow-hidden domes. There are no longer any buffalo for the trapper to hunt during the lull; but what buffalo formerly were to the hunter, rabbit are to-day. Shields and tepee covers, moccasins, caps and coats, thongs and meat, the buffalo used to supply. These are now supplied by "wahboos—little white chap," which is the Indian name for rabbit.

And there is no midwinter lull for "wahboos." While the "little white chap" runs, the long-haired, owlish-eyed lynx of the Northern forest runs too. So do all the lynx's feline cousins, the big yellowish cougar of the mountains slouching along with his head down and his tail lashing and a footstep as light and sinuous and silent as the motion of a snake; the short-haired lucifee gorging himself full of "little white chaps" and stretching out to sleep on a limb in a dapple of sunshine and shadow so much like the lucifee's skin not even a wolf would detect the sleeper; the bunchy bob-cat bounding and skimming over the snow for all the world like a bouncing football done up in gray fur—all members of the cat tribe running wherever the "little white chaps" run.

So when the lull fell on the hunt and the mink trapping was well over and marten had not yet begun, Koot gathered up his traps, and getting a supply of provisions at the fur post, crossed the white wastes of prairie to lonely swamp ground where dwarf alder and willow and cottonwood and poplar and pine grew in a tangle. A few old logs dovetailed into a square made the wall of a cabin. Over these he stretched the canvas of his tepee for a roof at a sharp enough angle to let the heavy snow-fall slide off from its own weight. Moss chinked up the logs. Snow banked out the wind. Pine boughs made the floor, two logs with pine boughs, a bed. An odd-shaped stump served as chair or table; and on the logs of the inner walls hung wedge-shaped slabs of cedar to stretch the skins. A caribou curtain or bear-skin across the entrance completed Koot's winter quarters for the rabbit-hunt.

Koot's genealogy was as vague as that of all old trappers hanging round fur posts. Part of him—that part which served best when he was on the hunting-field—was Ojibway. The other part, which made him improvise logs into chair and table and bed, was white man; and that served him best when he came to bargain with the chief factor over the pelts. At the fur post he attended the Catholic mission. On the hunting-field, when suddenly menaced by some great danger, he would cry out in the Indian tongue words that meant "O Great Spirit!" And it is altogether probable that at the mission and on the hunting-field, Koot was worshipping the same Being. When he swore—strange commentary on civilization—he always used white man's oaths, French patois or straight English.

Though old hermits may be found hunting alone through the Rockies, Idaho, Washington, and Minnesota, trappers do not usually go to the wilds alone; but there was so little danger in rabbit-snaring, that Koot had gone out accompanied by only the mongrel dog that had drawn his provisions from the fort on a sort of toboggan sleigh.

The snow is a white page on which the wild creatures write their daily record for those who can read. All over the white swamp were little deep tracks; here, holes as if the runner had sunk; there, padded marks as from the bound—bound—bound of something soft; then, again, where the thicket was like a hedge with only one breach through, the footprints had beaten a little hard rut walled by the soft snow. Koot's dog might have detected a motionless form under the thicket of spiney shrubs, a form that was gray almost to whiteness and scarcely to be distinguished from the snowy underbrush but for the blink of a prism light—the rabbit's eye. If the dog did catch that one tell-tale glimpse of an eye which a cunning rabbit would have shut, true to the training of his trapper master he would give no sign of the discovery except perhaps the pricking forward of both ears. Koot himself preserved as stolid a countenance as the rabbit playing dead or simulating a block of wood. Where the footprints ran through the breached hedge, Koot stooped down and planted little sticks across the runway till there was barely room for a weasel to pass. Across the open he suspended a looped string hung from a twig bent so that the slightest weight in the loop would send it up with a death jerk for anything caught in the tightening twine.

All day long, Koot goes from hedge to hedge, from runway to runway, choosing always the places where natural barriers compel the rabbit to take this path and no other, travelling if he can in a circle from his cabin so that the last snare set will bring him back with many a zigzag to the first snare made. If rabbits were plentiful—as they always were in the fur country of the North except during one year in seven when an epidemic spared the land from a rabbit pest—Koot's circuit of snares would run for miles through the swamp. Traps for large game would be set out so that the circuit would require only a day; but where rabbits are numerous, the foragers that prey—wolf and wolverine and lynx and bob-cat—will be numerous, too; and the trapper will not set out more snares than he can visit twice a day. Noon—the Indian's hour of the short shadow—is the best time for the first visit, nightfall, the time of no shadow at all, for the second. If the trapper has no wooden door to his cabin, and in it—instead of caching in a tree—keeps fish or bacon that may attract marauding wolverine, he will very probably leave his dogs on guard while he makes the round of the snares.

Finding tracks about the shack when he came back for his noonday meal, Koot shouted sundry instructions into the mongrel's ear, emphasized them with a moccasin kick, picked up the sack in which he carried bait, twine, and traps, and set out in the evening to make the round of his snares, unaccompanied by the dog. Rabbit after rabbit he found, gray and white, hanging stiff and stark, dead from their own weight, strangled in the twine snares. Snares were set anew, the game strung over his shoulder, and Koot was walking through the gray gloaming for the cabin when that strange sense of feel told him that he was being followed. What was it? Could it be the dog? He whistled—he called it by name.

In all the world, there is nothing so ghostly silent, so deathly quiet as the swamp woods, muffled in the snow of midwinter, just at nightfall. By day, the grouse may utter a lonely cluck-cluck, or the snowbuntings chirrup and twitter and flutter from drift to hedge-top, or the saucy jay shriek some scolding impudence. A squirrel may chatter out his noisy protest at some thief for approaching the nuts which lie cached under the rotten leaves at the foot of the tree, or the sun-warmth may set the melting snow showering from the swan's-down branches with a patter like rain. But at nightfall the frost has stilled the drip of thaw. Squirrel and bird are wrapped in the utter quiet of a gray darkness. And the marauders that fill midnight with sharp bark, shrill trembling scream, deep baying over the snow are not yet abroad in the woods. All is shadowless—stillness—a quiet that is audible.

Koot turned sharply and whistled and called his dog. There wasn't a sound. Later when the frost began to tighten, sap-frozen twigs would snap. The ice of the swamp, frozen like rock, would by-and-bye crackle with the loud echo of a pistol-shot—crackle—and strike—and break as if artillery were firing a fusillade and infantry shooters answering sharp. By-and-bye, moon and stars and Northern Lights would set the shadows dancing; and the wail of the cougar would be echoed by the lifting scream of its mate. But now, was not a sound, not a motion, not a shadow, only the noiseless stillness, the shadowless quiet, and the feel, the feel of something back where the darkness was gathering like a curtain in the bush.

It might, of course, be only a silly long-ears loping under cover parallel to the man, looking with rabbit curiosity at this strange newcomer to the swamp home of the animal world. Koot's sense of feel told him that it wasn't a rabbit; but he tried to persuade himself that it was, the way a timid listener persuades herself that creaking floors are burglars. Thinking of his many snares, Koot smiled and walked on. Then it came again, that feel of something coursing behind the underbrush in the gloom of the gathering darkness. Koot stopped short—and listened—and listened—listened to a snow-muffled silence, to a desolating solitude that pressed in on the lonely hunter like the waves of a limitless sea round a drowning man.

The sense of feel that is akin to brute instinct gave him the impression of a presence. Reason that is man's told him what it might be and what to do. Was he not carrying the snared rabbits over his shoulder? Some hungry flesh-eater, more bloodthirsty than courageous, was still hunting him for the food on his back and only lacked the courage to attack. Koot drew a steel-trap from his bag. He did not wish to waste a rabbit-skin, so he baited the spring with a piece of fat bacon, smeared the trap, the snow, everything that he had touched with a rabbit-skin, and walked home through the deepening dark to the little log cabin where a sharp "woof-woof" of welcome awaited him.

That night, in addition to the skins across the doorway, Koot jammed logs athwart; "to keep the cold out" he told himself. Then he kindled a fire on the rough stone hearth built at one end of the cabin and with the little clay pipe beneath his teeth sat down on the stump chair to broil rabbit. The waste of the rabbit he had placed in traps outside the lodge. Once his dog sprang alert with pricked ears. Man and dog heard the sniff—sniff—sniff of some creature attracted to the cabin by the smell of broiling meat, and now rummaging at its own risk among the traps. And once when Koot was stretched out on a bear-skin before the fire puffing at his pipe-stem, drying his moccasins and listening to the fusillade of frost rending ice and earth, a long low piercing wail rose and fell and died away. Instantly from the forest of the swamp came the answering scream—a lifting tumbling eldritch shriek.

"I should have set two traps," says Koot. "They are out in pairs."

Black is the flag of danger to the rabbit world. The antlered shadows of the naked poplar or the tossing arms of the restless pines, the rabbit knows to be harmless shadows unless their dapple of sun and shade conceals a brindled cat. But a shadow that walks and runs means to the rabbit a foe; so the wary trapper prefers to visit his snares at the hour of the short shadow.

It did not surprise the trapper after he had heard the lifting wail from the swamp woods the night before that the bacon in the trap lay untouched. The still hunter that had crawled through the underbrush lured by the dead rabbits over Koot's shoulder wanted rabbit, not bacon. But at the nearest rabbit snare, where a poor dead prisoner had been torn from the twine, were queer padded prints in the snow, not of the rabbit's making. Koot stood looking at the tell-tale mark. The dog's ears were all aprick. So was Koot's sense of feel, but he couldn't make this thing out. There was no trail of approach or retreat. The padded print of the thief was in the snow as if the animal had dropped from the sky and gone back to the sky.

Koot measured off ten strides from the rifled snare and made a complete circuit round it. The rabbit runway cut athwart the snow circle, but no mark like that shuffling padded print.

"It isn't a wolverine, and it isn't a fisher, and it isn't a coyote," Koot told himself.

The dog emitted stupid little sharp barks looking everywhere and nowhere as if he felt what he could neither see nor hear. Koot measured off ten strides more from this circuit and again walked completely round the snare. Not even the rabbit runways cut this circle. The white man grows indignant when baffled, the Indian superstitious. The part that was white man in Koot sent him back to the scene in quick jerky steps to scatter poisoned rabbit meat over the snow and set a trap in which he readily sacrificed a full-grown bunny. The part that was Indian set a world of old memories echoing, memories that were as much Koot's nature as the swarth of his skin, memories that Koot's mother and his mother's ancestors held of the fabulous man-eating wolf called the loup-garou, and the great white beaver father of all beavers and all Indians that glided through the swamp mists at night like a ghost, and the monster grisly that stalked with uncouth gambols through the dark devouring benighted hunters.

This time when the mongrel uttered his little sharp barkings that said as plainly as a dog could speak, "Something's somewhere! Be careful there—oh!—I'll be on to you in just one minute!" Koot kicked the dog hard with plain anger; and his anger was at himself because his eyes and his ears failed to localize, to real-ize, to visualize what those little pricks and shivers tingling down to his finger-tips meant. Then the civilized man came uppermost in Koot and he marched off very matter of fact to the next snare.

But if Koot's vision had been as acute as his sense of feel and he had glanced up to the topmost spreading bough of a pine just above the snare, he might have detected lying in a dapple of sun and shade something with large owl eyes, something whose pencilled ear-tufts caught the first crisp of the man's moccasins over the snow-crust. Then the ear-tufts were laid flat back against a furry form hardly differing from the dapple of sun and shade. The big owl eyes closed to a tiny blinking slit that let out never a ray of tell-tale light. The big round body mottled gray and white like the snowy tree widened—stretched—-flattened till it was almost a part of the tossing pine bough. Only when the man and dog below the tree had passed far beyond did the pencilled ears blink forward and the owl eyes open and the big body bunch out like a cat with elevated haunches ready to spring.

But by-and-bye the man's snares began to tell on the rabbits. They grew scarce and timid. And the thing that had rifled the rabbit snares grew hunger-bold. One day when Koot and the dog were skimming across the billowy drifts, something black far ahead bounced up, caught a bunting on the wing, and with another bounce disappeared among the trees.

Koot said one word—"Cat!"—and the dog was off full cry.

Ever since he had heard that wailing call from the swamp woods, he had known that there were rival hunters, the keenest of all still hunters among the rabbits. Every day he came upon the trail of their ravages, rifled snares, dead squirrels, torn feathers, even the remains of a fox or a coon. And sometimes he could tell from the printings on the white page that the still hunter had been hunted full cry by coyote or timber-wolf. Against these wolfish foes the cat had one sure refuge always—a tree. The hungry coyote might try to starve the bob-cat into surrender; but just as often, the bob-cat could starve the coyote into retreat; for if a foolish rabbit darted past, what hungry coyote could help giving chase? The tree had even defeated both dog and man that first week when Koot could not find the cat. But a dog in full chase could follow the trail to a tree, and a man could shoot into the tree.

As the rabbits decreased, Koot set out many traps for the bob-cats now reckless with hunger, steel-traps and deadfalls and pits and log pens with a live grouse clucking inside. The midwinter lull was a busy season for Koot.

Towards March, the sun-glare has produced a crust on the snow that is almost like glass. For Koot on his snow-shoes this had no danger; but for the mongrel that was to draw the pelts back to the fort, the snow crust was more troublesome than glass. Where the crust was thick, with Koot leading the way snow-shoes and dog and toboggan glided over the drifts as if on steel runners. But in midday the crust was soft and the dog went floundering through as if on thin ice, the sharp edge cutting his feet. Koot tied little buckskin sacks round the dog's feet and made a few more rounds of the swamp; but the crust was a sign that warned him it was time to prepare for the marten-hunt. To leave his furs at the fort, he must cross the prairie while it was yet good travelling for the dog. Dismantling the little cabin, Koot packed the pelts on the toboggan, roped all tightly so there could be no spill from an upset, and putting the mongrel in the traces, led the way for the fort one night when the snow-crust was hard as ice.

The moon came up over the white fields in a great silver disk. Between the running man and the silver moon moved black skulking forms—the foragers on their night hunt. Sometimes a fox loped over a drift, or a coyote rose ghostly from the snow, or timber-wolves dashed from wooded ravines and stopped to look till Koot fired a shot that sent them galloping.

In the dark that precedes daylight, Koot camped beside a grove of poplars—that is, he fed the dog a fish, whittled chips to make a fire and boil some tea for himself, then digging a hole in the drift with his snow-shoe, laid the sleigh to windward and cuddled down between bear-skins with the dog across his feet.

Daylight came in a blinding glare of sunshine and white snow. The way was untrodden. Koot led at an ambling run, followed by the dog at a fast trot, so that the trees were presently left far on the offing and the runners were out on the bare white prairie with never a mark, tree or shrub, to break the dazzling reaches of sunshine and snow from horizon to horizon. A man who is breaking the way must keep his eyes on the ground; and the ground was so blindingly bright that Koot began to see purple and yellow and red patches dancing wherever he looked on the snow. He drew his capote over his face to shade his eyes; but the pace and the sun grew so hot that he was soon running again unprotected from the blistering light.

Towards the afternoon, Koot knew that something had gone wrong. Some distance ahead, he saw a black object against the snow. On the unbroken white, it looked almost as big as a barrel and seemed at least a mile away. Lowering his eyes, Koot let out a spurt of speed, and the next thing he knew he had tripped his snow-shoe and tumbled. Scrambling up, he saw that a stick had caught the web of his snow-shoe; but where was the barrel for which he had been steering? There wasn't any barrel at all—the barrel was this black stick which hadn't been fifty yards away. Koot rubbed his eyes and noticed that black and red and purple patches were all over the snow. The drifts were heaving and racing after each other like waves on an angry sea. He did not go much farther that day; for every glint of snow scorched his eyes like a hot iron. He camped at the first bluff and made a poultice of cold tea leaves which he laid across his blistered face for the night.

Any one who knows the tortures of snow-blindness will understand why Koot did not sleep that night. It was a long night to the trapper, such a very long night that the sun had been up for two hours before its heat burned through the layers of his capote into his eyes and roused him from sheer pain. Then he sprang up, put up an ungantled hand and knew from the heat of the sun that it was broad day. But when he took the bandage off his eyes, all he saw was a black curtain one moment, rockets and wheels and dancing patches of purple fire the next.

Koot was no fool to become panicky and feeble from sudden peril. He knew that he was snow-blind on a pathless prairie at least two days away from the fort. To wait until the snow-blindness had healed would risk the few provisions that he had and perhaps expose him to a blizzard. The one rule of the trapper's life is to go ahead, let the going cost what it may; and drawing his capote over his face, Koot went on.

The heat of the sun told him the directions; and when the sun went down, the crooning west wind, bringing thaw and snow-crust, was his compass. And when the wind fell, the tufts of shrub-growth sticking through the snow pointed to the warm south. Now he tied himself to his dog; and when he camped beside trees into which he had gone full crash before he knew they were there, he laid his gun beside the dog and sleigh. Going out the full length of his cord, he whittled the chips for his fire and found his way back by the cord.

On the second day of his blindness, no sun came up; nor could he guide himself by the feel of the air, for there was no wind. It was one of the dull dead gray days that precedes storms. How would he get his directions to set out? Memory of last night's travel might only lead him on the endless circling of the lost. Koot dug his snow-shoe to the base of a tree, found moss, felt it growing on only one side of the tree, knew that side must be the shady cold side, and so took his bearings from what he thought was the north.

Koot said the only time that he knew any fear was on the evening of the last day. The atmosphere boded storm. The fort lay in a valley. Somewhere between Koot and that valley ran a trail. What if he had crossed the trail? What if the storm came and wiped out the trail before he could reach the fort? All day, whisky-jack and snow-bunting and fox scurried from his presence; but this night in the dusk when he felt forward on his hands and knees for the expected trail, the wild creatures seemed to grow bolder. He imagined that he felt the coyotes closer than on the other nights. And then the fearful thought came that he might have passed the trail unheeding. Should he turn back?

Afraid to go forward or back, Koot sank on the ground, unhooded his face and tried to force his eyes to see. The pain brought biting salty tears. It was quite useless. Either the night was very dark, or the eyes were very blind.

And then white man or Indian—who shall say which came uppermost?—Koot cried out to the Great Spirit. In mockery back came the saucy scold of a jay.

But that was enough for Koot—it was prompt answer to his prayer; for where do the jays quarrel and fight and flutter but on the trail? Running eagerly forward, the trapper felt the ground. The rutted marks of a "jumper" sleigh cut the hard crust. With a shout, Koot headed down the sloping path to the valley where lay the fur post, the low hanging smoke of whose chimneys his eager nostrils had already sniffed.

CHAPTER XVI

OTHER LITTLE ANIMALS BESIDES WAHBOOS THE RABBIT—BEING AN ACCOUNT OF MUSQUASH THE MUSK-RAT, SIKAK THE SKUNK, WENUSK THE BADGER, AND OTHERS

I

Musquash the Musk-rat

Every chapter in the trapper's life is not a "stunt."

There are the uneventful days when the trapper seems to do nothing but wander aimlessly through the woods over the prairie along the margin of rush-grown marshy ravines where the stagnant waters lap lazily among the flags, though a feathering of ice begins to rim the quiet pools early in autumn. Unless he is duck-shooting down there in the hidden slough where is a great "quack-quack" of young teals, the trapper may not uncase his gun. For a whole morning he lies idly in the sunlight beside some river where a roundish black head occasionally bobs up only to dive under when it sees the man. Or else he sits by the hour still as a statue on the mossy log of a swamp where a long wriggling—wriggling trail marks the snaky motion of some creature below the amber depths.

To the city man whose days are regulated by clockwork and electric trams with the ceaseless iteration of gongs and "step fast there!" such a life seems the type of utter laziness. But the best-learned lessons are those imbibed unconsciously and the keenest pleasures come unsought. Perhaps when the great profit-and-loss account of the hereafter is cast up, the trapper may be found to have a greater sum total of happiness, of usefulness, of real knowledge than the multi-millionaire whose life was one buzzing round of drive and worry and grind. Usually the busy city man has spent nine or ten of the most precious years of his youth in study and travel to learn other men's thoughts for his own life's work. The trapper spends an idle month or two of each year wandering through a wild world learning the technic of his craft at first hand. And the trapper's learning is all done leisurely, calmly, without bluster or drive, just as nature herself carries on the work of her realm.

On one of these idle days when the trapper seems to be slouching so lazily over the prarie comes a whiff of dank growth on the crisp autumn air. Like all wild creatures travelling up-wind, the trapper at once heads a windward course. It comes again, just a whiff as if the light green musk-plant were growing somewhere on a dank bank. But ravines are not dank in the clear fall days; and by October the musk-plant has wilted dry. This is a fresh living odour with all the difference between it and dead leaves that there is between June roses and the dried dust of a rose jar. The wind falls. He may not catch the faintest odour of swamp growth again, but he knows there must be stagnant water somewhere in these prairie ravines; and a sense that is part feel, part intuition, part inference from what the wind told of the marsh smell, leads his footsteps down the browned hillside to the soggy bottom of a slough.

A covey of teals—very young, or they would not be so bold—flackers up, wings about with a clatter, then settles again a space farther ahead when the ducks see that the intruder remains so still. The man parts the flags, sits down on a log motionless as the log itself—and watches! Something else had taken alarm from the crunch of the hunter's moccasins through the dry reeds; for a wriggling trail is there, showing where a creature has dived below and is running among the wet under-tangle. Not far off on another log deep in the shade of the highest flags solemnly perches a small prairie-owl. It is almost the russet shade of the dead log. It hunches up and blinks stupidly at all this noise in the swamp.

"Oho," thinks the trapper, "so I've disturbed a still hunt," and he sits if anything stiller than ever, only stooping to lay his gun down and pick up a stone.

At first there is nothing but the quacking of the ducks at the far end of the swamp. A lapping of the water against the brittle flags and a water-snake has splashed away to some dark haunt. The whisky-jack calls out officious note from a topmost bough, as much as to say: "It's all right! Me—me!—I'm always there!—I've investigated!—it's all right!—he's quite harmless!" And away goes the jay on business of state among the gopher mounds.

Then the interrupted activity of the swamp is resumed, scolding mother ducks reading the riot act to young teals, old geese coming craning and craning their long necks to drink at the water's edge, lizards and water-snakes splashing down the banks, midgets and gnats sunning themselves in clouds during the warmth of the short autumn days, with a feel in the air as of crisp ripeness, drying fruit, the harvest-home of the year. In all the prairie region north and west of Minnesota—the Indian land of "sky-coloured water"—the sloughs lie on the prairie under a crystal sky that turns pools to silver. On this almost motionless surface are mirrored as if by an etcher's needle the sky above, feathered wind clouds, flag stems, surrounding cliffs, even the flight of birds on wing. As the mountains stand for majesty, the prairies for infinity, so the marsh lands are types of repose.

But it is not a lifeless repose. Barely has the trapper settled himself when a little sharp black nose pokes up through the water at the fore end of the wriggling trail. A round rat-shaped head follows this twitching proboscis. Then a brownish earth-coloured body swims with a wriggling sidelong movement for the log, where roosts the blinking owlet. A little noiseless leap! and a dripping musk-rat with long flat tail and webbed feet scrabbles up the moss-covered tree towards the stupid bird. Another moment, and the owl would have toppled into the water with a pair of sharp teeth clutched to its throat. Then the man shies a well-aimed stone!

Splash! Flop! The owl is flapping blindly through the flags to another hiding-place, while the wriggle-wriggle of the waters tells where the marsh-rat has darted away under the tangled growth. From other idle days like these, the trapper has learned that musk-rats are not solitary but always to be found in colonies. Now if the musk-rat were as wise as the beaver to whom the Indians say he is closely akin, that alarmed marauder would carry the news of the man-intruder to the whole swamp. Perhaps if the others remembered from the prod of a spear or the flash of a gun what man's coming meant, that news would cause terrified flight of every musk-rat from the marsh. But musquash—little beaver, as the Indians call him—is not so wise, not so timid, not so easily frightened from his home as amisk,[44] the beaver. In fact, nature's provision for the musk-rat's protection seems to have emboldened the little rodent almost to the point of stupidity. His skin is of that burnt umber shade hardly to be distinguished from the earth. At one moment his sharp nose cuts the water, at the next he is completely hidden in the soft clay of the under-tangle; and while you are straining for a sight of him through the pool, he has scurried across a mud bank to his burrow.

Hunt him as they may, men and boys and ragged squaws wading through swamps knee-high, yet after a century of hunting from the Chesapeake and the Hackensack to the swamps of "sky-coloured water" on the far prairie, little musquash still yields 6,000,000 pelts a year with never a sign of diminishing. A hundred years ago, in 1788, so little was musk-rat held in esteem as a fur, the great North-West Company of Canada sent out only 17,000 or 20,000 skins a year. So rapidly did musk-rat grow in favour as a lining and imitation fur that in 1888 it was no unusual thing for 200,000 musk-rat-skins to be brought to a single Hudson's Bay Company fort. In Canada the climate compels the use of heavier furs than in the United States, so that the all-fur coat is in greater demand than the fur-lined; but in Canada, not less than 2,000,000 musk-rat furs are taken every year. In the United States the total is close on 4,000,000. In one city alone, St. Paul, 50,000 musk-rat-skins are cured every year. A single stretch of good marsh ground has yielded that number of skins year after year without a sign of the hunt telling on the prolific little musquash. Multiply 50,000 by prices varying from 7 cents to 75 cents and the value of the musk-rat-hunt becomes apparent.

What is the secret of the musk-rat's survival while the strong creatures of the chase like buffalo and timber-wolf have been almost exterminated? In the first place, settlers can't farm swamps; so the musk-rat thrives just as well in the swamps of New Jersey to-day as when the first white hunter set foot in America. Then musquash lives as heartily on owls and frogs and snakes as on water mussels and lily-pads. If one sort of food fails, the musk-rat has as omnivorous powers of digestion as the bear and changes his diet. Then he can hide as well in water as on land. And most important of all, musk-rat's family is as numerous as a cat's, five to nine rats in a litter, and two or three litters a year. These are the points that make for little musquash's continuance in spite of all that shot and trap can do.

Having discovered what the dank whiff, half animal, half vegetable, signified, the trapper sets about finding the colony. He knows there is no risk of the little still-hunter carrying alarm to the other musk-rats. If he waits, it is altogether probable that the fleeing musk-rat will come up and swim straight for the colony. On the other hand, the musk-rat may have scurried overland through the rushes. Besides, the trapper observed tracks, tiny leaf-like tracks as of little webbed feet, over the soft clay of the marsh bank. These will lead to the colony, so the trapper rises and parting the rushes not too noisily, follows the little footprint along the margin of the swamp.

Fort MacPherson, now the most northerly post of the Hudson's Bay Company, beyond tree line; hence the houses are built of imported timber, with thatch roofs.

Here the track is lost at the narrow ford of an inflowing stream, but across the creek lies a fallen poplar littered with—what? The feathers and bones of a dead owlet. Balancing himself—how much better the moccasins cling than boots!—the trapper crosses the log and takes up the trail through the rushes. But here musquash has dived off into the water for the express purpose of throwing a possible pursuer off the scent. But the tracks betrayed which way musquash was travelling; so the trapper goes on, knowing if he does not find the little haycock houses on this side, he can cross to the other.

Presently, he almost stumbles over what sent the musk-rat diving just at this place. It is the wreck of a wolverine's ravage—a little wattled dome-shaped house exposed to that arch-destroyer by the shrinking of the swamp. So shallow has the water become, that a wolverine has easily waded and leaped clear across to the roof of the musk-rat's house. A beaver-dam two feet thick cannot resist the onslaught of the wolverine's claws; how much less will this round nest of reeds and grass and mosses cemented together with soft clay? The roof has been torn from the domed house, leaving the inside bare and showing plainly the domestic economy of the musk-rat home, smooth round walls inside, a floor or gallery of sticks and grasses, where the family had lived in an air chamber above the water, rough walls below the water-line and two or three little openings that must have been safely under water before the swamp receded. Perhaps a mussel or lily bulb has been left in the deserted larder. From the oozy slime below the mid-floor to the topmost wall will not measure more than two or three feet. If the swamp had not dried here, the stupid little musk-rats that escaped the ravager's claws would probably have come back to the wrecked house, built up the torn roof, and gone on living in danger till another wolverine came. But a water doorway the musk-rat must have. That he has learned by countless assaults on his house-top, so when the marsh retreated the musk-rats abandoned their house.

All about the deserted house are runways, tiny channels across oozy peninsulas and islands of the musk-rat's diminutive world such as a very small beaver might make. The trapper jumps across to a dry patch or mound in the midst of the slimy bottom and prods an earth bank with a stick. It is as he thought—hollow; a musk-rat burrow or gallery in the clay wall where the refugees from this house had scuttled from the wolverine. But now all is deserted. The water has shrunk—that was the danger signal to the musk-rat; and there had been a grand moving to a deeper part of the swamp. Perhaps, after all, this is a very old house not used since last winter.

Going back to the bank, the trapper skirts through the crush of brittle rushes round the swamp. Coming sharply on deeper water, a dank, stagnant bayou, heavy with the smell of furry life, the trapper pushes aside the flags, peers out and sees what resembles a prairie-dog town on water—such a number of wattled houses that they had shut in the water as with a dam. Too many flags and willows lie over the colony for a glimpse of the tell-tale wriggling trail across the water; but from the wet tangle of grass and moss comes an oozy pattering.

If it were winter, the trapper could proceed as he would against a beaver colony, staking up the outlet from the swamp, trenching the ice round the different houses, breaking open the roofs and penning up any fugitives in their own bank burrows till he and his dog and a spear could clear out the gallery. But in winter there is more important work than hunting musk-rat. Musk-rat-trapping is for odd days before the regular hunt.

Opening the sack which he usually carries on his back, the trapper draws out three dozen small traps no larger than a rat or mouse trap. Some of these he places across the runways without any bait; for the musk-rat must pass this way. Some he smears with strong-smelling pomatum. Some he baits with carrot or apple. Others he does not bait at all, simply laying them on old logs where he knows the owlets roost by day. But each of the traps—bait or no bait—he attaches to a stake driven into the water so that the prisoner will be held under when he plunges to escape till he is drowned. Otherwise, he would gnaw his foot free of the trap and disappear in a burrow.

If the marsh is large, there will be more than one musk-rat colony. Having exhausted his traps on the first, the trapper lies in wait at the second. When the moon comes up over the water, there is a great splashing about the musk-rat nests; for autumn is the time for house-building and the musk-rats work at night. If the trapper is an Eastern man, he will wade in as they do in New Jersey; but if he is a type of the Western hunter, he lies on the log among the rushes, popping a shot at every head that appears in the moonlit water. His dog swims and dives for the quarry. By the time the stupid little musk-rats have taken alarm and hidden, the man has twenty or thirty on the bank. Going home, he empties and resets the traps.

Thirty marten traps that yield six martens do well. Thirty musk-rat traps are expected to give thirty musk-rats. Add to that the twenty shot, and what does the day's work represent? Here are thirty skins of a coarse light reddish hair, such as lines the poor man's overcoat. These will sell for from 7 to 15 cents each. They may go roughly for $3 at the fur post. Here are ten of the deeper brown shades, with long soft fur that lines a lady's cloak. They are fine enough to pass for mink with a little dyeing, or imitation seal if they are properly plucked. These will bring 25 or 30 cents—say $2.50 in all. But here are ten skins, deep, silky, almost black, for which a Russian officer will pay high prices, skins that will go to England, and from England to Paris, and from Paris to St. Petersburg with accelerating cost mark till the Russian grandee is paying $1 or more for each pelt. The trapper will ask 30, 40, 50 cents for these, making perhaps $3.50 in all. Then this idle fellow's day has totaled up to $9, not a bad day's work, considering he did not go to the university for ten years to learn his craft, did not know what wear and tear and drive meant as he worked, did not spend more than a few cents' worth of shot. But for his musk-rat-pelts the man will not get $9 in coin unless he lives very near the great fur markets. He will get powder and clothing and food and tobacco whose first cost has been increased a hundredfold by ship rates and railroad rates, by keel-boat freight and pack-horse expenses and portage charges past countless rapids. But he will get all that he needs, all that he wants, all that his labour is worth, this "lazy vagabond" who spends half his time idling in the sun. Of how many other men can that be said?

But what of the ruthless slaughter among the little musk-rats? Does humanity not revolt at the thought? Is this trapping not after all brutal butchery?

Animal kindliness—if such a thing exists among musk-rats—could hardly protest against the slaughter, seeing the musk-rats themselves wage as ruthless a war against water-worm and owlet as man wages against musk-rats. It is the old question, should animal life be sacrificed to preserve human life? To that question there is only one answer. Linings for coats are more important life-savers than all the humane societies of the world put together. It is probable that the first thing the prehistoric man did to preserve his own life when he realized himself was to slay some destructive animal and appropriate its coat.

II

Sikak the Skunk

Sikak the skunk it is who supplies the best imitations of sable. But cleanse the fur never so well, on a damp day it still emits the heavy sickening odour that betrays its real nature. That odour is sikak's invincible defence against the white trapper. The hunter may follow the little four-abreast galloping footprints that lead to a hole among stones or to rotten logs, but long before he has reached the nesting-place of his quarry comes a stench against which white blood is powerless. Or the trapper may find an unexpected visitor in one of the pens which he has dug for other animals—a little black creature the shape of a squirrel and the size of a cat with white stripings down his back and a bushy tail. It is then a case of a quick deadly shot, or the man will be put to rout by an odour that will pollute the air for miles around and drive him off that section of the hunting-field. The cuttlefish is the only other creature that possesses as powerful means of defence of a similar nature, one drop of the inky fluid which it throws out to hide it from pursuers burning the fisherman's eyes like scalding acid. As far as white trappers are concerned, sikak is only taken by the chance shots of idle days. Yet the Indian hunts the skunk apparently utterly oblivious of the smell. Traps, poison, deadfalls, pens are the Indian weapons against the skunk; and a Cree will deliberately skin and stretch a pelt in an atmosphere that is blue with what is poison to the white man.

The only case I ever knew of white trappers hunting the skunk was of three men on the North Saskatchewan. One was an Englishman who had been long in the service of the Hudson's Bay Company and knew all the animals of the north. The second was the guide, a French-Canadian, and the third a Sandy, fresh "frae oot the land o' heather." The men were wakened one night by the noise of some animal scrambling through the window into their cabin and rummaging in the dark among the provisions. The Frenchman sprang for a light and Sandy got hold of his gun.

"Losh, mon, it's a wee bit beastie a' strip't black and white wi' a tail like a so'dier's cocade!"

That information brought the Englishman to his feet howling, "Don't shoot it! Don't shoot it! Leave that thing alone, I tell you!"

But Sandy being a true son of Scotia with a Presbyterian love of argument wished to debate the question.

"An' what for wu'd a leave it eating a' the oatmeal? I'll no leave it rampagin' th' eatables—I wull be pokin' it oot!—shoo!—shoo!"

At that the Frenchman flung down the light and bolted for the door, followed by the English trader cursing between set teeth that before "that blundering blockhead had argued the matter" something would happen.

Something did happen.

Sandy came through the door with such precipitate haste that the topmost beam brought his head a mighty thwack, roaring out at the top of his voice that the deil was after him for a' the sins that iver he had committed since he was born.

III

Wenusk the Badger

Badger, too, is one of the furs taken by the trapper on idle days. East of St. Paul and Winnipeg, the fur is comparatively unknown, or if known, so badly prepared that it is scarcely recognisable for badger. This is probably owing to differences in climate. Badger in its perfect state is a long soft fur, resembling wood marten, with deep overhairs almost the length of one's hand and as dark as marten, with underhairs as thick and soft and yielding as swan's-down, shading in colour from fawn to grayish white. East of the Mississippi, there is too much damp in the atmosphere for such a long soft fur. Consequently specimens of badger seen in the East must either be sheared of the long overhairs or left to mat and tangle on the first rainy day. In New York, Quebec, Montreal, and Toronto—places where the finest furs should be on sale if anywhere—I have again and again asked for badger, only to be shown a dull matted short fawnish fur not much superior to cheap dyed furs. It is not surprising there is no demand for such a fur and Eastern dealers have stopped ordering it. In the North-West the most common mist during the winter is a frost mist that is more a snow than a rain, so there is little injury to furs from moisture. Here the badger is prime, long, thick, and silky, almost as attractive as ermine if only it were enhanced by as high a price. Whether badger will ever grow in favour like musk-rat or 'coon, and play an important part in the returns of the fur exporters, is doubtful. The world takes its fashions from European capitals; and European capitals are too damp for badger to be in fashion with them. Certainly, with the private dealers of the North and West, badger is yearly becoming more important.

Like the musk-rat, badger is prime in the autumn. Wherever the hunting-grounds of the animals are, there will the hunting-grounds of the trapper be. Badgers run most where gophers sit sunning themselves on the clay mounds, ready to bolt down to their subterranean burrows on the first approach of an enemy. Eternal enemies these two are, gopher and badger, though they both live in ground holes, nest their lairs with grasses, run all summer and sleep all winter, and alike prey on the creatures smaller than themselves—mice, moles, and birds. The gopher, or ground squirrel, is smaller than the wood squirrel, while the badger is larger than a Manx cat, with a shape that varies according to the exigencies of the situation. Normally, he is a flattish, fawn-coloured beast, with a turtle-shaped body, little round head, and small legs with unusually strong claws. Ride after the badger across the prairie and he stretches out in long, lithe shape, resembling a baby cougar, turning at every pace or two to snap at your horse, then off again at a hulking scramble of astonishing speed. Pour water down his burrow to compel him to come up or down, and he swells out his body, completely filling the passage, so that his head, which is downward, is in dry air, while his hind quarters alone are in the water. In captivity the badger is a business-like little body, with very sharp teeth, of which his keeper must beware, and some of the tricks of the skunk, but inclined, on the whole, to mind his affairs if you will mind yours. Once a day regularly every afternoon out of his lair he emerges for the most comical sorts of athletic exercises. Hour after hour he will trot diagonally—because that gives him the longest run—from corner to corner of his pen, rearing up on his hind legs as he reaches one corner, rubbing the back of his head, then down again and across to the other corner, where he repeats the performance. There can be no reason for the badger doing this, unless it was his habit in the wilds when he trotted about leaving dumb signs on mud banks and brushwood by which others of his kind might know where to find him at stated times.

Sunset is the time when he is almost sure to be among the gopher burrows. In vain the saucy jay shrieks out a warning to the gophers. Of all the prairie creatures, they are the stupidest, the most beset with curiosity to know what that jay's shriek may mean. Sunning themselves in the last rays of daylight, the gophers perch on their hind legs to wait developments of what the jay announced. But the badger's fur and the gopher mounds are almost the same colour. He has pounced on some playful youngsters before the rest see him. Then there is a wild scuttling down to the depths of the burrows. That, too, is vain; for the badger begins ripping up the clay bank like a grisly, down—down—in pursuit, two, three, five feet, even twelve.

Then is seen one of the most curious freaks in all the animal life of the prairie. The underground galleries of the gophers connect and lead up to different exits. As the furious badger comes closer and closer on the cowering gophers, the little cowards lose heart, dart up the galleries to open doors, and try to escape through the grass of the prairie. But no sooner is the badger hard at work than a gray form seems to rise out of the earth, a coyote who had been slinking to the rear all the while; and as the terrified gophers scurry here, scurry there, coyote's white teeth snap!—snap! He is here—there—everywhere—pouncing—jumping—having the fun of his life, gobbling gophers as cats catch mice. Down in the bottom of the burrow, the badger may get half a dozen poor cooped huddling prisoners; but the coyote up on the prairie has devoured a whole colony.

Do these two, badger and coyote, consciously hunt together? Some old trappers vow they do—others just as vehemently that they don't. The fact remains that wherever the badger goes gopher-hunting on an unsettled prairie, there the coyote skulks reaping reward of all the badger's work. The coincidence is no stranger than the well-known fact that sword-fish and thrasher—two different fish—always league together to attack the whale.

One thing only can save the gopher colony, and that is the gun barrel across yon earth mound where a trapper lies in wait for the coming of the badger.

IV

The 'Coon

Sir Alexander MacKenzie reported that in 1798 the North-West Company sent out only 100 raccoon from the fur country. Last year the city of St. Paul alone cured 115,000 'coon-skins. What brought about the change? Simply an appreciation of the qualities of 'coon, which combines the greatest warmth with the lightest weight and is especially adapted for a cold climate and constant wear. What was said of badger applies with greater force to 'coon. The 'coon in the East is associated in one's mind with cabbies, in the West with fashionably dressed men and women. And there is just as wide a difference in the quality of the fur as in the quality of the people. The cabbies' 'coon coat is a rough yellow fur with red stripes. The Westerner's 'coon is a silky brown fur with black stripes. One represents the fall hunt of men and boys round hollow logs, the other the midwinter hunt of a professional trapper in the Far North. A dog usually bays the 'coon out of hiding in the East. Tiny tracks, like a child's hand, tell the Northern hunter where to set his traps.

Wahboos the rabbit, musquash the musk-rat, sikak the skunk, wenusk the badger, and the common 'coon—these are the little chaps whose hunt fills the idle days of the trapper's busy life. At night, before the rough stone hearth which he has built in his cabin, he is still busy by fire-light preparing their pelts. Each skin must be stretched and cured. Turning the skin fur side in, the trapper pushes into the pelt a wedge-shaped slab of spliced cedar. Into the splice he shoves another wedge of wood which he hammers in, each blow widening the space and stretching the skin. All pelts are stretched fur in but the fox. Tacking the stretched skin on a flat board, the trapper hangs it to dry till he carries all to the fort; unless, indeed, he should need a garment for himself—cap, coat, or gantlets—in which case he takes out a square needle and passes his evenings like a tailor, sewing.

CHAPTER XVII
THE RARE FURS—HOW THE TRAPPER TAKES SAKWASEW THE MINK, NEKIK THE OTTER, WUCHAK THE FISHER, AND WAPISTAN THE MARTEN
I

Sakwasew the Mink

There are other little chaps with more valuable fur than musquash, whose skin seldom attains higher honour than inside linings, and wahboos, whose snowy coat is put to the indignity of imitating ermine with a dotting of black cat for the ermine's jet tip. There are mink and otter and fisher and fox and ermine and sable, all little fellows with pelts worth their weight in coin of the realm.

On one of those idle days when the trapper seems to be doing nothing but lying on his back in the sun, he has witnessed a curious, but common, battle in pantomime between bird and beast. A prairie-hawk circles and drops, lifts and wheels again with monotonous silent persistence above the swamp. What quarry does he seek, this lawless forager of the upper airs still hunting a hidden nook of the low prairie? If he were out purely for exercise, like the little badger when it goes rubbing the back of its head from post to post, there would be a buzzing of wings and shrill lonely callings to an unseen mate.

But the circling hawk is as silent as the very personification of death. Apparently he can't make up his mind for the death-drop on some rat or frog down there in the swamp. The trapper notices that the hawk keeps circling directly above the place where the waters of the swamp tumble from the ravine in a small cataract to join a lower river. He knows, too, from the rich orange of the plumage that the hawk is young. An older fellow would not be advertising his intentions in this fashion. Besides, an older hawk would have russet-gray feathering. Is the rascally young hawk meditating a clutch of talons round some of the unsuspecting trout that usually frequent the quiet pools below a waterfall. Or does he aim at bigger game? A young hawk is bold with the courage that has not yet learned the wisdom of caution. That is why there are so many more of the brilliant young red hawks in our museums than old grizzled gray veterans whose craft circumvents the specimen hunter's cunning. Now the trapper comes to have as keen a sense of feel for all the creatures of the wilds as the creatures of the wilds have for man; so he shifts his position that he may find what is attracting the hawk.

Down on the pebbled beach below the waterfalls lies an auburn bundle of fur, about the size of a very long, slim, short-legged cat, still as a stone—some member of the weasel family gorged torpid with fish, stretched out full length to sleep in the sun. To sleep, ah, yes, and as the Danish prince said, "perchance to dream"; for all the little fellows of river and prairie take good care never to sleep where they are exposed to their countless enemies. This sleep of the weasel arouses the man's suspicion. The trapper draws out his field-glass. The sleeper is a mink, and its sleep is a sham with beady, red eyes blinking a deal too lively for real death. Why does it lie on its back rigid and straight as if it were dead with all four tiny paws clutched out stiff? The trapper scans the surface of the swamp to see if some foolish musk-rat is swimming dangerously near the sleeping mink.

Presently the hawk circles lower—lower!—Drop, straight as a stone! Its talons are almost in the mink's body, when of a sudden the sleeper awakens—awakens—with a leap of the four stiff little feet and a darting spear-thrust of snapping teeth deep in the neck of the hawk! At first the hawk rises tearing furiously at the clinging mink with its claws. The wings sag. Down bird and beast fall. Over they roll on the sandy beach, hawk and mink, over and over with a thrashing of the hawk's wings to beat the treacherous little vampire off. Now the blood-sucker is on top clutching—clutching! Now the bird flounders up craning his neck from the death-grip. Then the hawk falls on his back. His wings are prone. They cease to flutter.

Running to the bank the trapper is surprised to see the little blood-sucker making off with the prey instead of deserting it as all creatures akin to the weasel family usually do. That means a family of mink somewhere near, to be given their first lesson in bird-hunting, in mink-hawking by the body of this poor, dead, foolish gyrfalcon.

By a red mark here, by a feather there, crushed grass as of something dragged, a little webbed footprint on the wet clay, a tiny marking of double dots where the feet have crossed a dry stone, the trapper slowly takes up the trail of the mink. Mink are not prime till the late fall. Then the reddish fur assumes the shades of the russet grasses where they run until the white of winter covers the land. Then—as if nature were to exact avengement for all the red slaughter the mink has wrought during the rest of the year—his coat becomes dark brown, almost black, the very shade that renders him most conspicuous above snow to all the enemies of the mink world. But while the trapper has no intention of destroying what would be worthless now but will be valuable in the winter, it is not every day that even a trapper has a chance to trail a mink back to its nest and see the young family.

But suddenly the trail stops. Here is a sandy patch with some tumbled stones under a tangle of grasses and a rivulet not a foot away. Ah—there it is—a nest or lair, a tiny hole almost hidden by the rushes! But the nest seems empty. Fast as the trapper has come, the mink came faster and hid her family. To one side, the hawk had been dropped among the rushes. The man pokes a stick in the lair but finds nothing. Putting in his hand, he is dragging out bones, feathers, skeleton musk-rats, putrid frogs, promiscuous remnants of other quarries brought to the burrow by the mink, when a little cattish s-p-i-t! almost touches his hand. His palm closes over something warm, squirming, smaller than a kitten with very downy fur, on a soft mouse-like skin, eyes that are still blind and a tiny mouth that neither meows nor squeaks, just spits!—spits!—spits!—in impotent viperish fury. All the other minklets, the mother had succeeded in hiding under the grasses, but somehow this one had been left. Will he take it home and try the experiment of rearing a young mink with a family of kittens?

The trapper calls to mind other experiments. There was the little beaver that chewed up his canoe and gnawed a hole of escape through the door. There were the three little bob-cats left in the woods behind his cabin last year when he refrained from setting out traps and tied up his dog to see if he could not catch the whole family, mother and kittens, for an Eastern museum. Furtively at first, the mother had come to feed her kittens. Then the man had put out rugs to keep the kittens warm and lain in wait for the mother; but no sooner did she see her offspring comfortably cared for, than she deserted them entirely, evidently acting on the proverb that the most gracious enemy is the most dangerous, or else deciding that the kits were so well off that she was not needed. Adopting the three little wild-cats, the trapper had reared them past blind-eyes, past colic and dumps and all the youthful ills to which live kittens are heirs, when trouble began. The longing for the wilds came. Even catnip green and senna tea boiled can't cure that. So keenly did the gipsy longing come to one little bob that he perished escaping to the woods by way of the chimney flue. The second little bob succeeded in escaping through a parchment stop-gap that served the trapper as a window. And the third bobby dealt such an ill-tempered gash to the dog's nose that the combat ended in instant death for the cat.

Thinking over these experiments, the trapper wisely puts the mink back in the nest with words which it would have been well for that litle ball of down to have understood. He told it he would come back for it next winter and to be sure to have its best black coat on. For the little first-year minks wear dark coats, almost as fine as Russian sable. Yes—he reflects, poking it back to the hole and retreating quickly so that the mother will return— better leave it till the winter; for wasn't it Koot who put a mink among his kittens, only to have the little viper set on them with tooth and claw as soon as its eyes opened? Also mink are bad neighbours to a poultry-yard. Forty chickens in a single night will the little mink destroy, not for food but—to quote man's words—for the zest of the sport. The mink, you must remember, like other pot-hunters, can boast of a big bag.

The trapper did come back next fall. It was when he was ranging all the swamp-lands for beaver-dams. Swamp lands often mean beaver-dams; and trappers always note what stops the current of a sluggish stream. Frequently it is a beaver colony built across a valley in the mountains, or stopping up the outlet of a slough. The trapper was sleeping under his canoe on the banks of the river where the swamp tumbled out from the ravine. Before retiring to what was a boat by day and a bed by night, he had set out a fish net and some loose lines—which the flow of the current would keep in motion—below the waterfall. Carelessly, next day, he threw the fish-heads among the stones. The second morning he found such a multitude of little tracks dotting the rime of the hoar frost that he erected a tent back from the waterfalls, and decided to stay trapping there till the winter. The fish-heads were no longer thrown away. They were left among the stones in small steel-traps weighted with other stones, or attached to a loose stick that would impede flight. And if the poor gyrfalcon could have seen the mink held by the jaws of a steel-trap, hissing, snarling, breaking its teeth on the iron, spitting out all the rage of its wicked nature, the bird would have been avenged.

And as winter deepened, the quality of minks taken from the traps became darker, silkier, crisper, almost brown black in some of the young, but for light fur on the under lip. The Indians say that sakwasew the mink would sell his family for a fish, and as long as fish lay among the stones, the trapper gathered his harvest of fur: reddish mink that would be made into little neck ruffs and collar pieces, reddish brown mink that would be sewed into costly coats and cloaks, rare brownish black mink that would be put into the beautiful flat scarf collars almost as costly as a full coat. And so the mink-hunt went on merrily for the man till the midwinter lull came at Christmas. For that year the mink-hunt was over.

II

Nekik the Otter

Sakwasew was not the only fisher at the pool below the falls. On one of those idle days when the trapper sat lazily by the river side, a round head slightly sunburned from black to russet had hobbled up to the surface of the water, peered sharply at the man sitting so still, paddled little flipper-like feet about, then ducked down again. Motionless as the mossed log under him sits the man; and in a moment up comes the little black head again, round as a golf ball, about the size of a very large cat, followed by three other little bobbing heads—a mother otter teaching her babies to dive and swim and duck from the river surface to the burrows below the water along the river bank. Perhaps the trapper has found a dead fish along this very bank with only the choice portions of the body eaten—a sure sign that nekik the otter, the little epicure of the water world, has been fishing at this river.

With a scarcely perceptible motion, the man turns his head to watch the swimmers. Instantly, down they plunge, mother and babies, to come to the surface again higher up-stream, evidently working up-current like the beaver in spring for a glorious frolic in the cold clear waters of the upper sources. At one place on the sandy beach they all wade ashore. The man utters a slight "Hiss!" Away they scamper, the foolish youngsters, landward instead of to the safe water as the hesitating mother would have them do, all the little feet scrambling over the sand with the funny short steps of a Chinese lady in tight boots. Maternal care proves stronger than fear. The frightened mother follows the young otter and will no doubt read them a sound lecture on land dangers when she has rounded them back to the safe water higher up-stream.

Of all wild creatures, none is so crafty in concealing its lairs as the otter. Where did this family come from? They had not been swimming up-stream; for the man had been watching on the river bank long before they appeared on the surface. Stripping, the trapper dives in mid-stream, then half wades, half swims along the steepest bank, running his arm against the clay cliff to find a burrow. On land he could not do this at the lair of the otter; for the smell of the man-touch would be left on his trail, and the otter, keener of scent and fear than the mink, would take alarm. But for the same reason that the river is the safest refuge for the otter, it is the surest hunting for the man—water does not keep the scent of a trail. So the man runs his arm along the bank. The river is the surest hunting for the man, but not the safest. If an old male were in the bank burrow now, or happened to be emerging from grass-lined subterranean air chambers above the bank gallery, it might be serious enough for the exploring trapper. One bite of nekik the otter has crippled many an Indian. Knowing from the remnants of half-eaten fish and from the holes in the bank that he has found an otter runway, the man goes home as well satisfied as if he had done a good day's work.

And so that winter when he had camped below the swamp for the mink-hunt, the trapper was not surprised one morning to find a half-eaten fish on the river bank. Sakwasew the mink takes good care to leave no remnants of his greedy meal. What he cannot eat he caches. Even if he has strangled a dozen water-rats in one hunt, they will be dragged in a heap and covered. The half-eaten fish left exposed is not mink's work. Otter has been here and otter will come back; for as the frost hardens, only those pools below the falls keep free from ice. No use setting traps with fish-heads as long as fresh fish are to be had for the taking. Besides, the man has done nothing to conceal his tracks; and each morning the half-eaten fish lie farther off the line of the man-trail.

By-and-bye the man notices that no more half-eaten fish are on his side of the river. Little tracks of webbed feet furrowing a deep rut in the soft snow of the frozen river tell that nekik has taken alarm and is fishing from the other side. And when Christmas comes with a dwindling of the mink-hunt, the man, too, crosses to the other side. Here he finds that the otter tracks have worn a path that is almost a toboggan slide down the crusted snow bank to the iced edge of the pool. By this time nekik's pelt is prime, almost black, and as glossy as floss. By this time, too, the fish are scarce and the epicure has become ravenous as a pauper. One night when the trapper was reconnoitring the fish hole, he had approached the snow bank so noiselessly that he came on a whole colony of otters without their knowledge of his presence. Down the snow bank they tumbled, head-first, tail-first, slithering through the snow with their little paws braced, rolling down on their backs like lads upset from a toboggan, otter after otter, till the man learned that the little beasts were not fishing at all, but coasting the snow bank like youngsters on a night frolic. No sooner did one reach the bottom than up he scampered to repeat the fun; and sometimes two or three went down in a rolling bunch mixed up at the foot of a slide as badly as a couple of toboggans that were unpremeditatedly changing their occupants. Bears wrestle. The kittens of all the cat tribe play hide and seek. Little badger finds it fun to run round rubbing the back of his head on things; and here was nekik the otter at the favourite amusement of his kind—coasting down a snow bank.

If the trapper were an Indian, he would lie in wait at the landing-place and spear the otter as they came from the water. But the white man's craft is deeper. He does not wish to frighten the otter till the last had been taken. Coming to the slide by day, he baits a steel-trap with fish and buries it in the snow just where the otter will be coming down the hill or up from the pool. Perhaps he places a dozen such traps around the hole with nothing visible but the frozen fish lying on the surface. If he sets his traps during a snow-fall, so much the better. His own tracks will be obliterated and the otter's nose will discover the fish. Then he takes a bag filled with some substance of animal odour, pomatum, fresh meat, pork, or he may use the flesh side of a fresh deer-hide. This he drags over the snow where he has stepped. He may even use a fresh hide to handle the traps, as a waiter uses a serviette to pass plates. There must be no man-smell, no man-track near the otter traps. While the mink-hunt is fairly over by midwinter, otter-trapping lasts from October to May. The value of all rare furs, mink, otter, marten, ermine, varies with two things: (1) the latitude of the hunting-field; (2) the season of the hunt. For instance, ask a trapper of Minnesota or Lake Superior what he thinks of the ermine, and he will tell you that it is a miserable sort of weasel of a dirty drab brown not worth twenty-five cents a skin. Ask a trapper of the North Saskatchewan what he thinks of ermine; and he will tell you it is a pretty little whitish creature good for fur if trapped late enough in the winter and always useful as a lining. But ask a trapper of the Arctic about the ermine, and he describes it as the finest fur that is taken except the silver fox, white and soft as swan's-down, with a tail-tip like black onyx. This difference in the fur of the animal explains the wide variety of prices paid. Ermine not worth twenty-five cents in Wisconsin might be worth ten times as much on the Saskatchewan.

Fur press in use at Fort Good Hope, at the extreme north of Hudson's Bay Company's territory.

Old wedge press in use at Fort Resolution, of the sub-Arctics.

Types of Fur Presses.

So it is with the otter. All trapped between latitude thirty-five and sixty is good fur; and the best is that taken toward the end of winter when scarcely a russet hair should be found in the long over-fur of nekik's coat.

III

Wuchak the Fisher, or Pekan

Wherever the waste of fish or deer is thrown, there will be found lines of double tracks not so large as the wild-cat's, not so small as the otter's, and without the same webbing as the mink's. This is wuchak the fisher, or pekan, commonly called "the black cat"—who, in spite of his fishy name, hates water as cats hate it. And the tracks are double because pekan travel in pairs. He is found along the banks of streams because he preys on fish and fisher, on mink and otter and musk-rat, on frogs and birds and creatures that come to drink. He is, after all, a very greedy fellow, not at all particular about his diet, and, like all gluttons, easily snared. While mink and otter are about, the trapper will waste no steel-traps on pekan. A deadfall will act just as effectively; but there is one point requiring care. Pekan has a sharp nose. It is his nose that brings him to all carrion just as surely as hawks come to pick dead bones. But that same nose will tell him of man's presence. So when the trapper has built his pen of logs so that the front log or deadfall will crush down on the back of an intruder tugging at the bait inside, he overlays all with leaves and brush to quiet the pekan's suspicions. Besides, the pekan has many tricks akin to the wolverine. He is an inveterate thief. There is a well-known instance of Hudson's Bay trappers having a line of one hundred and fifty marten traps stretching for fifty miles robbed of their bait by pekan. The men shortened the line to thirty miles and for six times in succession did pekan destroy the traps. Then the men set themselves to trap the robber. He will rifle a deadfall from the slanting back roof where there is no danger; so the trapper overlays the back with heavy brush.

Pekan do not yield a rare fur; but they are always at run where the trapper is hunting the rare furs, and for that reason are usually snared at the same time as mink and otter.

IV

Wapistan the Marten

When Koot went blind on his way home from the rabbit-hunt, he had intended to set out for the pine woods. Though blizzards still howl over the prairie, by March the warm sun of midday has set the sap of the forests stirring and all the woodland life awakens from its long winter sleep. Cougar and lynx and bear rove through the forest ravenous with spring hunger. Otter, too, may be found where the ice mounds of a waterfall are beginning to thaw. But it is not any of these that the trapper seeks. If they cross his path, good—they, too, will swell his account at the fur post. It is another of the little chaps that he seeks, a little, long, low-set animal whose fur is now glistening bright on the deep dark overhairs, soft as down in the thick fawn underhairs, wapistan the marten.

When the forest begins to stir with the coming of spring, wapistan stirs too, crawling out from the hollow of some rotten pine log, restless with the same blood-thirst that set the little mink playing his tricks on the hawk. And yet the marten is not such a little viper as the mink. Wapistan will eat leaves and nuts and roots if he can get vegetable food, but failing these, that ravenous spring hunger of his must be appeased with something else. And out he goes from his log hole hunger-bold as the biggest of all other spring ravagers. That boldness gives the trapper his chance at the very time when wapistan's fur is best. All winter the trapper may have taken marten; but the end of winter is the time when wapistan wanders freely from cover. Thus the trapper's calendar would have months of musk-rat first, then beaver and mink and pekan and bear and fox and ermine and rabbit and lynx and marten, with a long idle midsummer space when he goes to the fort for the year's provisions and gathers the lore of his craft.

Wapistan is not hard to track. Being much longer and heavier than a cat with very short legs and small feet, his body almost drags the ground and his tracks sink deep, clear, and sharp. His feet are smaller than otter's and mink's, but easily distinguishable from those two fishers. The water animal leaves a spreading footprint, the mark of the webbed toes without any fur on the padding of the toe-balls. The land animal of the same size has clear cut, narrower, heavier marks. By March, these dotting foot-tracks thread the snow everywhere.

Coming on marten tracks at a pine log, the trapper sends in his dog or prods with a stick. Finding nothing, he baits a steel-trap with pomatum, covers it deftly with snow, drags the decoy skin about to conceal his own tracks, and goes away in the hope that the marten will come back to this log to guzzle on his prey and sleep.

If the track is much frequented, or the forest over-run with marten tracks, the trapper builds deadfalls, many of them running from tree to tree for miles through the forest in a circle whose circuit brings him back to his cabin. Remnants of these log traps may be seen through all parts of the Rocky Mountain forests. Thirty to forty traps are considered a day's work for one man, six or ten marten all that he expects to take in one round; but when marten are plentiful, the unused traps of to-day may bring a prize to-morrow.

The Indian trapper would use still another kind of trap. Where the tracks are plainly frequently used runways to watering-places or lair in hollow tree, the Indian digs a pit across the marten's trail. On this he spreads brush in such roof fashion that though the marten is a good climber, if once he falls in, it is almost impossible for him to scramble out. If a poor cackling grouse or "fool-hen" be thrust into the pit, the Indian is almost sure to find a prisoner. This seems to the white man a barbarous kind of trapping; but the poor "fool-hen," hunted by all the creatures of the forest, never seems to learn wisdom, but invites disaster by popping out of the brush to stare at every living thing that passes. If she did not fall a victim in the pit, she certainly would to her own curiosity above ground. To the steel-trap the hunter attaches a piece of log to entangle the prisoner's flight as he rushes through the underbush. Once caught in the steel jaws, little wapistan must wait—wait for what? For the same thing that comes to the poor "fool-hen" when wapistan goes crashing through the brush after her; for the same thing that comes to the baby squirrels when wapistan climbs a tree to rob the squirrel's nest, eat the young, and live in the rifled house; for the same thing that comes to the hoary marmot whistling his spring tune just outside his rocky den when wapistan, who has climbed up, pounces down from above. Little death-dealer he has been all his life; and now death comes to him for a nobler cause than the stuffing of a greedy maw—for the clothing of a creature nobler than himself—man.

The otter can protect himself by diving, even diving under snow. The mink has craft to hide himself under leaves so that the sharpest eyes cannot detect him. Both mink and otter furs have very little of that animal smell which enables the foragers to follow their trail. What gift has wapistan, the marten, to protect himself against all the powers that prey? His strength and his wisdom lie in the little stubby feet. These can climb.

A trapper's dog had stumbled on a marten in a stump hole. A snap of the marten's teeth sent the dog back with a jump. Wapistan will hang on to the nose of a dog to the death; and trappers' dogs grow cautious. Before the dog gathered courage to make another rush, the marten escaped by a rear knot-hole, getting the start of his enemy by fifty yards. Off they raced, the dog spending himself in fury, the marten keeping under the thorny brush where his enemy could not follow, then across open snow where the dog gained, then into the pine woods where the trail ended on the snow. Where had the fugitive gone? When the man came up, he first searched for log holes. There were none. Then he lifted some of the rocks. There was no trace of wapistan. But the dog kept baying a special tree, a blasted trunk, bare as a mast pole and seemingly impossible for any animal but a squirrel to climb. Knowing the trick by which creatures like the bob-cat can flatten their body into a resemblance of a tree trunk, the trapper searched carefully all round the bare trunk. It was not till many months afterward when a wind storm had broken the tree that he discovered the upper part had been hollow. Into this eerie nook the pursued marten had scrambled and waited in safety till dog and man retired.

In one of his traps the man finds a peculiarly short specimen of the marten. In the vernacular of the craft this marten's bushy tail will not reach as far back as his hind legs can stretch. Widely different from the mink's scarcely visible ears, this fellow's ears are sharply upright, keenly alert. He is like a fox, where the mink resembles a furred serpent. Marten moves, springs, jumps like an animal. Mink glides like a snake. Marten has the strong neck of an animal fighter. Mink has the long, thin, twisting neck which reptiles need to give them striking power for their fangs. Mink's under lip has a mere rim of white or yellow. Marten's breast is patched sulphur. But this short marten with a tail shorter than other marten differs from his kind as to fur. Both mink and marten fur are reddish brown; but this short marten's fur is almost black, of great depth, of great thickness, and of three qualities: (1) There are the long dark overhairs the same as the ordinary marten, only darker, thicker, deeper; (2) there is the soft under fur of the ordinary marten, usually fawn, in this fellow deep brown; (3) there is the skin fur resembling chicken-down, of which this little marten has such a wealth—to use a technical expression—you cannot find his scalp. Without going into the old quarrel about species, when a marten has these peculiarities, he is known to the trapper as sable.

Whether he is the American counterpart to the Russia sable is a disputed point. Whether his superior qualities are owing to age, climate, species, it is enough for the trapper to know that short, dark marten yields the trade— sable.

CHAPTER XVIII
UNDER THE NORTH STAR—WHERE FOX AND ERMINE RUN
I

Of Foxes, Many and Various—Red, Cross, Silver, Black, Prairie, Kit or Swift, Arctic, Blue, and Gray

Wherever grouse and rabbit abound, there will foxes run and there will the hunter set steel-traps. But however beautiful a fox-skin may be as a specimen, it has value as a fur only when it belongs to one of three varieties—Arctic, black, and silver. Other foxes—red, cross, prairie, swift, and gray—the trapper will take when they cross his path and sell them in the gross at the fur post, as he used to barter buffalo-hides. But the hunter who traps the fox for its own sake, and not as an uncalculated extra to the mink-hunt or the beaver total, must go to the Far North, to the land of winter night and midnight sun, to obtain the best fox-skins.

It matters not to the trapper that the little kit fox or swift at run among the hills between the Missouri and Saskatchewan is the most shapely of all the fox kind, with as finely pointed a nose as a spitz dog, ears alert as a terrier's and a brush, more like a lady's gray feather boa than fur, curled round his dainty toes. Little kit's fur is a grizzled gray shading to mottled fawn. The hairs are coarse, horsey, indistinctly marked, and the fur is of small value to the trader; so dainty little swift, who looks as if nature made him for a pet dog instead of a fox, is slighted by the hunter, unless kit persists in tempting a trap. Rufus the red fellow, with his grizzled gray head and black ears and whitish throat and flaunting purplish tinges down his sides like a prince royal, may make a handsome mat; but as a fur he is of little worth. His cousin with the black fore feet, the prairie fox, who is the largest and strongest and scientifically finest of all his kind, has more value as a fur. The colour of the prairie fox shades rather to pale ochre and yellow that the nondescript grizzled gray that is of so little value as a fur. Of the silver-gray fox little need be said. He lives too far south—California and Texas and Mexico—to acquire either energy or gloss. He is the one indolent member of the fox tribe, and his fur lacks the sheen that only winter cold can give. The value of the cross fox depends on the markings that give him his name. If the bands, running diagonally over his shoulders in the shape of a cross, shade to grayish blue he is a prize, if to reddish russet, he is only a curiosity.

The Arctic and black and silver foxes have the pelts that at their worst equal the other rare furs, at their best exceed the value of all other furs by so much that the lucky trapper who takes a silver fox has made his fortune. These, then, are the foxes that the trapper seeks and these are to be found only on the white wastes of the polar zone.

That brings up the question—what is a silver fox? Strange as it may seem, neither scientist nor hunter can answer that question. Nor will study of all the park specimens in the world tell the secret, for the simple reason that only an Arctic climate can produce a silver fox; and parks are not established in the Arctics yet. It is quite plain that the prairie fox is in a class by himself. The uniformity of his size, his strength, his habits, his appearance, distinguish him from other foxes. It is quite plain that the little kit fox or swift is of a kind distinct from other foxes. His smallness, the shape of his bones, the cast of his face, the trick of sitting rather than lying, that wonderful big bushy soft tail of which a peacock might be vain—all differentiate him from other foxes. The same may be said of the Arctic fox with a pelt that is more like white wool than hairs of fur. He is much smaller than the red. His tail is bushier and larger than the swift, and like all Arctic creatures, he has the soles of his feet heavily furred. All this is plain and simple classification. But how about Mr. Blue Fox of the same size and habit as the white Arctic? Is he the Arctic fox in summer clothing? Yes, say some trappers; and they show their pelts of an Arctic fox taken in summer of a rusty white. But no, vow other trappers—that is impossible, for here are blue fox-skins captured in the depths of midwinter with not a white hair among them. Look closely at the skins. The ears of one blue fox are long, perfect, unbitten by frost or foe—he was a young fellow; and he is blue. Here is another with ears almost worn to stubs by fights and many winters' frosts—he is an old fellow; and he, too, is blue. Well, then, the blue fox may sometimes be the white Arctic fox in summer dress; but the blue fox who is blue all the year round, varying only in the shades of blue with the seasons, is certainly not the white Arctic fox.

The same difficulty besets distinction of silver fox from black. The old scientists classified these as one and the same creature. Trappers know better. So do the later scientists who almost agree with the unlearned trapper's verdict—there are as many species as there are foxes. Black fox is at its best in midwinter, deep, brilliantly glossy, soft as floss, and yet almost impenetrable—the very type of perfection of its kind. But with the coming of the tardy Arctic spring comes a change. The snows are barely melted in May when the sheen leaves the fur. By June, the black hairs are streaked with gray; and the black fox is a gray fox. Is it at some period of the transition that the black fox becomes a silver fox, with the gray hairs as sheeny as the black and each gray hair delicately tipped with black? That question, too, remains unanswered; for certainly the black fox trapped when in his gray summer coat is not the splendid silver fox of priceless value. Black fox turning to a dull gray of midsummer may not be silver fox; but what about gray fox turning to the beautiful glossy black of midwinter? Is that what makes silver fox? Is silver fox simply a fine specimen of black caught at the very period when he is blooming into his greatest beauty? The distinctive difference between gray fox and silver is that gray fox has gray hairs among hairs of other colour, while silver fox has silver hair tipped with glossiest black on a foundation of downy gray black.

Even greater confusion surrounds the origin of cross and red and gray. Trappers find all these different cubs in one burrow; but as the cubs grow, those pronounced cross turn out to be red, or the red becomes cross; and what they become at maturity, that they remain, varying only with the seasons.[45] It takes many centuries to make one perfect rose. Is it the same with the silver fox? Is he a freak or a climax or the regular product of yearly climatic changes caught in the nick of time by some lucky trapper? Ask the scientist that question, and he theorizes. Ask the trapper, and he tells you if he could only catch enough silver foxes to study that question, he would quit trapping. In all the maze of ignorance and speculation, there is one anchored fact. While animals turn a grizzled gray with age, the fine gray coats are not caused by age. Young animals of the rarest furs—fox and ermine—are born in ashy colour that turns to gray while they are still in their first nest.

To say that silver fox is costly solely because it is rare is sheerest nonsense. It would be just as sensible to say that labradorite, which is rare, should be as costly as diamonds. It is the intrinsic beauty of the fur, as of the diamonds, that constitutes its first value. The facts that the taking of a silver fox is always pure luck, that the luck comes seldom, that the trapper must have travelled countless leagues by snow-shoe and dog train over the white wastes of the North, that trappers in polar regions are exposed to more dangers and hardships than elsewhere and that the fur must have been carried a long distance to market—add to the first high value of silver fox till it is not surprising that little pelts barely two feet long have sold for prices ranging from $500 to $5,000. For the trapper the way to the fortune of a silver fox is the same as the road to fortune for all other men—by the homely trail of every-day work. Cheers from the fort gates bid trappers setting out for far Northern fields God-speed. Long ago there would have been a firing of cannon when the Northern hunters left for their distant camping-grounds; but the cannon of Churchill lie rusting to-day and the hunters who go to the sub-Arctics and the Arctics no longer set out from Churchill on the bay, but from one of the little inland MacKenzie River posts. If the fine powdery snow-drifts are glossed with the ice of unbroken sun-glare, the runners strap iron crampets to their snow-shoes, and with a great jingling of the dog-bells, barking of the huskies, and yelling of the drivers, coast away for the leagueless levels of the desolate North. Frozen river-beds are the only path followed, for the high cliffs—almost like ramparts on the lower MacKenzie—shut off the drifting east winds that heap barricades of snow in one place and at another sweep the ground so clear that the sleighs pull heavy as stone. Does a husky fag? A flourish of whips and off the laggard scampers, keeping pace with the others in the traces, a pace that is set for forty miles a day with only one feeding time, nightfall when the sleighs are piled as a wind-break and the frozen fish are doled out to the ravenous dogs. Gun signals herald the hunter's approach to a chance camp; and no matter how small and mean the tepee, the door is always open for whatever visitor, the meat pot set simmering for hungry travellers. When the snow crust cuts the dogs' feet, buckskin shoes are tied on the huskies; and when an occasional dog fags entirely, he is turned adrift from the traces to die. Relentless as death is Northern cold; and wherever these long midwinter journeys are made, gruesome traditions are current of hunter and husky.

I remember hearing of one old husky that fell hopelessly lame during the north trip. Often the drivers are utter brutes to their dogs, speaking in curses which they say is the only language a husky can understand, emphasized with the blows of a club. Too often, as well, the huskies are vicious curs ready to skulk or snap or bolt or fight, anything but work. But in this case the dog was an old reliable that kept the whole train in line, and the driver had such an affection for the veteran husky that when rheumatism crippled the dog's legs the man had not the heart to shoot such a faithful servant. The dog was turned loose from the traces and hobbled lamely behind the scampering teams. At last he fell behind altogether, but at night limped into camp whining his joy and asking dumbly for the usual fish. In the morning when the other teams set out, the old husky was powerless to follow. But he could still whine and wag his tail. He did both with all his might, so that when the departing driver looked back over his shoulder, he saw a pair of eyes pleading, a head with raised alert ears, shoulders straining to lift legs that refused to follow, and a bushy tail thwacking—thwacking—thwacking the snow!

"You ought to shoot him," advised one driver.

"You do it—you're a dead sure aim," returned the man who had owned the dog.

But the other drivers were already coasting over the white wastes. The owner looked at his sleighs as if wondering whether they would stand an additional burden. Then probably reflecting that old age is not desirable for a suffering dog in a bitingly keen frost, he turned towards the husky with his hand in his belt. Thwack—thwack went the tail as much as to say: "Of course he wouldn't desert me after I've hauled his sleigh all my life! Thwack—thwack! I'd get up and jump all around him if I could; there isn't a dog-gone husky in all polar land with half as good a master as I have!"

The man stopped. Instead of going to the dog he ran back to his sleigh, loaded his arms full of frozen fish and threw them down before the dog. Then he put one caribou-skin under the old dog, spread another over him and ran away with his train while the husky was still guzzling. The fish had been poisoned to be thrown out to the wolves that so often pursue Northern dog trains.

Once a party of hunters crossing the Northern Rockies came on a dog train stark and stiff. Where was the master who had bidden them stand while he felt his way blindly through the white whirl of a blizzard for the lost path? In the middle of the last century, one of that famous family of fur traders, a MacKenzie, left Georgetown to go north to Red River in Canada. He never went back to Georgetown and he never reached Red River; but his coat was found fluttering from a tree, a death signal to attract the first passer-by, and the body of the lost trader was discovered not far off in the snow. Unless it is the year of the rabbit pest and the rabbit ravagers are bold with hunger, the pursuing wolves seldom give full chase. They skulk far to the rear of the dog trains, licking up the stains of the bleeding feet, or hanging spectrally on the dim frosty horizon all night long. Hunger drives them on; but they seem to lack the courage to attack. I know of one case where the wolves followed the dog trains bringing out a trader's family from the North down the river-bed for nearly five hundred miles. What man hunter would follow so far?

The farther north the fox hunter goes, the shorter grow the days, till at last the sun, which has rolled across the south in a wheel of fire, dwindles to a disk, the disk to a rim—then no rim at all comes up, and it is midwinter night, night but not darkness. The white of endless unbroken snow, the glint of icy particles filling the air, the starlight brilliant as diamond points, the Aurora Borealis in curtains and shafts and billows of tenuous impalpable rose-coloured fire—all brighten the polar night so that the sun is unmissed. This is the region chiefly hunted by the Eskimo, with a few white men and Chippewyan half-breeds. The regular Northern hunters do not go as far as the Arctics, but choose their hunting-ground somewhere in the region of "little sticks," meaning the land where timber growth is succeeded by dwarf scrubs.

The hunting-ground is chosen always from the signs written across the white page of the snow. If there are claw-marks, bird signs of Northern grouse or white ptarmigan or snow-bunting, ermine will be plentiful; for the Northern birds with their clogged stockings of feet feathers have a habit of floundering under the powdery snow; and up through that powdery snow darts the snaky neck of stoat, the white weasel-hunter of birds. If there are the deep plunges of the white hare, lynx and fox and mink and marten and pekan will be plentiful; for the poor white hare feeds all the creatures of the Northern wastes, man and beast. If there are little dainty tracks—oh, such dainty tracks that none but a high-stepping, clear-cut, clean-limbed, little thoroughbred could make them!—tracks of four toes and a thumb claw much shorter than the rest, with a padding of five basal foot-bones behind the toes, tracks that show a fluff on the snow as of furred foot-soles, tracks that go in clean, neat, clear long leaps and bounds—the hunter knows that he has found the signs of the Northern fox.

Here, then, he will camp for the winter. Camping in the Far North means something different from the hastily pitched tent of the prairie. The north wind blows biting, keen, unbroken in its sweep. The hunter must camp where that wind will not carry scent of his tent to the animal world. For his own sake, he must camp under shelter from that wind, behind a cairn of stones, below a cliff, in a ravine. Poles have been brought from the land of trees on the dog sleigh. These are put up, criss-crossed at top, and over them is laid, not the canvas tent, but a tent of skins, caribou, wolf, moose, at a sharp enough angle to let the snow slide off. Then snow is banked deep, completely round the tent. For fire, the Eskimo depends on whale-oil and animal grease. The white man or half-breed from the South hoards up chips and sticks. But mainly he depends on exercise and animal food for warmth. At night he sleeps in a fur bag. In the morning that bag is frozen stiff as boards by the moisture of his own breath. Need one ask why the rarest furs, which can only be produced by the coldest of climates, are so costly?

Having found the tracks of the fox, the hunter sets out his traps baited with fish or rabbit or a bird-head. If the snow be powdery enough, and the trapper keen in wild lore, he may even know what sort of a fox to expect. In the depths of midwinter, the white Arctic fox has a wool fur to his feet like a brahma chicken. This leaves its mark in the fluffy snow. A ravenous fellow he always is, this white fox of the hungry North, bold from ignorance of man, but hard to distinguish from the snow because of his spotless coat. The blue fox being slightly smaller than the full-grown Arctic, lopes along with shorter leaps by which the trapper may know the quarry; but the blue fox is just as hard to distinguish from the snow as his white brother. The gray frost haze is almost the same shade as his steel-blue coat; and when spring comes, blue fox is the same colour as the tawny moss growth. Colour is blue fox's defence. Consequently blue foxes show more signs of age than white—stubby ears frozen low, battle-worn teeth, dulled claws.

The chances are that the trapper will see the black fox himself almost as soon as he sees his tracks; for the sheeny coat that is black fox's beauty betrays him above the snow. Bushy tail standing straight out, every black hair bristling erect with life, the white tail-tip flaunting a defiance, head up, ears alert, fore feet cleaving the air with the swift ease of some airy bird—on he comes, jump—jump—jump—more of a leap than a lope, galloping like a wolf, altogether different from the skulking run of little foxes, openly exulting in his beauty and his strength and his speed! There is no mistaking black fox. If the trapper does not see the black fox scurrying over the snow, the tell-tale characteristics of the footprints are the length and strength of the leaps. Across these leaps the hunter leaves his traps. Does he hope for a silver fox? Does every prospector expect to find gold nuggets? In the heyday of fur company prosperity, not half a dozen true silver foxes would be sent out in a year. To-day I doubt if more than one good silver fox is sent out in half a dozen years. But good white fox and black and blue are prizes enough in themselves, netting as much to the trapper as mink or beaver or sable.

II

The White Ermine

All that was said of the mystery of fox life applies equally to ermine. Why is the ermine of Wisconsin and Minnesota and Dakota a dirty little weasel noted for killing forty chickens in a night, wearing a mahogany-coloured coat with a sulphur strip down his throat, while the ermine of the Arctics is as white as snow, noted for his courage, wearing a spotless coat which kings envy, yes, and take from him? For a long time the learned men who study animal life from museums held that the ermine's coat turned white from the same cause as human hair, from senility and debility and the depleting effect of an intensely trying climate. But the trappers told a different story. They told of baby ermine born in Arctic burrows, in March, April, May, June, while the mother was still in white coat, babies born in an ashy coat something like a mouse-skin that turned to fleecy white within ten days. They told of ermine shedding his brown coat in autumn to display a fresh layer of iron-gray fur that turned sulphur white within a few days. They told of the youngest and smallest and strongest ermine with the softest and whitest coats. That disposed of the senility theory. All the trapper knows is that the whitest ermine is taken when the cold is most intense and most continuous, that just as the cold slackens the ermine coat assumes the sulphur tinges, deepening to russet and brown, and that the whitest ermine instead of showing senility, always displays the most active and courageous sort of deviltry.

Summer or winter, the Northern trapper is constantly surrounded by ermine and signs of ermine. There are the tiny claw-tracks almost like frost tracery across the snow. There is the rifled nest of a poor grouse—eggs sucked, or chickens murdered, the nest fouled so that it emits the stench of a skunk, or the mother hen lying dead from a wound in her throat. There is the frightened rabbit loping across the fields in the wildest, wobbliest, most woe-begone leaps, trying to shake something off that is clinging to his throat till over he tumbles—the prey of a hunter that is barely the size of rabbit's paw. There is the water-rat flitting across the rocks in blind terror, regardless of the watching trapper, caring only to reach safety—water—water! Behind comes the pursuer—this is no still hunt but a straight open chase—a little creature about the length of a man's hand, with a tail almost as long, a body scarcely the thickness of two fingers, a mouth the size of a bird's beak, and claws as small as a sparrow's. It gallops in lithe bounds with its long neck straight up and its beady eyes fastened on the flying water-rat. Splash—dive—into the water goes the rat! Splash—dive—into the water goes the ermine! There is a great stirring up of the muddy bottom. The water-rat has tried to hide in the under-tangle; and the ermine has not only dived in pursuit but headed the water-rat back from the safe retreat of his house. Up comes a black nose to the surface of the water. The rat is foolishly going to try a land race. Up comes a long neck like a snake's, the head erect, the beady eyes on the fleeing water-rat—then with a splash they race overland. The water-rat makes for a hole among the rocks. Ermine sees and with a spurt of speed is almost abreast when the rat at bay turns with a snap at his pursuer. But quick as flash, the ermine has pirouetted into the air. The long writhing neck strikes like a serpent's fangs and the sharp fore teeth have pierced the brain of the rat. The victim dies without a cry, without a struggle, without a pain. That long neck was not given the ermine for nothing. Neither were those muscles massed on either side of his jaws like bulging cheeks.

In winter the ermine's murderous depredations are more apparent. Now the ermine, too, sets itself to reading the signs of the snow. Now the ermine becomes as keen a still hunter as the man. Sometimes a whirling snow-fall catches a family of grouse out from furze cover. The trapper, too, is abroad in the snow-storm; for that is the time when he can set his traps undetected. The white whirl confuses the birds. They run here, there, everywhere, circling about, burying themselves in the snow till the storm passes over. The next day when the hunter is going the rounds of these traps, along comes an ermine. It does not see him. It is following a scent, head down, body close to ground, nose here, there, threading the maze which the crazy grouse had run. But stop, thinks the trapper, the snow-fall covered the trail. Exactly—that is why the little ermine dives under snow just as it would under water, running along with serpentine wavings of the white powdery surface till up it comes again where the wind has blown the snow-fall clear. Along it runs, still intent, quartering back where it loses the scent—along again till suddenly the head lifts—that motion of the snake before it strikes! The trapper looks. Tail feathers, head feathers, stupid blinking eyes poke through the fluffy snow-drift. And now the ermine no longer runs openly. There are too many victims this time—it may get all the foolish hidden grouse; so it dives and if the man had not alarmed the stupid grouse, ermine would have darted up through the snow with a finishing stab for each bird.

By still hunt and open hunt, by nose and eye, relentless as doom, it follows its victims to the death. Does the bird perch on a tree? Up goes the ermine, too, on the side away from the bird's head. Does the mouse thread a hundred mazes and hide in a hole? The ermine threads every maze, marches into the hidden nest and takes murderous possession. Does the rat hide under rock? Under the rock goes the ermine. Should the trapper follow to see the outcome of the contest, the ermine will probably sit at the mouth of the rat-hole, blinking its beady eyes at him. If he attacks, down it bolts out of reach. If he retires, out it comes looking at this strange big helpless creature with bold contempt.

The keen scent, the keen eyes, the keen ears warn it of an enemy's approach. Summer and winter, its changing coat conceals it. The furze where it runs protects it from fox and lynx and wolverine. Its size admits it to the tiniest of hiding-places. All that the ermine can do to hunt down a victim, it can do to hide from an enemy. These qualities make it almost invincible to other beasts of the chase. Two joints in the armour of its defence has the little ermine. Its black tail-tip moving across snow betrays it to enemies in winter: the very intentness on prey, its excess of self-confidence, leads it into danger; for instance, little ermine is royally contemptuous of man's tracks. If the man does not molest it, it will follow a scent and quarter and circle under his feet; so the man has no difficulty in taking the little beast whose fur is second only to that of the silver fox. So bold are the little creatures that the man may discover their burrows under brush, in rock, in sand holes, and take the whole litter before the game mother will attempt to escape. Indeed, the plucky little ermine will follow the captor of her brood. Steel rat traps, tiny deadfalls, frosted bits of iron smeared with grease to tempt the ermine's tongue which the frost will hold like a vice till the trapper comes, and, most common of all, twine snares such as entrap the rabbit, are the means by which the ermine comes to his appointed end at the hands of men.

The quality of the pelt shows as wide variety as the skin of the fox; and for as mysterious reasons. Why an ermine a year old should have a coat like sulphur and another of the same age a coat like swan's-down, neither trapper nor scientist has yet discovered. The price of the perfect ermine-pelt is higher than any other of the rare furs taken in North America except silver fox; but it no longer commands the fabulous prices that were certainly paid for specimen ermine-skins in the days of the Georges in England and the later Louis in France. How were those fabulously costly skins prepared? Old trappers say no perfectly downy pelt is ever taken from an ermine, that the downy effect is produced by a trick of the trade—scraping the flesh side so deftly that all the coarse hairs will fall out, leaving only the soft under-fur.

CHAPTER XIX
WHAT THE TRAPPER STANDS FOR

Waging ceaseless war against beaver and moose, types of nature's most harmless creatures, against wolf and wolverine, types of nature's most destructive agents, against traders who were rivals and Indians who were hostiles, the trapper would almost seem to be himself a type of nature's arch-destroyer.

Beautiful as a dream is the silent world of forest and prairie and mountain where the trapper moves with noiseless stealth of the most skilful of all the creatures that prey. In that world, the crack of the trapper's rifle, the snap of the cruel steel jaws in his trap, seem the only harsh discords in the harmony of an existence that riots with a very fulness of life. But such a world is only a dream. The reality is cruel as death. Of all the creatures that prey, man is the most merciful.

Ordinarily, knowledge of animal life is drawn from three sources. There are park specimens, stuffed to the utmost of their eating capacity and penned off from the possibility of harming anything weaker than themselves. There are the private pets fed equally well, pampered and chained safely from harming or being harmed. There are the wild creatures roaming natural haunts, some two or three days' travel from civilization, whose natures have been gradually modified generation by generation from being constantly hunted with long-range repeaters. Judging from these sorts of wild animals, it certainly seems that the brute creation has been sadly maligned. The bear cubs lick each other's paws with an amatory singing that is something between the purr of a cat and the grunt of a pig. The old polars wrestle like boys out of school, flounder in grotesque gambols that are laughably clumsy, good-naturedly dance on their hind legs, and even eat from their keeper's hand. And all the deer family can be seen nosing one another with the affection of turtle-doves. Surely the worst that can be said of these animals is that they shun the presence of man. Perhaps some kindly sentimentalist wonders if things hadn't gone so badly out of gear in a certain historic garden long ago, whether mankind would not be on as friendly relations with the animal world as little boys and girls are with bears and baboons in the fairy books. And the scientist goes a step further, and soberly asks whether these wild things of the woods are not kindred of man after all; for have not man and beast ascended the same scale of life? Across the centuries, modern evolution shakes hands with old-fashioned transmigration.

To be sure, members of the deer family sometimes kill their mates in fits of blind rage, and the innocent bear cubs fall to mauling their keeper, and the old bears have been known to eat their young. These things are set down as freaks in the animal world, and in nowise allowed to upset the influences drawn from animals living in unnatural surroundings, behind iron bars, or in haunts where long-range rifles have put the fear of man in the animal heart.

Now the trapper studies animal life where there is neither a pen to keep the animal from doing what it wants to do, nor any rifle but his own to teach wild creatures fear. Knowing nothing of science and sentiment, he never clips facts to suit his theory. On the truthfulness of his eyes depends his own life, so that he never blinks his eyes to disagreeable facts.

Looking out on the life of the wilds clear-visioned as his mountain air, the trapper sees a world beautiful as a dream but cruel as death. He sees a world where to be weak, to be stupid, to be dull, to be slow, to be simple, to be rash are the unpardonable crimes; where the weak must grow strong, keen of eye and ear and instinct, sharp, wary, swift, wise, and cautious; where in a word the weak must grow fit to survive or—perish!The slow worm fills the hungry maw of the gaping bird. Into the soft fur of the rabbit that has strayed too far from cover clutch the swooping talons of an eagle. The beaver that exposes himself overland risks bringing lynx or wolverine or wolf on his home colony. Bird preys on worm, mink on bird, lynx on mink, wolf on lynx, and bear on all creatures that live from men and moose down to the ant and the embryo life in the ant's egg. But the vision of ravening destruction does not lead the trapper to morbid conclusions on life as it leads so many housed thinkers in the walled cities; for the same world that reveals to him such ravening slaughter shows him that every creature, the weakest and the strongest, has some faculty, some instinct, some endowment of cunning, or dexterity or caution, some gift of concealment, of flight, of semblance, of death—that will defend it from all enemies. The ermine is one of the smallest of all hunters, but it can throw an enemy off the scent by diving under snow. The rabbit is one of the most helpless of all hunted things, but it can take cover from foes of the air under thorny brush, and run fast enough to outwind the breath of a pursuer, and double back quick enough to send a harrying eagle flopping head over heels on the ground, and simulate the stillness of inanimate objects surrounding it so truly that the passer-by can scarcely distinguish the balls of fawn fur from the russet bark of a log. And the rabbit's big eyes and ears are not given it for nothing.Poet and trapper alike see the same world, and for the same reason. Both seek only to know the truth, to see the world as it is; and the world that they see is red in tooth and claw. But neither grows morbid from his vision; for that same vision shows each that the ravening destruction is only a weeding out of the unfit. There is too much sunlight in the trapper's world, too much fresh air in his lungs, too much red blood in his veins for the morbid miasmas that bring bilious fumes across the mental vision of the housed city man.

And what place in the scale of destruction does the trapper occupy? Modern sentiment has almost painted him as a red-dyed monster, excusable, perhaps, because necessity compels the hunter to slay, but after all only the most highly developed of the creatures that prey. Is this true? Arch-destroyer he may be; but it should be remembered that he is the destroyer of destroyers.

Animals kill young and old, male and female.

The true trapper does not kill the young; for that would destroy his next year's hunt. He does not kill the mother while she is with the young. He kills the grown males which—it can be safely said—have killed more of each other than man has killed in all the history of trapping. Wherever regions have been hunted by the pot-hunter, whether the sportsman for amusement or the settler supplying his larder, game has been exterminated. This is illustrated by all the stretch of country between the Platte and the Saskatchewan. Wherever regions have been hunted only by the trapper, game is as plentiful as it has ever been. This is illustrated by the forests of the Rockies, by the No-Man's Land south of Hudson Bay and by the Arctics. Wherever the trapper has come destroying grisly and coyote and wolverine, the prong horn and mountain-sheep and mountain-goat and wapiti and moose have increased.But the trapper stands for something more than a game warden, something more than the most merciful of destroyers. He destroys animal life—a life which is red in tooth and claw with murder and rapine and cruelty—in order that human life may be preserved, may be rendered independent of the elemental powers that wage war against it.It is a war as old as the human race, this struggle of man against the elements, a struggle alike reflected in Viking song of warriors conquering the sea, and in the Scandinavian myth of pursuing Fenris wolf, and in the Finnish epic of the man-hero wresting secrets of life-bread from the earth, and in Indian folk-lore of a Hiawatha hunting beast and treacherous wind. It is a war in which the trapper stands forth as a conqueror, a creature sprung of earth, trampling all the obstacles that earth can offer to human will under his feet, finding paths through the wilderness for the explorer who was to come after him, opening doors of escape from stifled life in crowded centres of population, preparing a highway for the civilization that was to follow his own wandering trail through the wilds.

APPENDIX

When in Labrador and Newfoundland a few years ago, the writer copied the entries of an old half-breed woman trapper's daily journal of her life. It is fragmentary and incoherent, but gives a glimpse of the Indian mind. It is written in English. She was seventy-five years old when the diary opened in December, 1893. Her name was Lydia Campbell and she lived at Hamilton Inlet. Having related how she shot a deer, skinning it herself, made her snow-shoes and set her rabbit snares, she closes her first entry with:

"Well, as I sed, I can't write much at a time now, for i am getting blind and some mist rises up before me if i sew, read or write a little while."

Lydia Campbell's mother was captured by Eskimo. She ran away when she had grown up, to quote her own terse diary, "crossed a river on drift sticks, wading in shallows, through woods, meeting bears, sleeping under trees—seventy miles flight—saw a French boat—took off skirt and waved it to them—came—took my mother on board—worked for them—with the sealers—camped on the ice.

"As there was no other kind of women to marrie hear, the few English men each took a wife of that sort and they never was sorry that they took them, for they was great workers and so it came to pass that I was one of the youngest of them." [Meaning, of course, that she was the daughter of one of these marriages.]

"Our young man pretended to spark the two daughters of Tomas. He was a one-armed man, for he had shot away one arm firing at a large bird.... He double-loaded his gun in his fright, so the por man lost one of his armes,... he was so smart with his gun that he could bring down a bird flying past him, or a deer running past he would be the first to bring it down."

"They was holden me hand and telling me that I must be his mother now as his own mother is dead and she was a great friend of mine although we could not understand each other's language sometimes, still we could make it out with sins and wonders."

"April 7, 1894.—Since I last wrote on this book, I have been what people call cruising about here. I have been visiting some of my friends, though scattered far apart, with my snow-shoes and axe on my shoulders. The nearest house to this place is about five miles up a beautiful river, and then through woods, what the french calls a portage—it is what I call pretty. Many is the time that I have been going with dogs and komatick 40 or 50 years ago with my husband and family to N. W. River, to the Hon. Donald A. Smith and family to keep N. Year or Easter."

"My dear old sister Hannah Mishlin who is now going on for 80 years old and she is smart yet, she hunts fresh meat and chops holes in the 3 foot ice this very winter and catches trout with her hook, enough for her household, her husband not able to work, he has a bad complaint."

"You must please excuse my writing and spelling for I have never been to school, neither had I a spelling book in my young day—me a native of this country, Labrador, Hamilton's Inlet, Esquimaux Bay—if you wish to know who I am, I am old Lydia Campbell, formerly Lydia Brooks, then Blake, after Blake, now Campbell. So you see ups and downs has been my life all through, and now I am what I am—prais the Lord."

"I have been hunting most every day since Easter, and to some of my rabbit snares and still traps, cat traps and mink traps. I caught 7 rabbits and 1 marten and I got a fix and 4 partridges, about 500 trout besides household duties—never leave out morning and Evening prayers and cooking and baking and washing for 5 people—3 motherless little children—with so much to make for sale out of seal skin and deer skin shoes, bags and pouches and what not.... You can say well done old half-breed woman in Hamilton's Inlet. Good night, God bless us all and send us prosperity.

"Yours ever true,

"LYDIA CAMPBELL."

"We are going to have an evening worship, my poor old man is tired, he has been a long way to-day and he shot 2 beautyful white partridges. Our boy heer shot once spruce partridge."

"Caplin so plentiful boats were stopped, whales, walrusses and white bears."

"Muligan River, May 24, 1894.—They say that once upon a time the world was drowned and that all the Esquimaux were drownded but one family and he took his family and dogs and chattels and his seal-skin boat and Kiak and Komaticks and went on the highest hill that they could see, and stayed there till the rain was over and when the water dried up they descended down the river and got down to the plains and when they could not see any more people, they took off the bottoms of their boots and took some little white [seal] pups and sent the poor little things off to sea and they drifted to some islands far away and became white people. Then they done the same as the others did and the people spread all over the world. Such was my poor father's thought.... There is up the main river a large fall, the same that the American and English gentlemen have been up to see. [Referring to Mr. Bryant, of Philadelphia, who visited Grand Falls.] Well there is a large whirlpool or hole at the bottom of the fall. The Indians that frequent the place say that there is three women—Indians—that lives under that place or near to it I am told, and at times they can hear them speaking to each other louder than the roar of the falls." [The Indians always think the mist of a waterfall signifies the presence of ghosts.]

"I have been the cook of that great Sir D. D. Smith that is in Canada at this time. [In the days when Lord Strathcona was chief trader at Hamilton Inlet.] He was then at Rigolet Post, a chief trader only, now what is he so great! He was seen last winter by one of the women that belong to this bay. She went up to Canada ... and he is gray headed and bended, that is Sir D. D. Smith."

"August 1, 1894.—My dear friends, you will please excuse my writing and spelling—the paper sweems by me, my eyesight is dim now———"

THE END

FOOTNOTES:

[1] Whom Bradbury and Irving and Chittenden have all conspired to make immortal.

[2] While Lewis and Clark were on the Upper Missouri, the former had reached a safe footing along a narrow pass, when he heard a voice shout, "Good God, captain, what shall I do?" Turning, Lewis saw Windsor had slipped to the verge of a precipice, where he lay with right arm and leg over it, the other arm clinging for dear life to the bluff. With his hunting-knife he cut a hole for his right foot, ripped off his moccasins so that his toes could have the prehensile freedom of a monkey's tail, and thus crawled to safety like a fly on a wall.

[3] Whether they actually reached the shores of the bay on this trip is still a dispute among French-Canadian savants.

[4] 1685-'87; the same Le Moyne d'Iberville who died in Havana after spending his strength trying to colonize the Mississippi for France—one instance which shows how completely the influence of the fur trade connected every part of America, from the Gulf to the pole, as in a network irrespective of flag.

[5] The men employed in mere rafting and barge work in contradistinction to the trappers and voyageurs.

[6] This was probably the real motive of the Hudson's Bay Company sending Hearne to explore the Coppermine in 1769-'71. Hearne, unfortunately, has never reaped the glory for this, owing to his too-ready surrender of Prince of Wales Fort to the French in La Perouse's campaign of 1782.

[7] To the mouth of the MacKenzie River in 1789, across the Rockies in 1793, for which feats he was knighted.

[8] Of the Lewis and Clark expedition.

[9] Either the Nor' Westers or the Mackinaws, for the H. B. C. were not yet so far south.

[10] In it were the two original partners, Clark, the Chouteaus of Missouri fame, Andrew Henry, the first trader to cross the northern continental divide, and others of whom Chittenden gives full particulars.

[11] This on the testimony of a North-West partner, Alexander Henry, a copy of whose diary is in the Parliamentary Library, Ottawa. Both Coues

and Chittenden, the American historians, note the corroborative testimony of Henry's journal.

[12] Henceforth known as the South-West Company, in distinction to the North-West.

[13] The modern Winnipeg.

[14] MacKay, MacDougall, and the two Stuarts.

[15] Franchère, one of the scribbling clerks whom Thorn so detested, says this man was Weekes, who almost lost his life entering the Columbia. Irving, who drew much of his material from Franchère, says Lewis, and may have had special information from Mr. Astor; but all accounts—Franchère's, and Ross Cox's, and Alexander Ross's—are from the same source, the Indian interpreter, who, in the confusion of the massacre, sprang overboard into the canoes of the squaws, who spared him on account of his race. Franchère became prominent in Montreal, Cox in British Columbia, and Ross in Red River Settlement of Winnipeg, where the story of the fur company conflict became folk-lore to the old settlers. There is scarcely a family but has some ancestor who took part in the contest among the fur companies at the opening of the nineteenth century, and the tale is part of the settlement's traditions.

[16] A partner in trade with Crooks, both of whom lost everything going up the Missouri in Lisa's wake.

[17] Doings in the North-West camp have only become known of late from the daily journals of two North-West partners—MacDonald of Garth, whose papers were made public by a descendant of the MacKenzies, and Alexander Henry, whose account is in the Ottawa Library.

[18] A son of the English officer of the Eighty-fourth Regiment in the American War of Independence.

[19] Jane Barnes, an adventuress from Portsmouth, the first white woman on the Columbia.

[20] In justice to the many descendants of the numerous clan MacTavish in the service of the fur companies, this MacTavish should be distinguished from others of blameless lives.

[21] Some say seventy-four.

[22] The enormous returns made up largely of the Astoria capture. The unusually large guard was no doubt owing to the War of 1812.

[23] An antecedent of the late Sir Roderick Cameron of New York.

[24] More of the voyageurs' romance; named because of a voice heard calling and calling across the lake as voyageurs entered the valley—said to be the spirit of an Indian girl calling her lover, though prosaic sense explains it was the echo of the voyageurs' song among the hills.

[25] Continental soldiers disbanded after the Napoleonic wars.

[26] A law that could not, of course, be enforced, except as to the building of permanent forts, in regions beyond the reach of law's enforcement.

[27] For example, the Deschamps of Red River.

[28] Chittenden.

[29] Larpenteur, who was there, has given even a more circumstantial account of this terrible tragedy.

[30] Radisson and Groseillers, from regions westward of Duluth.

[31] Especially the Château de Ramezay, where great underground vaults were built for the storing of pelts in case of attack from New Englander and Iroquois. These vaults may still be seen under Château de Ramezay.

[32] This is no exaggeration. Smith's trappers, who were scattered from Fort Vancouver to Monterey, the Astorians, Major Andrew Henry's party—had all been such wide-ranging foresters.

[33] Fitzpatrick was late in reaching the hunting-ground this year, owing to a disaster with Smith on the way back from Santa Fé.

[34] By law the Hudson's Bay had no right in this region from the passing of the act forbidding British traders in the United States. But, then, no man had a right to steal half a million of another's furs, which was the record of the Rocky Mountain men.

[35] A death almost similar to that on the shores of Hudson Bay occurred in the forests of the Boundary, west of Lake Superior, a few years ago. In this case eight wolves were found round the body of the dead trapper, and eight holes were empty in his cartridge-belt—which tells its own story.

[36] In further confirmation of Montagnais's bear, the chief factor's daughter, who told me the story, was standing in the fort gate when the Indian came running back with a grisly pelt over his shoulder. When he saw her his hands went up to conceal the price he had paid for the pelt.

[37] This phase of prairie life must not be set down to writer's license. It is something that every rider of the plains can see any time he has patience to rein up and sit like a statue within field-glass distance of the gopher-burrows about nightfall when the badgers are running.

[38] Would not such critics think twice before passing judgment if they recalled that General Parker was a full-blood Indian; that if Johnston had not married Wabogish's daughter and if Johnston's daughter had not preferred to marry Schoolcraft instead of going to her relatives of the Irish nobility, Longfellow would have written no Hiawatha? Would they not hesitate before slurring men like Premier Norquay of Manitoba and the famous MacKenzies, those princes of fur trade from St. Louis to the Arctic, and David Thompson, the great explorer? Do they forget that Lord Strathcona, one of the foremost peers of Britain, is related to the proudest race of plain-rangers that ever scoured the West, the Bois-Brûlés? The writer knows the West from only fifteen years of life and travel there; yet with that imperfect knowledge cannot recall a single fur post without some tradition of an unfamed Pocahontas.

[39] The spelling of the name with an apostrophe in the charter seems to be the only reason for the company's name always having the apostrophe, whereas the waters are now known simply as Hudson Bay.

[40] To the Indian mind the hand-to-hand duels between white traders were incomprehensible pieces of folly.

[41] It need hardly be explained that it is the prairie Indian and not the forest Ojibway who places the body on high scaffolding above the ground; hence the woman's dilemma.

[42] The flag was hoisted on Sundays to notify the Indians there would be no trade.

[43] Governor Norton will, of course, be recalled as the most conspicuous for his brutality.

[44] Amisk, the Chippewyan, umisk, the Cree, with much the same sound. A well-known trader told the writer that he considered the variation in Indian language more a matter of dialect than difference in meaning, and that while he could speak only Ojibway he never had any difficulty in understanding and being understood by Cree, Chippewyan, and Assiniboine. For instance, rabbit, "the little white chap," is wahboos on the Upper Ottawa, wapus on the Saskatchewan, wapauce on the MacKenzie.

[45] That is, as far as trappers yet know.